Keep the Quality

SCOTTISH WOOLLENS

SCOTTISH WOOLLENS

PUBLISHED BY

SINCE 1797
Johnstons
of Elgin

"The market-girls an' fishermen,
The shepherds an' the sailors, too,
They 'eard old songs turn up again,
But kep' it quiet – same as you!"

🏵   🏵   🏵   🏵

"Here's tae us, who's like us!"

🏵   🏵   🏵   🏵

"For who wou'd leave unbrib'd Hibernia's land
Or change the rocks of Scotland for the Strand."

🏵   🏵   🏵   🏵

"Then while time serves, and we are but decaying,
Come, my Corinna, come! let's go a-Maying"

ISBN 978-0-9525329-1-0

Copyright Johnstons of Elgin, 2016
The right of Ian Urquhart to be identified as the editor of this edition has been asserted
in accordance with the Copyright, Designs and Patents Act 1988

Set in Miller Daily and designed by Think Publishing Ltd, London and Glasgow
Printed and bound using FSC paper stocks by Bell & Bain Ltd, Glasgow

Published by Johnstons of Elgin, Newmill, Elgin, Moray, IV30 4AF, Scotland, Great Britain
www.johnstonscashmere.com

FOREWORD TO 2016
SPECIAL EDITION

This volume is a reprint of a book published in 1956. That book was created by bringing together newsletters published from 1931 and 1956. Almost all the newsletters were written by Edward Stroud Harrison, senior partner then Chairman of Johnstons of Elgin from 1920 to 1966. E.S. Harrison trained as a textile designer and was also an artist becoming FSA. He penned most of the drawings in this book. He was my late wife's grandfather. I was his neighbour for almost ten years and knew him well. He was also Lord Provost (Mayor) of the City and Royal Burgh of Elgin and one of very few people to be granted the Freedom of Elgin. We hope you enjoy reading and learning about our fascinating industry those many years ago. At that time, the description "District Check" was used – these would now be known as "Estate Tweeds". These are covered in another book published by Johnstons of Elgin, Scottish Estate Tweeds. Measurement of weight is shown as either lbs. or pounds and one equates to 0.454 kilogram, and height is measured in feet, one equates to 0.305 metres.

EDITED BY
IAN URQUHART,
Director,
Johnstons of Elgin,
since 1981.
Chairman,
since 2001.

FOREWORD TO 1956 EDITION

It was noted that it would be evident to the discerning reader that most of the newsletters were the work of a single hand, namely Edward Stroud Harrison. It was a labour of love for him yet there was admiration and gratitude to him for undertaking the great amount of research that went into the production of each newsletter. The industry, as the National Association of Scottish Woollen Manufacturers, recorded their thanks to him.

CONTENTS

CONTENTS – *Continued*

LIST OF COLOUR ILLUSTRATIONS

BLACK AND WHITE PLATES AT END OF VOLUME

PREFACE TO 1956 EDITION

When our experiment in journalism, "Scottish Woollens", proved a totally unexpected success and had arrived at its destination, we thought it might be usefully preserved in a more permanent form. A file full of leaflets is not convenient and, worse still, is exceedingly vulnerable to the attacks of borrowers. We therefore decided to publish the complete set of papers in a book. We concluded also that no attempt should be made to change the original leaflets, even those in which we recorded some domestic aspects of the war. The articles, apart from two contributed by authorities outside our trade, were anonymous. We concluded they should so remain though we were tempted to index all our friends whose contributions had produced our success. Of our illustrators, two have died – W. R. Lawson, the originator of our emblem, the lamb – and Robert Burns, R.S.A. These were the youngest and the oldest, each in his own very different way a sad loss to Scottish Art. As to us, the Editor, like all editors, we had to fill in odd spaces where text and illustrations were needed at the last moment, but we are most grateful for all the skilled and willing help we received.

A quite unexpected series of compliments came our way. Our original ambition rose no higher than a possible edition of a thousand. But it was not many years before we ran up to 6000 and nearly all our earlier numbers were reprinted – some several times. Our subscribers by request included Government Departments, libraries at the National level, and Universities both at home and overseas, so we feel much less modest than we did some years ago and we hope our new volume will be useful.

E.S. HARRISON.

MEMBERS OF THE NATIONAL ASSOCIATION
OF SCOTTISH WOOLLEN MANUFACTURERS, 1956

THOS. M. ADIE & SONS
VOE, SHETLAND

WM. ARCHIBALD, SON & CO. LTD.
STRUDE MILLS, ALVA

AUCHENTROIG HOMESPUNS
BUCHLYVIE, By STIRLING

D. BALLANTYNE, BROS., & CO. LTD.
MARCH STREET MILLS, PEEBLES

HENRY BALLANTYNE & SONS, LTD.
TWEEDVALE MILLS, WALKERBURN

BECKETT & ROBERTSON
ST RONAN'S MILL, INNERLEITHEN

ALEX. BEGG & CO. LTD.
TWEED MILLS, AYR

ARTHUR BELL (SCOTCH TWEEDS) LTD.
BUCCLEUCH MILL, LANGHOLM

BLACK & BORTHWICK, LTD.
164 HOWARD STREET, GLASGOW, C.1

BLENKHORN, RICHARDSON & CO. LTD.
EASTFIELD MILLS, HAWICK

JAMES BOYD & SON
NEW BONGATE MILLS, JEDBURGH

BROWN, ALLAN & CO.
RIVERSIDE MILLS, SELKIRK

BROWN BROS. (GALASHIELS) LTD.
BUCKHOLM MILLS, GALASHIELS

WM. BROWN, SONS & CO. LTD.
WILDERBANK MILL, GALASHIELS

JAMES BROWNLEE & SONS
VICTORIA DYEWORKS, GALASHIELS

CLAN WOOLLENS (EXPORT) LTD.
INDUSTRIAL ESTATE, LARKHALL

COLOURCRAFT (GALASHIELS) LTD.
NETHERDALE MILL, GALASHIELS

CORBIE LYNN MILL, LTD.
SELKIRK

THE RONALD COWLEY CO.
21 KING STREET, DUNDEE

CREE MILLS, LTD.
NEWTON STEWART, WIGTOWNSHIRE

J. & J. CROMBIE, LTD.
GRANDHOLM WORKS, WOODSIDE, ABERDEEN

ARTHUR DICKSON & CO. LTD.
COMELYBANK MILL, GALASHIELS

FRIEDLANDER (GT. BRIT.) LTD.
WATT ROAD, HILLINGTON, GLASGOW, S.W.2

GALLOWAY REELS
15-19 CAVENDISH PLACE, LONDON, W.1

EDWARD GARDINER & SONS, LTD.
TWEED MILLS, SELKIRK

GIBSON & LUMGAIR, LTD.
ST MARY'S MILLS, SELKIRK

JOHN GLADSTONE & CO. LTD.
BEECHBANK WORKS, GALASHIELS

GLEN CREE, LTD.
NEWTON STEWART, WIGTOWNSHIRE

A. HALL & SONS, LTD.
LANGLANDS MILLS, NEWTOWN ST BOSWELLS

HAMILTON WEAVING CO.
32 BURNBANK ROAD, HAMILTON

HEATHER MILLS CO. LTD.
HEATHER MILLS, SELKIRK

HOLMES & ALLAN
FIELDEN MILLS, 199 FIELDEN STREET, BRIDGETON, GLASGOW

HUNTER & CO. (GALASHIELS) LTD.
ABBOTSFORD MILLS, GALASHIELS

T. M. HUNTER, LTD.
SUTHERLAND WOOL MILLS, BRORA

EBENEZER Y. JOHNSTON, LTD.
TWEED MILL, GALASHIELS

JAMES JOHNSTON & CO. OF ELGIN, LTD.
NEWMILL, ELGIN

JAMES JOHNSTON & CO.
15 COCHRANE STREET, GLASGOW, C.1

KEDDIE, GORDON & CO. LTD.
ROSEBANK MILL, GALASHIELS

KEMP, BLAIR & CO. LTD.
GALA DYEWORKS, GALASHIELS

G. & G. KYNOCH, LTD.
ISLA BANK MILLS, KEITH

LAIDLAW & FAIRGRIEVE, LTD.
LADHOPE MILLS, GALASHIELS

ROBERT LAIDLAW & SONS, LTD.
SEAFIELD MILLS, KEITH

JOHN LAWSON & SONS, LTD.
LOANHEAD MILLS, KILMARNOCK

GEORGE LEES & CO. LTD.
GALABANK MILLS, GALASHIELS

LEITHEN MILLS SPINNING CO.
LEITHEN MILLS, INNERLEITHEN

PETER MACARTHUR & CO. LTD.
207 INGRAM STREET, GLASGOW, C.1

MACDONALD'S TWEEDS, LTD.
ARGYLL TWEED MILLS, OBAN

HUGH McGILL, LTD.
CROOKEDHOLM MILL, HURLFORD, KILMARNOCK

MACLEOD TWEEDS
GLENALBYN, CARSE ROAD, INVERNESS

S. H. McKINNON & CO. LTD.
KELVINHOSIERY WORKS, 16–22 MONTROSE STREET, GLASGOW, C.1

A. & J. MACNAB, LTD.
SLATEFORD, EDINBURGH, 11

A. & J. MACNAUGHTON
PITLOCHRY

WALTER MERCER & SON, LTD.
STOW MILLS, STOW, MIDLOTHIAN

MUNRO & CO. LTD.
RESTALRIG FACTORY, EDINBURGH, 7

R. G. NEILL & SON, LTD.
GLENESK MILL, LANGHOLM

NETHERDALE HANDLOOM WEAVERS, LTD.
GLENFIELD MILL, GALASHIELS

ROBERT NOBLE & CO. LTD.
GLEBE MILLS, HAWICK

ADAM PATERSON & SONS, LTD.
WEST MILLS, HADDINGTON

J. & D. PATON & CO. LTD
GRAMPIAN MILLS, TILLICOULTRY

PATONS & BALDWINS, LTD.
SPINNERS, ALLOA

JAMES PORTEOUS & CO. LTD
MEADOW MILL, ALVA

JAMES PRINGLE, LTD.
HOLM TWEED MILLS, INVERNESS

G. RAE & SON (WOOLLENS) LTD.
TWEED MILLS, GALASHIELS

REID & TAYLOR, LTD.
WOOLLEN MANUFACTURERS, LANGHOLM

REID & WELSH, LTD.
LOSSIEBANK MILL, ELGIN

J. C. RENNIE & CO. LTD.
MILLADEN, MINTLAW, ABERDEENSHIRE

GEORGE ROBERTS & CO. LTD
FOREST MILL, SELKIRK

G. & H. ROBERTS, LTD.
SPINNERS, DALRY, AYRSHIRE

A WORD OF INTRODUCTION

 COTLAND, from its climate, has always been a sheep country. Sheep, indeed, seem to have followed the ice northward as it retreated towards the Pole after the last glacial epoch, and so from very early times the use of wool for clothing developed, but how the crafts of spinning and of weaving started is still a mystery and probably will so remain.

The object of these leaflets is not to deal with antiquarian imaginings, but to give interesting and useful information to those of us who deal in woollen cloths for our daily bread. During the tour of North America by our Delegates of the Scottish Woollen Manufacturers' Association in March and April of this year, they were continually asked such questions as: "What is a Scotch Tweed?"; "How are we to know Scotch cloths?"; "Who started tartans?"; "What are District Checks – Bannockburns, Gunclub Checks, Glenurquharts?"; "What makes the difference between a woollen and a worsted cloth?" "What are Cashmeres and Vicunas?"; "Why does a worsted get shiny sooner than a woollen cloth?" In fact, everywhere they were asked for information on every possible aspect of the trade; information that would be both interesting and useful to salesmen dealing in our woollen cloths. So when the Delegates came home, they recommended that we should send out a series of leaflets giving information on all sorts of points that might be of interest and to invite suggestions from salesmen who may wish to learn about any special subject. This is the first of the series, and it is our idea to send out a leaflet about every three months. So as to enable any salesmen who might wish to keep our leaflets for reference, we are making them uniform in size, punching them for filing, and to any one who wishes we shall send a file cover in which to store them. If the series rouses enough interest to be continued, it should, little by little, collect quite a large quantity of information on the bypaths of history, for there is a lot of human interest wrapped up in the development of human clothing.

Another point we would like to make is this. Obviously, the object of issuing these leaflets is not disinterest. We wish to rouse and maintain interest in our Scottish Woollens. We are whole-hearted believers in the goodness of our cloths, but our leaflets aim to give absolutely accurate information on every subject on which we touch, and to collect and to correct this information we are going to use all the old experience gathered by all the workers in our old, intricate and highly skilled industry. We aim at something quite different from ordinary advertisement. Something more akin to a scientific publication.

The first subject we deal with is the word "tweed". It is a word that has passed into the English language completely. It is particularly attached to Scotland, and is applied to woollen suiting and coating cloths of various stages of roughness, from the coarsest homespuns down to finer but not very dressy cloths. In the medium and rougher types, we have something just perfect for outdoor sportswear for temperate climates. All sportsmen have a love for ancient clothes, and good tweeds cannot be beaten for this purpose. They are almost everlasting. The non-conducting property of woollen-spun material – we shall deal with the difference between woollen and worsted spinning later – makes good tweeds a protection alike from heat and cold, the most equable wear possible. The applicability of colour renders it possible to choose colourings that will blend with any background. Modern machinery and knowledge have given us weights of cloths suited to any climate where it is possible to wear anything warmer than cotton or linen. Our Scottish Industry has suffered by the fame of its old staple productions. In countries outside our own islands, the word has stood for the earlier and rougher types of cloth, and tweeds have been taken for the only production of the Scotch mills. In consequence, overseas buyers have quite unnecessarily sought outside of Scotland for the finer, lighter, more elaborate cloths required by modern fashions.

The modern journalist and advertiser have found that labels are almost necessary, so we now have a vast flock of names for cloths – practically all pure inventions or contortions of ordinary language or ordinary words suggesting the raw materials used in the cloths or suggesting nothing at all. These names for the most part are mere up starts of unknown parentage, but the older names are aristocratic and can trace their descent from some true meaning and origin in the utilities that form the basis of all languages, and the Scottish National word "tweed" is one of these.

In weaving, the simplest structure is the interlacing of two sets of threads, over one under one.

This is the foundation weave of most primitive cloths and is typical of the Irish woollens such as Donegals. Curiously enough, the Navaho Indians have evolved an unbalanced version of this primitive weave in which only one set of threads shows on the surface, and in which they have worked out most beautiful and elaborate designs for their blankets. The Scotch weavers, seeking a denser and heavier cloth, evolved the idea of the twill in which the threads cross over two under two and at the same time move forward to the right or left.

We cannot claim this weave as the sole and only property of Scotland. It is a logical outcome of the growth of the craft and has been used over all the world in weaving, which, being based in necessity – like the potter's art – is one

of the most ancient and most widespread of all arts. This construction, known by such names as the "two and two twill", the "Cassimere twill" or, in Scotland, as the "common twill", became the everyday weave in Scotland, and so Scotch cloths came to be called "twills," or in the Scotch form of the word, "tweel". This word "tweel", in fact, became applied even to the thread used in the weaving, as any lover of our old Scotch songs may well remember: "And ye maun reel the tweel, John," said Mistress Grumly.

Now the Scottish Woollen Trade being an ancient craft, having its roots in the everyday needs of the people, is remarkably little centralised, as is always apt to be the case where a trade has been introduced full-fledged from outside as was the English Woollen Trade. Both population and sheep were more dense in the south – or perhaps as there were few of either compared with modern ideas, we had better say both sheep and people were more common in the south. Moreover, at the beginning of the nineteenth century, the Highlands had only recently emerged from barbarism. So when the time came for the old crafts to turn into industries and want power, it was natural enough that it was in the Tweed Valley that the greatest concentration of the Woollen Trade was found. Although the river had long been the much-disputed and fought for border in the days before we finally annexed England, it was on the Scottish side of the Borders that the trade developed. Thus it happened that the early export trade in Scottish Woollens began from the Valley of the Tweed, and the cloths became associated in the minds of oursouthern customers with the Tweed.

Why should the people of London, let us say, have ever heard about our river? It is only a small stream, after all, perhaps eighty miles – say a three hours' run from where its shining springs bubble up amidst the low green hills, empty save for the sheep and the lonely cottages of the shepherds, down to its mouth at Berwick where it flows into the North Sea. It is a hurried stream, no longer navigable a mile from its mouth and so carrying no commercial fame.

About the second half of the eighteenth centur,y the effects of the Union with England began to tell on Scotland. For centuries, the energies of Scotland had been spent on defence against the attacks of her powerful neighbour, and now they were released and blossomed forth in one of the most magnificent of National revivals. In literature, Burns and Sir Walter Scott were the great manifestations, and Scott's researches in the great stores of Border song and story and his own novels and poems had made the Tweed famous beyond any other stream. The fame of Sir Walter is difficult to appreciate at this distance of time. One little anecdote is suggestive. In the Paris Exhibition of Pictures – now known as the Salon – in 1831 over forty of the pictures took their subjects from Sir Walter's works.

Then came a curious and happy error. About 1840, a quantity of tweel was invoiced by Watsons of Hawick to James Locke, a London merchant. The writing of the word "tweel" was hurried, and it is pleasant to think of the London merchant having spent the evening before dreaming over some entrancing Border story by the Great Wizard, and with the silvery waters of the Tweed humming in his ears next day, he misread the invoice absent-mindedly, and cast the glamour of romance over our Scottish cloths and called them "tweed".

OUR MOTTO

Our Delegation reported to us in these words: "We were anxiously seeking for some motto or slogan that would crystallise in a phrase the stored-up traditions and aims of our trade, and we could find nothing that satisfied us. For two days at Rochester we were nobly entertained by the Clothiers, and on the second day we and our other hosts were guests at a lunch of which the details were most charmingly conceived, in a factory where no detail is ever overlooked — it is superfluous to be more exact. Across the entrance was the magic sign, 'Keep the Quality Up'. Instantly, we looked at one another and smiled — and being good Scotsmen, we took it with us, for which we tender our apologies and our sincerest thanks."

WORSTEDS *versus* WOOLLENS

COTLAND makes woollens, England makes worsteds – more or less! According to the "Century Dictionary", worsted "is a variety of woollen yarn or thread spun from long stapled wool which has been combed and, in the spinning, has been twisted harder than is usual". We are further told that it is called after Worstead, a little village in Norfolk where it was first made. The "Century" is a pleasant book, pleasantly illustrated both with pictures and quotations. In this example, it quotes Chaucer's "Canterbury Tales", the "Prologue," line 262: "Of double worstet was his semi-cope." Chaucer probably died in 1400, so that is already pretty old, and if our reference sends any of our readers back to the "Prologue" to see that incomparable procession passing before his eyes, he should lay some votive offering at the shrine of "Scottish Woollens" for having rendered him so good a service. The line is from the portrait of the Friar, "a wantown and a merye", who was the best of beggars in his house and who "for thogh a widwe hadde noght a sho, so plesaunt was his 'In Principio' yet wolde he have a ferthing, er he wente". A well-to-do cleric. Of course, had not all the Scottish woollen manufacturers been engaged at that time raiding on the Borders, or farther north killing each other, he would have been wearing "Scottish Woollens".

In our first essay, we promised not to write as antiquarians, so we are not going to give a long history of spinning bristling with dates – if such sticky things can be said to bristle – but deal at once with the practical differences between worsteds and woollens. The fundamental difference is the method of preparing the wool for the spinning, and this difference brings in its train a vast number of major and minor consequences that we shall examine in the course of these papers.

At this point in our story, we wish to pause for a short digression. "Scottish Woollens" No. 1 has had a surprising reception, both from our friends for whom the series was started, and from the press. We have had many letters, and our No. 1 was honoured by being reprinted in whole or in part in the trade journals of two continents, and occasionally in papers not devoted to the Woollen Trade. We have had much advice – the good we have taken or shall take – and we want just as much more as people will send to us. On one piece of advice we wish particularly to comment - very flattering and very encouraging – but just now we are not going to follow it. We are urged to publish monthly or even weekly. We are not following this advice for two reasons. We have said in No. 1 that we aim at more than a trade circular. We want our essays to be authoritative and solid. To produce these essays takes a wonderful lot of work. They are being written by practical men actually in the trade, and not by journalists accustomed to rapid writing. Moreover, an "Expert" – horrid title! – has only to start writing on his own subject to discover what a lot of references he has to verify. Our second reason is that these are serious essays, and for their thorough digestion, they require more than the casual glance given to a weekly trade letter. To be quite honest, there is another reason. Up here in Bonnie Scotland, we don't like to see our "siller" spent too quickly!

The difference, then, is that for making worsted yarn the wool is combed; for making woollen yarn, the wool is carded. The word "comb" is plain English, and in its technical sense its meaning is not changed. The wool is literally combed by various mechanical means, and the obvious consequence of combing either wool or your hair is that you disentangle it and remove short or broken fibres. The fibres in the worsted thread are therefore the longer fibres of the wool only, and they are laid parallel in the thread, disentangled completely.

The word "card" requires more explanation, for its connection with plain English is remote. In carding, all the wool is used. There is no removal of long or short fibres. The wool is carefully and methodically tangled as might be said, although minor tangles are all removed in so doing. The wool is carefully scraped, between two flat, hard boards covered with strong, wire teeth embedded in leather and called "cards", until all the fibres are thoroughly blended into an equally dense mass. This process is now replaced mechanically by rotary machinery. The result is that in the combed yarn the wool lies more or less like the wires in a big electric cable, giving an even, smooth

thread, whereas the carded wool is tangled and confusedly mixed in all directions.

This fundamental difference of structure runs right through the resultant cloths, affecting their appearance, their lustre, their wearing properties, their range of weights, their touch, their actual warmth, and their shrinking and felting, influencing the qualities of wools used for each. The two processes affect the whole industrial organisation, and is, in fact, the reason for the great difference between the Scottish Woollen Trade on one side and the English Worsted Trade on the other – a difference penetrating deeply into the social and national characteristics of the two peoples.

It is always dangerous to generalise, for there is always someone with knowledge ready to trip you up on some important exception. There are many exceptions, and we have so little space that we must generalise, but we shall be careful not to be misleading. Broadly speaking, long wools are most suitable for combing, and short wools for carding. It is equally true that any wool can be carded, but there are many wools that cannot be combed, although, as machinery improves, all processes tend to widen their scope.

As a primitive and old-fashioned example of the appreciation of this question of length of fibre – or of "staple" as it is called – we heard an interesting story from an old and very "skilly" carder. As a boy, he had worked in a primitive little northern mill with a water-wheel long ago swept away by modern progress. The wool of the district that the farmers brought in to be made into blankets and homespuns for their own use was long Blackface. The future carder was set up with an axe and a block of wood: he had to make the fleeces into a thick, rough rope and then chop it into lengths of four or five inches, a primitive preparatory method called by the quaint descriptive name of "brothering". This shortening of the long fibres enabled the long wool to blend better with the short parts of the fleece.

It follows then that there is more variety of raw material available for woollen cloths than for worsted cloths, and this unrestricted choice of raw material is one of the great sources of strength in the Scottish Woollen Trade. Every wool can be used by the Scottish manufacturer: the coarsest Blackface grown on our own Highland hills, most of which finds its way into the American carpet mills, where it is used in its "unbrotherly" state; beautiful crimpy English Downs, so run after for the finer knitting yarns because of their bulkiness; fine Merinos from their native Spain or from their adopted Australia; silky Chinese Cashmeres or camels' wools; Crossbreds from New Zealand and South America; the illbred wools of Chili and Peru, and the finest, most aristocratic of all wools from the same country, Vicuna; Mohairs from Anatolia and Tasmania and the Cape; rabbits, guanacos, llamas, alpacas – an endless procession of four-legged beasts, enough to fill half the room in Noah's Ark. In fact, there is no country outside the Tropics that does not furnish materials for the woollen spinner.

We have only room in this introduction to the subject of worsteds versus woollens to touch lightly on the most immediately practical results arising out of these structural differences. Let us start with warmth, one of the most important features of clothing. Air is one of the best insulators in nature. In the untidy structure of the woollen thread, it is quite evident that there is far more air included than in the neat and orderly build of the worsted thread, where one fibre lies smoothly against another. So important is this feature of included air that modern scientific manufacturers working on this fact have produced cloths that enclose, as it were, little blobs of air in their cellular construction, and have evolved warm cloths from such naturally low insulating materials as linen and cotton.

Countless implications arise out of this. The warmth of feathers, of down quilts, of the cotton wadding faced with silk used in China where there is little wool; of thin walls built of hollow brick; of furs; of a still day as compared with a windy day; of snow, which differs from water only in its bulk. Think of the comfort and warmth of a thatched roof made of layers of little straw tubes filled with air. See how Alpine and Arctic plants have evolved downy surfaces to protect themselves in winter with a blanket of air kept motionless by the frozen surface above. Everywhere throughout all Nature and in all the Arts where the passage of these elusive thermal units must be checked, still air is the surest, the most common and the cheapest! Remember it is heat that is the active element – cold is only the absence of heat. Clothing and shelter are needed to protect us from heat and cold alike. It is woollen cloth the Arab uses for his great picturesque burnous, which acts as cloak by day and blanket by night. It is woollen cloth the Navaho Indian makes for his most intemperate country. It is sheep and goat skins that clothe the shepherds of the Mediterranean hills now as in the days of Homer, and it is still wool and skin that shields the Arctic explorer from the cold or keeps in the warmth of his own body or of his small lamp.

And as a sort of practical anti-climax to all this, every one accustomed to wearing a suit of Scottish Woollens knows the unpleasant chilliness of a worsted suit.

In two points the combing process has a very real advantage, which also arises directly out of structure. Owing to the orderly arrangement of the fibres, a much smaller thread may be spun, and because the fibres are lying smoothly parallel to one another, each fibre takes its full share of tensile strain and produces a thread – theoretically at any rate – of the utmost strength of which the raw material is capable. From this follows the implication that wool cloths of the very lightest weights are for practical purposes made of combed or at least partly of combed yarns.

One more point of advantage in combed yarn is its superior brightness – not of colour, where the advantage is in some respects with carded yarns – but brightness of lustre. This depends not only, or even chiefly, on the lustre of the individual fibres composing a thread, but on the angle of reflection. The effect of lustre shows only where the elements of the reflecting surface are able to reflect the light in one direction, a feature admirably developed by the parallel structure of the combed yarn. The pattern on a white linen damask tablecloth is a very perfect example, as the whole design depends entirely on lustre. As you sit at table and look to your right, the pattern may show dark on a light ground. As you glance in front of you while engaged with your plate there is no pattern. You turn to exchange a word with your neighbour on your left and, behold! – the pattern is light upon a dark ground. So you come to all the wonderful array of damasks, brocades and shot effects; to the queer opaque transparency of opals and tiger stones; the dazzle of a smooth wet road before the windscreen of your car, and so onward into all that wonderland of light and unreal colour, which we shall explore a little when we speak of colour itself.

One real and practical drawback goes with this superior lustre of the worsted thread. A worsted cloth glazes much more, and much more quickly, than a woollen cloth.

Although very little combing is done in Scotland, quite a large weight of combed yarn is consumed, for Scottish manufacturers have recognised the extra scope the use of worsted yarns has given to their work. They make regular worsted suitings, although, for the most part, with a difference: the Scottish methods of cloth-making tend to influence the construction, finish and general manipulation of the cloths. Within the last few years, Scottish work has developed greatly in the direction of very light-weight dress goods in which many beautiful effects are obtained by the combination of combed and carded yarns.

There is the curious tough yet soft handle given by combing. The partial loss of spring that gives worsteds the advantage over woollens for trouserings and – in so different a purpose – hair belting for machinery. There is the very marked effect on the milling or felting of a cloth that makes woollen yarns essential for printers' cloths and many upholstery purposes, an aspect that will be dealt with later when we write on felting. It seems to us that a generation will pass before "Scottish Woollens" can hope to touch on all the interesting and useful subjects our survey opens up.

So to sum up the points we have been able to touch upon: for ladies' cloths, woollens are for some purposes best; in men's suitings, woollens are best for most purposes; for overcoatings, woollens are supreme almost to the exclusion of worsteds; and for such cloths as exist purely for their warmth and their clothing capacity, such as blankets and steamer rugs, woollens are the only wear.

At this point, Ladies and Gentlemen, we bow and give you the National Scottish Toast to be drunk with full honours:

"Here's tae us, wha's like us!"

Note. Our illustrations, The Spinning Wheel and the Cards, are drawn from old Scottish examples in the National Museum of Antiquities in Edinburgh, the threads from magnified samples of yarn.

DYEING – ANCIENT AND MODERN

E are going to put the cart before the horse in our "Scottish Woollens" Nos. 3 and 4. We are going to deal with the technical side of dyeing in No. 3, and outline the principles of colour itself in No. 4. Also, as the subjects are really almost one, we hope to shorten the interval between the papers and send out No. 4 within a couple of months. A knowledge of colour rules and dyeing is not an absolutely essential part of the make-up of a designer – not even very necessary as compared with a cultivated taste and natural love of beauty. But colour is so important to our Scottish Woollens that it forms one of the greatest attractions in our National products because of the wonderful variety of its application, and the exquisite delicacy and the brilliant purity that the Scottish process can display.

What we have said about the knowledge of colour laws being comparatively needless to the designer is sure to provoke attack if we do not carry our explanation a little further. Even in these days of almost universal technical instruction, the "practical" man who has worked at his trade is apt to despise the knowledge gained in the schools. In the early days of technical instruction, too much was claimed for class work, which, although necessary and useful, can never replace practical experience and ancient craft. How better can the matter be put than this: "There is no excellent beauty that hath not some strangeness in the proportion. A man cannot tell whether Apelles or Albert Dürer were the more trifler; whereof the one would make a personage by geometrical proportions; the other by taking the best parts of divers faces to make one excellent. Such personages, I think, would please nobody but the painter that made them. Not but I think a painter may make a better face than ever was; but he must do it by a kind of felicity, as a musician who maketh an excellent air in music, and not by rule." Bacon published his essay "Of Beauty" in 1625. How could the point of view be more perfectly presented – "by a kind of felicity, and not by rule." It is a big claim to put forward, but there is no doubt that whether it may be racial, or climatic, or a matter of upbringing, in Scotland we have that "kind of felicity" for colour and design to a degree not yet attained by any other country in the world.

Man has loved colour from earliest times. Julius Caesar narrates that in Britain our ancestors stained their bodies blue with woad or weld. The Bible tells of garments dyed with the juices of grapes and berries, and the coveted coat of Joseph showed what a large range of colours the designers had. Analysis of mummy cloths shows that the Egyptians were learned in the use of the metallic salts of aluminium and iron, and that they dyed scarlet on wool treated with alum, with the bodies of insects known as kermes, the Mediterranean equivalent of cochineal. The juice of a species of shellfish made Royal Tyrian Purple dye, whence the term, "born in the purple". Indigo has been used in the East for thousands of years, yet today it is still a standard for maximum fastness to light, although it is made synthetically and the method of application improved. The Romans procured the

INDIGO OR ANIL

yellow dye "saffron" from crocus plants, and early peoples produced several kinds of red shades with madder root, using different metallic salts to vary the shade, a process improved into the great modern Turkey Red trade of the Clyde Valley. Other vegetable dyes remained, or still remain, of great importance to industry. Logwood or Campeachy wood, which, with chromium or iron salts, yields a beautiful black, is not yet completely displaced by synthetic dyes of greater fastness but inferior tone. Cutch, extracted from the acacia and the areca of India, dyes brown, and is used by the herring fishers to produce the picturesque brown nets and sails, so loved of artists, partly for its colour, partly as a preservative. Cudbear and orchil, made from certain of the lichens of Europe, Africa and South America, produce shades of red and yellow. Yellows are well represented. Flavine is made from quercitron bark from one of the American oaks, *Quercus tinctoria*, and fustic from a South American tree, *Moms tinctoria*. Amongst the animal dyes, cochineal is much the most important, and for long was the most beautiful and brilliant red known. As we write, we have before us a translation, dated London 1789, from the French of Hellot on the "Art of Dyeing", in which the author speaks of having "a small quantity from Amsterdam undoubtedly 130 years old; they are, nevertheless, as entirely perfect as if they had but just arrived from Vera Cruz". The author goes on to speak of the wild cochineal gathered by the Indians in the woods of Old and New Mexico from the cactus plants.

It is very tempting to quote from such old books. There is a lot of interest in the sidelights: sales of shipwrecked lots "by some mischance damaged with sea water, at Cadiz"; the buying of tin from Cornwall for the preparation of the bath; and how the Levant bought scarlet cloths from Carcassonne and Languedoc, dyed in the piece, "five pieces of cloth at the same time."

In these days dyeing was a separate trade of great skill. As with the old painters, the dyers had to prepare all their dyes from the raw materials, a slow and uncertain process. Good dyeing was looked upon as so important that "true" and "false" dyeing was recognised and classified by the French Governments of the eighteenth century, and very closely regulated. Some day perhaps we may be allowed to go back along these interesting old tracks and alleys of ancient commerce, but not till we have cleared a lot of ground.

It is interesting to study how the early Scots gained the variety of dyes necessary for the colouring of the tartans for their plaids and kilts. We find at first these colours were all indigenous, natural products. The bark of the alder tree and the dockroot produced black. Tops of the currant bush with alum, bilberries (known in Scotland as blaeberries), dulse, and crotal were used for browns. Dulse is a common shore seaweed, also used as food, and sold by the fishwives of our coast towns along with oysters and fresh herring. Crotal is the common name for several kinds of lichens that grow on the rocks. It is to them that real Harris Tweeds chiefly owe their characteristic smell. Cup moss yielded purple; dandelions, magenta; blueberries and alum with club moss produced blue; wild cress, violet; whin or gorse bark, broom and knapweed gave a green; bracken – the coarse rough fern that covers many miles of our Highland hills and supplies bedding for crofters' cattle – and heather supplied a yellow; and white crotal was used for red. In later years, the hues of the tartans have become darker, but there is still a demand for vegetable shades.

We are all familiar with Fair Isle garments. The colours and designs catch the eye quickly, and we wonder from where on earth came colours like these; from where on earth came the courage to wear them!

It is difficult to resist the temptation to quote, but truly where something has been well said it is fatuous to try to substitute our own words. R. L. Stevenson in his "Random Memories" writes at greater length of the Fair Isle than we can quote, and our readers must read the rest of that charming essay for themselves:

Cochineal—Male & Female

"Halfway between Orkney and Shetland there lies a certain isle; on the one hand the Atlantic, on the other hand the North Sea bombard its pillared cliffs; sore-eyed, short-lived, inbred fishers and their families herd in its few huts; in the graveyard pieces of wreck-wood stand for monuments; there is nowhere a more inhospitable spot." Here was wrecked the flagship of Philip's Invincible Armada in 1588, and here for months the Duke of Medina Sidonia and his men lived.

"All the folk of the north isles are great artificers of knitting: the Fair-Islanders alone dye their fabrics in the Spanish manner. To this day gloves and night caps, innocently decorated, may be seen for sale in the Shetland warehouse at Edinburgh, or on the Fair Isle itself in the catechist's house; and to this day they tell the story of the Duke of Medina Sidonia's adventure." Words written many years before Europe and America "discovered" the Fair Isle, and sold by the hundred thousand mechanically produced imitations of these "innocently decorated" articles.

The discovery of a synthetic dyestuff, a mauve, by William Henry Perkin, in 1856, was epochmaking in its effect on dyeing. Perkin, a young chemist, was trying to discover a new method of producing quinine when he found this colouring matter. By consulting several dyers, he was encouraged to make further investigations, and later started to manufacture "Perkin's mauve", the first aniline dyestuff.

It may be noted that an issue of postage stamps in Queen Victoria's reign was coloured by this dyestuff. This included the penny stamp with the oval portrait of the Queen, which remained longer in use than any other stamp in the whole history of philately.

Perkin's mauve was soon followed by others, of which the most memorable was called magenta. This gives us a useful date to remember. On 4th June 1859, the Austrians in full retreat before the French made a determined stand at Magenta. Just a few days later was fought Solferino, another doubtful battle of extreme bloodiness, also commemorated in the naming of a dye. This short and confused war ended in the destruction of the Austrian rule in Lombardy, and the Riviera Coast, Nice, and Savoy were handed over to the French as the price of their help in the liberation of Italy.

The next important discovery was the diazo reaction in 1876 by Peter Griess. This made the manufacture of a large range of colours possible, dyes adapted for both cotton and wool, and even today the number of new colours of this "azo" group seems unlimited.

Then came the synthesis of alizarine to supplant the old madder root, which placed at the disposal of the dyer a large range of colours of superior fastness to the natural dyes. The Scottish Woollen Industry was quick to grasp their importance, which did much to foster the Scotch Tweed Trade and keep for it the highest reputation for quality. Science continued her march, and about 1887 "azo" dyes were actually produced on the fibre, involving a new principle in dyeing, and converting willy-nilly those dyers who used this process into actual colour makers.

Then came the improvement of the alizarine dyes, which had involved a two-bath process, by the introduction of the metachrome colours, a single-bath process. These demanded that to get successful results, the dyer must understand the chemical reactions taking place in the dye-bath.

In 1901, as the result of much research, a new family of vat colours was added to the market. These compared favourably with the sole vat dye, indigo, as regards fastness, and required a sound knowledge of the necessary chemistry to apply these.

The vat colours presented a difficulty, too, in that they were insoluble in water and required special preparation to render them soluble, but in 1920, an attempt to remove this drawback of insolubility proved successful by the manufacture of Caledon Jade Green, a triumph of British colour chemistry. It is curious that though Nature for the most part has chosen garments of green and blue, these have proved the most elusive for the colour-maker.

This resume illustrates that dyeing has been greatly simplified, yet latterly the demand upon the chemical knowledge of the dyer has increased. The various fibres are dyed in several stages of their manufacture from the raw material to the woven cloth, and with many hundred dyestuffs on the market, the status of the dyer has been raised. True, the old secrecy of recipes has passed away, but no recipe, however perfect, has made a dyer.

No dyed shade is absolutely fast, for fastness is only relative, but good dyed shades are fast compared with most "natural" colours. "Natural" colours of wools and hairs are rarely even fairly fast. You have only to remember the faded locks on dark sheep, or the light golden colour of the ends of children's hair at the seaside. A story is told of one of our old Scots dyers put "on the mat" for a complaint of fading of a slate grey: "If the Loard canna dye a cuddy a guid fast shade, hoo dae ye expect me tae manage it?"

The range of fastness for which the dyer must cater is wide and varied. A lady's evening dress is never exposed to daylight, and the only process it may pass through is dry-cleaning, and thus quite a fugitive dye may be fast enough for such fabrics. On the contrary, a naval uniform is exposed to the most severe conditions – sunlight, sea air – and even the fastest colours known gradually suffer with such exposure. Again, dyed linings do not require to stand the severe laundry treatment of shirtings, and so different sections of the dyeing industry have different standards of fastness.

The chemist has greatly changed the dyer's trade, has indeed destroyed widespread industries and created new ones. The old plants, anil and pastel, have long ceased to fill the fields of Languedoc and Provence. Indigo in Burma has been destroyed and synthesised aniline has taken its place. Cochineal and kermes insects with their wingless wives live undisturbed on the cactus of Mexico, and the dwarf oaks and ilex groves of the Mediterranean, and alizarine reds reign in their stead, distilled from plants that lived long ago when coal was green.

THE PRINCIPLES OF COLOUR

 COLOUR has always been a great source of joy to man. Far away in the dim background of influences and emotions that make up our composite nature, this love of colour has its beginnings, so fundamental that it seems to extend back almost beyond the birth of mankind. It seems almost to be an essential ingredient of animal nature. It goes back perhaps even further, for who can penetrate these dim beginnings when by imperceptible degrees life emerged from chaos?

Possibly this love of colour might be traced in animal and man alike to the development of protective necessity – possibly to that inutilitarian emotional side of our nature which delights in beauty and does not calculate the cost. But has not beauty truly its foundations in utility? Is not beauty the active principle as it were of all utility? The ultimate utility in fact? A curious and interesting line of speculation leading yet to great practical beneficial vistas of perfection to be occupied by future generations. The separation of beauty from utility is but a phase in the evolution of our ideas.

One of the pleasures of editing these papers is the contacts they produce with those who read them. Our last paper produced quite a number of interesting comments and requests for further information, particularly on the little-known subject of the old Highland vegetable dyes. We are tempted to promise a further paper on this subject some day. One of our dyers pointed out to us that our reference to Caledon Jade Green was not up to date. The name was later combined by the inventor with Solway, and the wool dye is called Soledon. He also points out that in these days science has overtaken Nature, and in light shades of blue alizarine dyes exist that are even faster than indigo. This question of standards of fastness is still in the tentative stage, and amongst the most important work on the subject is that of the U.S. Bureau of Standards, but there is still a long road to travel before true standards can be established.

Colour is a phenomenon of light. We can have no colour without light. White light contains all colours and may be broken up with a prism into its component parts as the shower forms the rainbow. It was a pleasant allegory of our designer to make colour the bridge for our lambkins to skip across the seas. We shall not here go into the question of wavelengths and the relationship between the visible rays of light, the heat rays, the wireless rays, excepting to say that they are all connected into one harmonious scale for which our hearing, seeing, feeling faculties act as receivers, some of one part, some of another part of the scale.

The light rays are divided into a perfectly graded rainbow consisting of red, orange, yellow, green, blue, violet. In the early days of colour investigation, those colours that could not be obtained by mixing were called primary, and those midway, as it were, between two primaries were called secondaries. The primaries are red, yellow and blue; the secondaries, the colours produced by mixing equal parts of two primaries: orange between red and yellow, green between yellow and blue, violet between blue and red. This classification belongs to the simple days when the full unity of wavelengths was either unknown or only dimly foreshadowed. For practical purposes, it is sufficient to account for all the ordinary visible phenomena of light and colour, and, though partial and incomplete, is accurate and useful as far as it goes.

As in all technical subjects, there is a great vocabulary of jargon, but we need not trouble over more than a very few words. We should remember primary and

secondary colours, and there is one other important word: complementary. A colour is complementary to another colour when its addition completes the prismatic series. Thus the complement of red is the combination of yellow and blue, which makes green; of yellow, red and blue, which makes purple; of blue, yellow and red, which makes orange. These were conveniently shown by the old investigators' "chromatic circle", by which device these pairs of complementary colours can be determined at a glance.

In the early days of colour investigation, it was found that the greatest effect of brilliance was obtained where a colour was contrasted with its complement, but that when mixed the result was dull; even grey could be made. More than this, the result of mixing such complementary coloured pigments – paints, dyes, any kind of colours – was to produce a shade darker than the component parts. In fact, with a little care, a dyer can produce a quite tolerable black on cloth or a printer on paper by the use of the complementary colours in combination.

On the other hand, in dealing with lights, the result of adding complementary colours is white. Red and green colour produces black; red and green light produces white. This at first seemed embarrassing behaviour until it became evident that one was subtraction and the other addition; that the coloured article reflected only the rays of its apparent colour and absorbed the others.

The action of dyestuffs is strange and is little understood. A certain process has the power to cause wool to absorb the yellow and blue rays of the white light of day. The cloth so treated can only reflect the red rays, and to us it seems to have been dyed red. Sometimes the process is stable and we call the colour fast, sometimes it changes and we call it fugitive. We do not know just what has happened, but the complex chemical structure we have laboriously built up in the wool has changed under the silent influence of the sun.

Now suppose we treat our red cloth with a chemical with the power of absorbing red only. That means that it reflects blue and yellow, so that our cloth if originally treated with this second chemical would be green. But, in this instance, the cloth already absorbs the red, so there are no red rays to reflect, and the result is the complete absence of reflection, or black. Without elaborating the argument further it is evident that the mixing of lights shows exactly the opposite effect because it is evidently a process of addition, and the adding of red to green will complete the composition of white light, just as the subtraction of green and red by absorbing all the rays produces black.

If we have made our argument clear, it will be evident that a coloured article can only reflect such rays as fall upon it, and that its apparent colour will be greatly influenced by the composition of the light. Thus to take an extreme case in the photographic dark-room, red paper is not distinguishable from white, nor green from black. This is the reason why evening dresses should always be chosen by artificial light, because practically all artificial lights show a great excess of red and yellow rays, so that all colours look "warmer" by artificial light than by daylight because of the absence of the blue rays in the light itself. Blues look dark and grey; reds look more intense; yellows paler and more brilliant. Our eyes are totally incapable of analysis of light – neither practice nor experience can enable us to analyse colours – and we have the strange phenomenon of colours that match by daylight and look quite different by artificial light.

The old colour chemists analysed a vast series of phenomena of colour contrasts and invented a beautiful abracadabra of magic words to describe them. These we shall pass by and shall sum them up in one law of contrasts – all and every kind of contrast – that things unlike each other look most unlike when placed side by side. A tall man and a short man, a colour and its complement. This has nothing to do with fashion. It may not be the fashion of the moment, but the utmost brilliance of red is obtained by contrasting it with green, or it may be dulled through an endless range of russet and brown to black by mixing it with green.

Here come in some interesting features shown by Scottish Woollens, and particularly the explanation of the wonderful early prominence of Scottish Cheviots when first the Woollen manufacturer began to discover mixtures, especially of the great group so typically Scottish, the Lovats. In a future paper, we shall deal with this interesting and important question, and sketch the origins and developments of some of the famous mixtures of the world. To produce a sparkling and lively mixture the original colours must, of course, be brilliant, but it is still more important that they must not be divided too minutely for the eye to see them separately, otherwise the result is simply dull, for one colour cancels out the other. For practical purposes of clothing, the fibres must be fine enough to spin to a yarn small enough to produce a cloth of the necessary weight or thickness; not so fine that the eye cannot distinguish the individual fibres near at hand; not so coarse as to be harsh to touch; of a good natural colour so as to be able to display the dyes well; of a lustre sufficient to reflect the light satisfactorily. Many wools have one or another of these points; none combine them all to such a degree as the fine Cheviot and Crossbred wools that are used for Scotch Cheviot suitings and coatings, and that is why we claim that they are paramount fundamentally, and, in spite of the whims of fashion, which now and then put them out of court, they are supreme and can only be temporarily displaced.

One of the most interesting fields for the study of colour mixing is colour printing. Any person interested in the subject can find endless enjoyment in the examination of colour prints of all sorts, puzzling out the complex overprintings of lithography and wood block work. Then there is the mathematical accuracy of the three colour process, with its light filters and complementary coloured inks, its half-tone screens that break the selected colours into rows of tiny spots. The process is also an interesting example of the value of international work in modern industry: Germany contributed the original scientific groundwork; Great Britain the early commercial development of the work; France the standardisation and production of the light filters; and the United States the mechanical perfection of the screens needed for successful and accurate printing.

Another interesting and curious effect is that colours tend to tint their surroundings with their complement. This is but a development of the effect of contrast, which makes a tall man look a giant amongst small men. The lovely twilight blues that fill the windows of a lighted room have no relationship to the actual outdoor colour, which is just neutral – a general absence of any special colour and quite unaffected whether the weather outside be wet or fine, blue sky or grey. The justly famous colour schemes of the Grand Canyon of the Colorado River again show the same effect, russet and red rocks, cobalt-blue shadows – again complements – imposed on the eye by the overpowering orange reflection of the blistering sun. We remember also a lovely scene of grey rocks in the Alps that developed into sheets of many-coloured flowers, which joined together to make a shimmering grey of the valley. An evening cycle run many years ago comes vividly back as a beautiful illustration. It was the valley of the Ettrick, beloved by Sir Walter Scott, the centenary of whose death this year has been the theme of countless memorial orations, not only in Scotland but throughout the world. Our road was already in shadow. The orange light of the setting sun touched the smooth sides of the opposite hills. The famous and lovely Ettrick meandered out and in from the cool shade of our side to the glowing landscape beyond, and everywhere as the stream flowed out into the vivid sunlight, it changed to an intense blue of piercing loveliness. In the offices of the mills where these papers are edited, a perpetual and cheerful effect of sunlight was procured by contrasting honey-coloured walls, light-toned woodwork, and mahogany furnishings in the inner office with a blue entrance lobby: blue stairs, blue rubber carpet, blue walls. The sun shines on the dullest day. A thousand such examples may be gathered from the works of Nature and of our artists, who use the rule with the subtlety of the great masters, or the blatancy of the successful designers of posters.

Even so very slight a sketch as this must not be finished without just a reference to the great group of iridescent effects. They have not so far been applied to the designing of Scottish Woollens, although there is no saying when the national energy and ingenuity may not sweep the world with the application of a new idea. This group is chiefly limited to primary and secondary colours – rainbow colours, in fact. Peacocks' feathers, lustre pottery and glass, the brilliant changing colours of some butterflies' wings, the shimmer of the dragonfly, the curious shifting colours of fire opals, the gay shades of the oil spilt on the wet asphalt of our city streets. These are caused by the breaking up of the light beams, either by the form of the reflecting surface or by the internal crystalline structure of the material through which the light is transmitted. These colours are even more illusive than our wool dyes. All colours are illusive. We know how they behave and we have great power over their manipulation, although we know little of their actual workings, but in these colours of iridescence we have nothing tangible at all – "such stuff as dreams are made on".

WOAD or PASTEL

19

TARTANS
PART I

Wool from the mountain, dyes from the vale,
　　Loom in the clachan, peat-fires bright;
To every strand of it some old tale –
　　Oh the tartan kilt is my delight!
Went to its spinning brave songs of Lorn;
　　Its hues from the berry and herb were spilt;
Lilts of the forest and glee of morn
　　Are in his walking who wears the kilt!

SKIRL of pipes down the road, then breaks on the ear the measured tramp. Here, they come! the bonnie Highland laddies, kilts swinging, ribbons flying, pipes playing. A sight to stir more than Scottish blood, it seems to conjure up the whole pageantry of Scottish History – visions of Bonnie Prince Charlie, Culloden Moor, the Thin Red Line, the Heights of Dargai rise to the eye of memory.

How are kilts and tartans regarded as the two things that are so inalienably and so essentially Scottish, the badge of all our tribe. It is a queer thing this nationalism. The kilt is only the historic wear of a section of the Nation, it is not even a garment peculiar to Scotland. Fewer than half of the Scottish people have the prescriptive right to any clan tartan. Still the heart of the exiled Lowlander warms to the sight of the tartan plaid, and he would deem his St Andrew's Night dinner incomplete without the accompaniment of the bagpipes and the presence of his kilted countrymen.

The answer to our question is to be found partly in the Jacobite tradition, partly in the Immortal Author of "Waverley", who has done so much to keep that tradition alive, partly in these intangible springs of human emotion to which no logic can apply.

There is still another element in the case. When James VI of Scotland, that sapient but somewhat grotesque monarch, was called in 1603 to reign over England as well as Scotland, Scotsmen were left without their time-honoured diversion of fighting with "the Auld Enemy", a strong National feeling developed that tended to heal the feuds between Highlander and Lowlander, and made the latter at least look for something to distinguish him from his little-loved neighbours across the Border. The Highlanders, having their own native garb and their tartans, and also being more aloof in their mountain fastnesses, were not concerned, but the Lowlander, who had little in his outward dress to differentiate him from the English, seized on the tartan as a National emblem, and the Lowland family tartans, such as the Scott, the Elliot and the Kennedy, seem to date from this period, or even considerably later.

"Who started tartans?" was a question frequently asked of the members of our Delegation that visited America in 1930. There is no direct answer possible. The word itself is of French or Spanish derivation, and its connection with the original meaning is probably the shimmer of the colours. The dictionary description is "a woollen or worsted cloth woven with lines or stripes of different colours crossing each other at right angles so as to form a definite pattern". This definite pattern is, in fact, a series of checks, and it might be as well to refer here to the confusion that arises in many minds as to the words "plaid" and "check". The word "plaid" is loosely applied, especially in America, to checks generally. A plaid is really a detached outer garment worn over the shoulder and somewhat resembles a shawl. The fact that the plaid is part of the Highland dress and is usually of a tartan or checked pattern accounts for the confusion. Checks, again, may be sub-divided into ground checks, the more solid bases that form the ground, and overchecks or large narrow checks, usually in tartans of white or bright colours but often black, superimposed on the ground pattern. The Gaelic word for tartans is "brecan", but as "tartans" they are known to the world.

The introduction of sheep into the Highlands is of relatively late date, and they were not to be found there in great numbers until within the last two centuries. This is peculiar, because Cheviot and Blackface or Mountain are two breeds of sheep that may be considered indigenous to Scotland, and, as wool is always susceptible to climatic influence, nowhere else in the world can these be grown in greater perfection as regards fineness and softness than in the north-western Highlands. One cause of the backward state of sheep breeding is the fact that the Highlanders were a warlike race. Their country was mountainous and inaccessible. A scanty living was wrung from the soil. Agriculture was despised as effeminate, and the mountain, the forest and the loch furnished the larder. By sudden descents on the Lowlands, they would occasionally replenish their store of cattle, but sheep are slow-moving animals, and, as quickness was essential to success in these raids, sheep were usually disregarded.

While the art of weaving in the Highlands dates at least from Druidic times, we must assume that up to five hundred years ago or later, woollen wear was only for the chieftains and their nearest of kin, while their poorer followers were clad in coarse linen shirts and depended for warmth on the skins of beasts.

But to return to tartans, their origin as well as that of the Highland garb is lost in the mists of unwritten history and the clouds of controversy. These controversies, very heated and very important to the Celt, we must disregard, and base our assumptions on more or less authentic history.

To begin with, although the art of woollen weaving was, even in the remote ages, practised pretty generally over the whole of Scotland, the sister art of dyeing, in woollens at least, was confined almost entirely to its Celtic population. On the Orkney and Shetland islands, as well as the far-off Faroes, where we have a purely Scandinavian population, attempts at colouring are to this day confined to the natural colours of the wool. The one curious exception is the Fair Isle, and there it was the result of an accident of history, which we touched upon in No. 3 of this series.

In south-eastern Scotland, with its chiefly Anglo-Saxon population, we find the same, and the Hodden Grey was merely a mixture of the natural black or grey wool with the larger bulk of white. Galashiels blacks and blues indeed did something to develop the dyers' art, but it was not until the advent of tweeds early in last century that any venture was made into the field of fancy colours.

On the other hand, in Celtic Scotland, from very early times we find evidences of colour dyeing and the traditional use of vegetable agents for producing these dyes, which have a fair range of blues, purples, crimson or red, browns, greens, and yellows, as well as black; they were obtained from such various materials, to give a few instances, as alder bark, crotal (a general name for several kinds of lichen that grow on the rocks), heather, whin bark, ragwort, wild cress, blaeberry and dandelion, and these colours can be seen today in the homespuns of North-Western Scotland, styled generically Harris. In Harris cloths they are, however, almost invariably in the form of mixtures – that is, the different colours are blended in the wool after dyeing, the mixing process taking place in the carding.

In tartans, the colour is always solid in the yarn, and the blending takes place in the woven design. Considerable skill has been shown in the blending or shading of colours one with the other, and great variety of pattern has been produced, always within the limits of a chequered design. There is no doubt at all about the traditional nature of these patterns. From very early times, evidently a record was handed down from one generation to the other, chiefly in the form of warping-sticks, the sticks on which the warp was rolled. This was carefully marked with the number of threads of each colour on the pattern across the web, and a similar method was used for checking the threads in the weft.

Each district or family – the terms are in some respects synonymous in the

Highlands – would gradually evolve a pattern and colours by which its clansmen could be recognised in war or peace. It is not possible to say when this idea was first put into practice, but it is recorded that clansmen were recognised in battle by their different tartans as early as the fourteenth century. Three centuries later, when we have a little more light in the form of authentic history, it is evident that the exact form and colours of the principal clans were pretty well established. The recognition of many of the clan tartans is of later date, but today they are sufficiently standardised and an error in the pattern or colour is as heinous in the eyes of a Highlander as false heraldry would be to the Lyon King at Arms.

Exact dates do not appear to us to be of great importance, nor can antiquity alone render sacred. Whether a particular tartan is one hundred or eight hundred years old, it seems sufficient that it is recognised as the tartan of a certain clan. His tartan has much the same significance for a Highlander than his uniform has for the soldier, but it is a closer, a more personal thing.

The Highland clans are divided, broadly speaking, into five or six main branches, each consisting of a number of clans and septs bound more or less by ties of kinship. The connection can be plainly traced in their armorial bearings, their badges, and also in their tartans. In the parent clan, as a rule, we find the simple form of the original tartan, and in its offshoots various modifications and alterations in colours, but always preserving the same design, or set as it is generally called. These modifications may be brought about by a change of colour or the introduction of an overcheck.

This system of the modification of a design has given rise to the expression "tartan heraldry".

While there is a good deal in this heraldry idea it cannot be pursued too far, for its development was never carried out on definite lines like true heraldry. It may be more properly likened to evolutionary development, by which naturally the younger branches of the family designed their tartans with the consciousness of their chief's tartan in their minds. It is significant, however, that it has been adopted to a certain extent by the Government in evolving the regimental tartans. We will not follow the subject any further at the moment, as we propose to deal with the variations of the tartans and their manufacture in a future number.

Tartans have at times had a wider significance than allegiance to the chieftain of a clan. There is an authentic tartan called the Jacobite, which was worn as an emblem of adherence to the Stuart Cause. It was to the Highland hills that Prince Charlie and the Old Pretender lifted their eyes for the help that was to re-establish them on the throne. Celtic Scotland was, with important exceptions, overwhelmingly with them. In the Highlands, every man was a potential soldier. In the Lowlands and northern England, more than a century of peace following the Union had somewhat subdued the fighting spirit of the ordinary man and wars were left to the professional soldier.

The risings of the 1715 and the 1745 and the culminating tragedy of Culloden have cast a glamour over the tartans, but the proscription of the wearing of the Highland dress that followed the latter rebellion has done more than anything else to preserve them. This oppressive Act, which was in force for thirty-five years, made the wearing of the tartan a penal offence. As is usual in history, oppression defeated its own ends. The law, rigorously and cruelly enforced at first and for many years, was finally repealed amid popular enthusiasm and without a dissentient vote in either of the Houses of Parliament, but in the meantime it had confirmed the Highlanders in their attachment to their historic garb and their tartans.

It is a curious commentary on this Act that the first Hanoverian King to visit Scotland, George IV, in 1822, should have received the homage of his northern subjects in a perfect riot of tartan, himself arrayed in full Highland dress of Royal Stewart tartan. Did it cross the mind of the now portly "First Gentleman of Europe" that seventy-seven years before, a younger and more romantic figure, similarly arrayed, had received the same homage on the same spot?

Sir Walter Scott, a Lowlander of the Lowlanders, who stage-managed the whole affair, himself donned the Garb of Old Gaul and set the seal of the Nation's approval on tartan as its emblem. But we regret to learn that it was the Campbell tartan that he sported, and not the Scott, that of his honoured Chief, the Duke of Buccleuch. Sir Walter was rather sceptical about the origins of the Lowland tartans, and was inclined to attribute them to the business acumen of the Edinburgh tartan merchants.

Any historical note, however brief, on Highland tartans would be incomplete without a reference to the Scottish regiments of the British Army, whose heroism has shed glory on the tartan on many a stricken field. Each of the Scottish regiments has its own tartan, but the five distinctively Highland regiments are kilted, while the Lowland regiments and the Highland Light Infantry wear the trews. The description and story of these tartans we must leave for the present. The subject is much too wide and too interesting to dismiss with a word at the end of such a paper as this. We shall therefore return to tartans in further numbers of "Scottish Woollens" and deal with more detailed aspects of this most interesting subject.

Note. Our illustration is from one of Sir Henry Raeburn's greatest portraits, "The MacNab", in the uniform of the Breadalbane Fencibles. It was painted about 1802, and at present belongs to Messrs John Dewar & Sons, Ltd., the Distillers of Perth, and hangs in their London Offices at Dewar House, in the Haymarket.

OUR SCOTTISH DISTRICT CHECKS
PART I

IT is always a matter of interest to watch the different phases of fashion, and the different subjects that interest those concerned in fashions. No one can usually say why or how some particular phase of fashions came into being or faded – "I came like water and like wind I go". A few generations ago, fashions, in clothes at any rate, moved slowly. Even within our memory, what Paris or London decreed today took six months or more to journey across the Atlantic, and another six months to reach the shores of the Pacific. Now there is but one season throughout the civilised world of dress, and what Paris designs today is already beginning to fade on the Californian beaches before the month is out. In the olden days, no one outside the small world of fashion paid any attention to such changes, and costume developed on National and not on fashionable lines. This new arrangement produces a terrible wear and tear of ideas, and our designers constantly have to retreat into the past for novelty. As for the writer of romance, so for the designer of fashions, Scotland is a favourite refuge. After long wandering amongst plain colours and jazzy disorder, the fashion makers have fallen back upon the somewhat barbaric orderliness of our Scottish District Checks. All the trade papers have been vying with one another in the invention of improbable legends about them, in which they have been aided and abetted by our own manufacturers; the plain truth being that remarkably little is known about the origins of these patterns because of their hidden and inconspicuous beginnings in the private annals of private families.

Before we go on with our subject, just a word on our last number. The verse that headed our preliminary essay on tartans has aroused great interest, and we are asked where it may be found. The verse is from Neil Munro's "The Kilt's My Delight," and is to be found in "The Poetry of Neil Munro", published in Edinburgh by the old Scottish House of Blackwood, a name familiar to all lovers of Sir Walter Scott. There are some good things both in Scots and in English in this slim volume of verses, which have been chosen and edited by John Buchan.

The District Checks belong to an interesting period in the history of Scotland, and to get their story right we must examine the circumstances out of which arose the development of modern Scotland. Scotland is not a rich country for the farmer. The parts that come under the plough by their very poverty have produced some of the finest agriculturists and stock breeders in the world. Before the Industrial Revolution, even southern Scotland with difficulty supported a not-very-numerous people in circumstances we would now consider on the poverty line. The wolf was never far from the door, and in a bad year many houses could not keep the door barred against him. In the north and west – the Highlands – things were even worse, for it had passed the wit of man to make an honest living in that "land of brown heath and shaggy wood" for more than the merest sprinkling of a population. Scotland has always been an exporter of her sons, a necessity that has developed into a national characteristic of roving so that there is no part of the world where the Scot is not to be found. In the Middle Ages, when nations waged wars on the very sensible principle of hiring men to fight for them, soldiering was the most common employment of the Highlander. For long the Scots supplied the Royal Bodyguard of France. In the niches of the great stairway of the Château de Blois, they still show you the names of the Guards – all Scottish names – scratched on the soft stone. The Southern Scots went out as traders and scholars; the Highlanders as soldiers of fortune.

Then came the Unions. First the Union of the Crowns, when our King James VI fell heir to the throne of England under the title of James I. Later, the Union of the Parliaments – a mariage de convenance, which for long seemed likely to end in the divorce court. It is curious that the very man who presided at the marriage was chosen to arrange the divorce, but by one of these unforeseen sudden developments in politics that have so often changed the development of nations, the proceedings for the dissolution of the Union were stopped, things settled down, and Scotland rose to a height of prosperity far beyond anything dreamed of by her most optimistic rulers.

Such great changes in the life of a nation can never happen without loss to someone. "Nothing for nothing" may be cruel, but it is inevitable. Someone must pay. This time, the payment had to be met by the Highlands. Their old trades were gone. Gradually an unsympathetic Government enforced law and order at home, built roads, and opened up these wild and inaccessible mountain regions. The old chieftains degenerated into landlords and became pale imitations of the great English landed families, imitating a social order built on very different foundations from those of the Scottish clan system. Even when the great Dr Johnson visited the Hebrides in 1773, he regretted to find that so many of the great families no longer lived in their ancient territories, but had gone to spend in London or Edinburgh the scanty incomes of their barren lands, incomes that, being largely in kind, were ample for the simple and barbaric lavishness of their accustomed hospitality, but were strained past breaking point to maintain their ancestral state in the wealthy society of the capitals.

The Union with England closed the armies of France – our old ally – against the Scot. The Old Scots Guards was replaced by the Swiss, so it was they and not we who "plunged forth among the pikes" that September day in 1793 when, in the streets of Paris, "there forms itself a piled heap of corpses, and the kennels begin to run red", and the poor remnants of the Red Guard that had survived the capture of the Tuileries were hewn in pieces one by one. "Let the traveller, as he passes through Lucerne, turn aside to look a little at their monumental Lion: not for Thorwaldsen's sake alone." Forgive me this digression.

By the beginning of the nineteenth century, the Highlands were reduced to desperate straits. Sir Walter Scott in his "Journal" gives some terrible pictures of the departure of shiploads of emigrants to the New World, a movement that a few years later culminated in the Highland Clearances. A movement, however grievous to the Highlands of Scotland, that furnished the English-speaking world with some of its finest pioneers and settlers. And so we come to the end of the first half of the nineteenth century. Scotland had changed extraordinarily in its social structure, although extraordinarily little in the character of its people. "Nature is often hidden, sometimes overcome, seldom extinguished" is as true of nations as of men. Sheep farming had replaced the primitive work of the Highlanders who had been deported from their old homes, some to the coast, some across the seas. Many parts of the country were almost totally depopulated by a movement as misguided as it was well intentioned. The next phase was the displacement of the sheep and the sheep farmers for deer, and the formation of the great deer forests and sporting estates. So great became the distress in these almost empty glens that many attempts were made by Parliament to help – not very successfully. The area was placed under the general supervision of the Congested Districts Board, a name surely applied with cynical humour to a district that never carried much population, but was now an almost uninhabited waste.

In this setting arose the great Highland sporting estates. The development owed much to Queen Victoria, who not only greatly admired the scenery, but, by her purchase of Balmoral, set the fashion for the Highlands. This connection of owner and tenant soon ripened into a great mutual love and sympathy between Her Majesty and the people of her estates, who transferred to the Little Lady the loyalty and affection that used to be commanded by their chiefs.

In the Highlands, money had always been scarce. Most payments were in kind and most privileges were repaid in service, so it was natural enough that the great estates should clothe their retainers. In the new developments of the country, many of the new owners have no right to any tartan, and moreover tartans are not very suitable for modern dress. The great scientific developments of the times interested such ardent minds as the Prince Consort in problems of protective colourings for his ghillies, keepers, foresters and so forth at Balmoral – and some tincture of the old clan spirit left it the fashion for owners and staff to be clothed alike in the costume of their forest. So came into being our District Checks.

In a later paper, we intend to trace this question of protective colouring in the development of mixtures, and give a page to the evolution of the Lovat Mixture, and the Elcho Mixture of the London Scottish Regiment. This idea, which originated in the minds of the sportsman Lord Lovat and the soldier Lord Elcho, has spread to the clothing of the armies of the world: the British Khaki, the German Field Grey, the Horizon Blue of the French are all alike the outcome of this social change in an obscure and unknown corner of the little Kingdom of Scotland, whose population even today is hardly greater than that of New York City.

In the Cheviots – the Borders – it had long been the habit of the shepherds to wear as their outer garment a long plaid or shawl, usually about four yards long and about a yard and a half wide, from which arises the common trade expression "six quarter wide". These plaids were almost always checked black and white – no special number of threads of each, but usually about a quarter of an inch. This pattern travelled north with the sheep and the shepherds, and became well known throughout the Highlands.

Perhaps I should explain that the word "glen" is the Gaelic for a valley. "Strath" is likewise a valley, but larger and more fertile. Naturally, in such a mountainous country as the Scottish Highlands, the population existed only in the valleys, so it is by the valley names that the Highland Districts were, and are, known.

As the idea of these special tweeds spread, they were naturally enough mostly made by our own mills in Elgin, as they were the oldest of the northern mills that developed more than a purely local trade. The first collection of the patterns was made by Fraser & Smith of Inverness, a firm that ceased to exist about forty years ago, when this part of their trade was carried on by the Edinburgh firm of the present editor's father, who introduced the definite name of District Checks and took up their general distribution seriously.

The District Checks follow a few main lines of development, as illustrated in our supplement, but their detailed consideration must be left to a further number of "Scottish Woollens". The Shepherd Check of the south is the foundation. The District Checks owe little or nothing to the tartans of the glens where they were first used. The Glenurquhart is one great development of the Shepherd – a stroke of genius that gave a new type to the woollen trade of the world – besides the type we give the Mar, which was adopted by King Edward when he was Prince of Wales for his Forest of Mar, just above the Royal Forest of Balmoral in the valley of the Dee. As a simple development of the Shepherd, we give the Glenfeshie. Then there is the great group of the Gunclubs, which linked our District Checks with the New World when the Coigach was adopted in 1874 as their uniform by the Gun Club of New York or Baltimore. I should be deeply indebted to anyone who could give me authentic information on this point.

Then there is a series of patterns that broke quite new ground, but that, from their natural limits, produced no further developments. These are illustrated by Prince Albert's Balmoral and the Erchless. There is also a group of regimental checks represented by the Scots Guards, which we illustrate. There are, of course, many others of varying degrees of interest and authenticity, and we shall return to these details in a further paper, when we shall sketch more definitely the stories of some of the principal patterns.

OUR SCOTTISH DISTRICT CHECKS
PART II

UR Scottish District Checks arose out of a modern social development acting on the ancient traditions and instincts that developed, in the first place, Heraldry – the Heraldry of Feudal Europe – and somewhat later the Highland tartans. A tradition that in its turn rose out of that defensive and offensive alliance of individuals that is one of the chief features that distinguish mankind from the lower orders of creation – the necessity of knowing our friends from our foes. That same instinct has its twentieth-century development in school and club colours, badges, marks, and national emblems, swastikas or black shirts or blue shirts, or a thousand other ornaments and disguises that please the barbarian child that is in us all.

The northern part of Scotland is divided from sea to sea by the Great Glen. From Inverness – which for a brief moment during the Great War became almost an American city, and was policed and kept in order by the United States Navy – the Great Glen runs south-west to the Atlantic at Fort William. It is little above sea level, and its floor is occupied by an almost continuous line of deep lochs. About half-way down the longest of these lochs, Loch Ness, the ancient ruined stronghold of Castle Urquhart dominates the waterway, and below it the brawling little river – the Enerick – ends its race down the wild glen that gives its name to the greatest of all the developments of woollen designing, the GLENURQUHART CHECK, or as it was called in the country of its birth the Glen Urquhart tartan. It is in its simple and original form a development of the Shepherd Check. Whilst the actual origin of the pattern may be, and probably was, accidental, for every one of us who has served his apprenticeship to the weaving and designing of our Scottish Woollens has got over the knuckles for mixing up the coloured threads of the Shepherd – the fixing and adopting of the definite device of the Glenurquhart is due to Caroline, Countess of Seafield, who, some time about the middle of the nineteenth century, adopted the form we illustrate in her Glen Urquhart estates, and there it was worn for many years by tenants, factors and gamekeepers alike. This device, combining two different patterns in one, was a stroke of genius, and has given the designers of the world a source of countless varieties of patterns that have clothed untold millions of well- and ill-dressed men and women all over the globe, wherever Western civilisation has made its touch felt. The Countess was a woman of great character, and, after the deaths of her husband and her son, ruled her wide estates for many years with beneficent tyranny. She was herself a handloom weaver and this is perhaps why tradition has credited her with the design. It seems certain that the actual designer was Elizabeth Macdougall, who lived at Lewiston, a small group of crofts at the foot of the Glen. She spun and dyed the yarn, and the first web was woven by William Fraser. It is an amusing detail of the story that as William did not easily understand her instructions for this outstanding novelty – in which he was very like his modern successors – she sketched her instructions with a stick on the mud in front of his cottage door, which suggests that elaborate apparatus is less important than ideas! Originally this great design was blue and white, but before long the present-day black replaced the original dark blue. The invention took place some time in the late 'forties of last century.

This, then, was the design chosen by Lord and Lady Seafield for their Glen Urquhart estates, and the original estate cloth was woven in a little mill, which, till quite recently, continued working in a quiet way. The mill still stands a little way up the Glen, but it is now only inhabited as a house. It is in itself interesting as one of the attempts to introduce industry and prosperity to these much harried lands after the last Stuart Rebellion of 1745. It was built by the Laird of Grant at the same time as the factory founded by the Honourable Commissioners for Annexed Estates at Invermorriston close by, and there are still preserved in the archives of Castle Grant the lists of women to whom the King's Commissioners distributed spinning wheels for the supply of yarns for the mill. It is difficult in these days of organised excursions, where streams of buses and motor cars pour continually through the glen, and excursion steamers pass up and down the loch, to remember that only a little more than a hundred and fifty years ago the King's Writ hardly ran in the valleys. The nineteenth century has seen great changes – not only in America, where the organisers of the Chicago Century of Progress Exhibition of this year had such difficulty in discovering the site of little Fort Dearborn, and where the comfortable tourist, in his palatial transcontinental dining-car, sees with a thrill the name Fort Sumner on the depot sheds, and remembers that almost within the memory of living man, this was the edge and frontier of civilisation.

Not many of the District Checks follow the Glenurquhart type. THE MAR we illustrate – brown and white with a green overcheck. Tradition – not too well authenticated – says it was designed by King Edward, when, as Prince of Wales, he used to shoot from Abergeldie House in the Forest of Mar. Mar is at the headwaters of the Dee, which flows down to the North Sea at Aberdeen, to which it gives its name. The Forest was acquired by the ancestors of the Duke of Fife, when the Earl of Mar was attainted and his estates forfeited for the part he took in the Jacobite Rising of 1715.

Just a little lower down the river from Mar lies Balmoral, which the Prince Consort bought in 1848 from the Farquharsons of Inverey, and where the royal couple built the new Balmoral Castle with all the enjoyment and enthusiastic interest that went to the making of many a frontier man's homestead: "Ever my heart becomes more fixed in this dear Paradise." The foundation-stone was laid on 28th September 1853, and there the ever-active brain of Prince Albert devised the BALMORAL TWEED, which we illustrate, and the Balmoral tartan, one of the very few tartans that can be absolutely "documented". The tweed is a very dark blue and white sprinkled with crimson – the blue so dark as to be almost black. It imitates very closely the texture and effect of these grey, granite mountains amongst which lies the Forest of Balmoral.

THE CARNEGIE is a very unusual treatment of a simple black-and-white Glenurquhart, three inches on the repeat. It is overchecked through the centre of the 2 and 2 part by a half-inch-wide strip of camel colour, a scheme that separates it very markedly from any other.

In their original form, our District Checks were made for real service on the hills – all men whose work exposes them to all weathers. Shepherds, keepers, guides, deep-sea fishermen all alike have no use for flimsy summer cloths, and all the original patterns were made in good, solid cloths of winter weights.

THE GLENFESHIE, one of the boldest and most invisible of all the Districts when seen in its proper environment, is the type of a considerable group. It is just the Shepherd Check with a brilliant scarlet overcheck. The Feshie is one of the bright clear streams that come down from the Cairngorm Mountains to join the Spey – a long and beautiful glen, the scene of many of Landseer's great paintings of deerstalking and highland landscape.

From 1834 till 1841, Glenfeshie was tenanted by the Right Honourable Edward Ellice, M.P., and General Balfour of Balbirnie, who rented the forest from Sir George Macpherson-Grant of Ballindalloch. The daughter of General Balfour married the son of Mr Ellice, and it is to the kindness of their son, Mr Edward C. Ellice, who was member for St Andrews Burghs, that we owe the record that we give. In those days, Glenfeshie Lodge had not been built and young Miss Balfour acted as hostess to the many interesting guests housed in a group of wooden huts sprinkled amongst the fine old pines that cover the narrow, level floor of the valley and restrain the turbulence of the river. In those days it was an inaccessible spot some eight miles from the nearest road, and nearer twelve from where the nearest stage-coach passed.

To quote her son's words, Mrs Ellice "was disturbed because she had no tartan, so she designed the plaid, which Mr Ellice and the gillies and keepers all wore from that time to the present date". The check – or mixture as it is called locally – was transplanted to Glengarry in the west when its designer and her family acquired the estates of Glengarry, but it also remains firmly rooted in its original soil. The ruined outline of the old mill, where the cloth was first made, is still to be traced – its Gaelic name rather beautiful, Druimnacailleach – but, like many a score of the cottages amongst our Northern mountains, is now silent and unroofed, inhabited only by rabbits, its garden marked by a few unfamiliar leaves soon to be obliterated by the encroaching forest, or the lovely empty spaces of the moorland.

It is said that Mrs Ellice introduced this simple and beautiful check to give the effect of the red and grey granites of Glenfeshie, but local tradition says the red check was introduced to distinguish the keepers and other men of the forest from the shepherds. How real and how far-reaching was the significance of these District Checks is well illustrated by Mr Alister Macpherson-Grant, who tells how his brother, the head of the family, was once accosted in Western Canada because he was wearing a cap of the Glenfeshie Mixture.

Entertainment in those days was much simpler than now. The young ladies sketched or picnicked – shooting not then being permissible for them. There were no near neighbours, and the evenings, which in these Northern glens start very early in the day, were spent singing and dancing to the pipes or the fiddle, which is more truly the national instrument. After all, is not Strathspey the very home of Highland dancing? Also, in those days, the sportsman had to work for his game – muzzle-loading guns and walking up your birds over dogs – and not the least delight that modern mechanised sport has lost in return for its vastly bigger bags is the delight of watching the work of the dogs. After a good day's work following the birds up and down the precipitous hills of Glenfeshie, the big wooden hut, which was the living-room, with its oil lamps and roaring log fire, makes a pleasant picture, with its whiskered sportsmen, and the ladies with their hooped skirts, and the dogs crowded round the fire. Songs and home-made ballads, old stories and new tales of the day's adventures. And if your bedroom was ill to find in the black darkness groping amongst the trees, the river and the wind made fine music to send you to sleep.

We can but take our patterns one by one, describe their main features, and add here and there such notes as we can to give a little of the background against which they appeared. Looked at from a distance, that nineteenth century was a strange period in our history, for the wealth whose sources had destroyed forever the old life of the Scottish Highlands supplied almost the only source of livelihood that remained.

THE ING is the Shepherd with a peculiar dull red-brown for black. THE BALLINDALLOCH the same, red-brown and white one way with a dull biscuit shade taking the place of the white in the cross threads. It has an overcheck the same size as the Glenfeshie Mixture, of dull olive-green. Till recently, it was used on the Strathspey estates of Sir George Macpherson-Grant of Ballindalloch.

THE ARDTORNISH, a West Coast check, is a 4 and 4 Shepherd of white and brown: olive-brown warp way, russet-brown weft way. THE GUISACHAN is remarkable as one of the very few not on a common twill ground, the warp 4 of black and 4 of white crossed with 4 of brown-and-yellow twist, and 4 of white, the weave a 4 x 4 diamond cut in the warp but not cut in the weft.

The two RUSSELL checks are peculiar in their colour effect. The check follows the style of the Glenfeshie, but, being crossed with two shades of drab, the dull brown overcheck gives the strange illusion of being wine coloured in the weft and russet in the warp, although they are actually the same. The Glenurquhart form of the Russell has the bold overcheck on each side of the 4 and 4 part of the check, the whole pattern being no less than 6½ inches.

THE GLENQUOICH is unique. It is a very small design, the warp ⅝-inch of white and ⅛-inch of black crossed in the weft with a dull warm drab for white, the black being used in both directions. Glenquoich, in the North-West Highlands, boasts the highest rainfall in Scotland – about 120 inches – and fittingly contains one of the biggest of our Hydro-Electric Schemes.

THE MINMORE, introduced by Mr Smith Grant in his Strathspey estates, is a very similar colour with a deep-green check. These two checks are the only examples we have seen of this method of varying the Shepherd ground.

THE COIGACH is again the representative of a large class. In it, the Shepherd has been varied by making its checks alternately black and strong red-brown, a very bold and original idea that, as we mentioned in our first article, forms a bond of union between Scotland and the United States through its adoption about 1874 as the club check of one of the American Gun Clubs. Perhaps it is because the original name of this fine design is quite a hard problem for those who are not a native of Bonnie Scotland that its new name of Gunclub became the world name for this, the third of the three great types that dominate the designing of the vast bulk of ordinary checked woollen cloths – the Shepherd, the Glenurquhart and the Gunclub.

THE DACRE is the Coigach boldly magnified by two. Its checks are ⅜-inch each. THE SEAFORTH, used by the Seaforth Highlanders as a tweed, is a beautiful scheme of two tones of russet on a white ground and overchecked with a brighter russet, one check bigger than the Glenfeshie Mixture, so as to fit the Gunclub ground. THE DUPPLIN is the Coigach with a scarlet overcheck, like the Seaforth THE STRATHSPEY the same, with a dark-blue overcheck.

THE LOCHMORE uses a greenish Lovat mixture to replace the black of the Coigach, and THE GAIRLOCH is the Coigach itself with a dull-yellow mixture replacing the white in the weft. THE GLENMORRISTON is the Coigach arrangement with dark blue and a light, slightly greenish Lovat mixture as the alternate colours. This valley of Glenmorriston is the next towards the west of Glen Urquhart and is part of the wide Seafield estates. Like the Glenurquhart

Check, the pattern belongs to the reign of Lady Caroline.

THE HAY or DUPPLIN is the same as the Strathspey, with a brown that is much lighter and yellower than the Coigach brown, so that its whole effect is different.

THE BROOKE, used on Lord Burton's estates, uses black-and-white twist and a light Lovat mixture as the alternate colours, and a skeleton overcheck of scarlet edging one of the Lovat checks. It is made with both silver-grey and white for the ground. The only other check we have seen using this type of overcheck is THE KINTAIL, the district in which Prince Charles Edward landed in '45. The alternate ground colours are a pale grey and a greenish drab.

THE ARNDILLY, from Strathspey, is a somewhat unusual and beautiful scheme. The ground a dull white – a "laid" white as it is called in the Highlands – and the alternate colours black and greenish fawn in the warp, black and reddish-fawn in the weft; the overcheck formed by replacing every third fawn check with a bar half dull peacock blue and half reseda green. It dates from before 1870, when it was introduced at Meggernie Castle in Glen Lyon by Ronald Stewart Menzies of Culdares, the father of the present owner, Colonel W. Stewart Menzies.

Though THE WYVIS is a Gunclub, it is so unlike the other Gunclubs as to require a special description. It is extremely bold, about 2¼ inches on the repeat. The ground is a deep fawn of the tint of withered bracken or dead beech leaves. The alternating colours are a solid, dull, browny-green moss shade and a sprinkled bar of twist yarns of bright green, moss shade and grey. Colonel Shoolbread, the owner, says it is very good on the hills. His note on the pattern so aptly covers a phase of these checks that it is tempting to quote: "Though I had no personal share in its designing and should not myself have chosen so large a check pattern, the mere size of the pattern possibly helps the invisibility of it on the hill – and, after all, nearly every bird and beast in the hill is brown of some shade or other, is it not?" Some time we hope to devote a number to this most interesting phase of "camouflage". The Wyvis was introduced about 45 years ago. Ben Wyvis, one of the most prominent of our Scottish mountains, dominates this forest and looks down upon Strathpeffer in Ross-shire. Strathpeffer was the base of the American Red Cross in our country during the Great War. It is a health resort of old standing, long famous for its mineral springs and pleasant climate, so with its many hotels transformed into hospitals, it formed an ideal place for such a purpose.

THE FANNICH is a check so unusual in construction as to demand special detail. The warp pattern is on 18 threads: white 6, Lovat Mixture 3, black 2, yellow 2, black 2, Lovat 3. The weft is a simple Gunclub repeating on 24 – white ground, black and Lovat the alternate colours.

THE SCOTS GUARD CHECK is one of the club checks chosen by the officers of several of our regiments for the members of their mess when out of uniform. In this, a bold basket effect is given by the reversing of the pattern, produced by two threads of light and two of dark warp and weft on our common twill weave. This is done by means of an overcheck of four threads, which reverses the position of the light and dark colours relative to the weave.

There is also a small edition in black and white of the original Glenurquhart where the same effect is used. It is about two-thirds of the size of the one illustrated, the alternate squares of the hairlines being reversed. This fine pattern is sometimes wrongly described as the Small Glen – a valley of Perthshire, far south of its native Glen Urquhart. Its proper name is simply THE SMALL GLENURQUHART.

Much the darkest of all Districts is THE CARNOUSIE. The ground is developed in black and black twisted with russet. It is about the size of the Small Glenurquhart, without the basket effect of the 2 and 2 part. Every alternate part of the 4 and 4 is sided with a bold crimson overcheck. Carnousie is on the Deveron, not far from Turriff in Aberdeenshire.

THE STRATHMASHIE is a large and very bold Glenurquhart, nearly 8 inches on the repeat. Using the colours of the Coigach, it is brown-and-white warp, black-and-white weft, the strong overchecking up the sides of the 4 and 4 part being ingeniously obtained by reversing the warp and weft colours. Its history is amusing. Some forty years ago, negotiations were started by one of our principal London tailors to arrange a check for the whole Brigade of Guards, instead of the individual regimental checks that we have enumerated. Finally, the negotiations failed, and, with good Scottish economy, the bold and excellent design was christened Strathmashie – a real place, but not the name of a forest.

There is a considerable list of variations of the 2 and 2 warp and weft effect. We have already referred to the Scots Guards – one of our illustrations. THE HORSE GUARDS use a brown-and-white ground overchecked every 3½ inches with six threads of bright navy. THE WELSH GUARDS, fawn ground with brown and red twist and an alternate 2-inch overcheck of light red and dark blue.

The Farquharsons of INVERCAULD – near neighbours of His Majesty at Balmoral – use a white ground with brown and drab twist overchecked every 2½ inches with bright tartan green. THE BATESON, from Shieldaig in the Gairloch district of Sutherland, is a strong red-brown and white, with pale yellow for white weft way. It is perhaps the most highly coloured in general effect of any – very invisible, nevertheless, in autumn in that country heavily overgrown with bracken.

The Malcolms of POLTALLOCH use a check in general aspect very like the Invercauld, but the overcheck is yellow crossed with red. THE GLENDOE estate in Inverness-shire uses a dull blue-grey and white ground with a very strong russet overcheck.

THE ERCHLESS is no longer used in the Forest of Erchless. It takes its name from Castle Erchless on the Beauly River to the west of Inverness. It is only a few miles from Strathpeffer. Castle Erchless is the seat of the head of the Chisholms, and the Forest extends over many miles of very high and rugged mountain country to the north. This most original design consists of a warp unit of 3 on the 4 thread weave, white, pale stone drab, and yellow, crossed by a weft of black twisted with white. It is a type that does not lend itself to great variation, and remains unique.

We have already touched on Prince Albert's BALMORAL, one of the few on an intricate weave. The warp arrangement is 1 of white, 2 of navy and white twist, Lord MINTO uses on his estates one of the darkest of the Districts, a deep, rich greenish mixture, almost as dark in its shade as the general effect of a holly tree.

THE DALHOUSIE, used by the Earl of Dalhousie, whose chief estate is not far south of Edinburgh, is quite unusual. It is a solid white warp crossed with a grey of a depth midway between black and white. The plain diagonal twill is broken every inch by reversing the twill for six threads. Every fourth reverse is dull green, and this dull green is checked with a corresponding bar of bright navy blue.

The Earl also has another very characteristic design for his northern estate of INVERMARK on the borders of Angus. It is an unusually heavy cloth even for a District. It is a true Glenurquhart, 3½ inches on the repeat. The ground is a strong olive-brown and white, the 4 and 4 part sided with a heavy navy overcheck, and also two threads of a bright, light scarlet – almost a carmine – down the centre of the 2 and 2 part.

THE KINLOCHEWE, from the head of Loch Maree, is of russet like the Seaforth, but is overchecked curiously by a thin check of one thread of black, and one of crimson in the white, crossed with a thin line of orange. These, being extra, throw the whole design out of position on the weave every alternate repeat of the pattern, and produce a marked and subtle effect. There is also a very handsome pattern, THE KINLOCHEWE GLENURQUHART. A pure Glenurquhart, 4½ inches overall, the dark colour of the warp black-and-yellow twist crossed with a dark camel's wool type of drab and white.

THE PRINCE OF WALES is a bold pattern of the Glenurquhart type. It is nine inches on the repeat, but, being a double arrangement, it hardly looks so large. The colours are the terra-cotta brown of the Ing and white. The general effect is a brownish pink. The 4 and 4 starts and ends with white and the dark slate overcheck is taken off the first and last brown expanded to six threads. The 2 and 2 starts and ends with dark so that a basket effect is produced. There is a not-very-well-authenticated story in our mills that it was made for King Edward VII when he was Prince.

THE BUCCLEUGH CHECK or TARTAN is the same as the Glenfeshie, but with sky blue for the red overcheck. The pattern is 5 by 6½ inches on the repeat. The ground is a Shepherd Check, ¼-inch of black and ¼-inch of white: the cloth a fine Saxony kilting. It was designed by Sir Richard Waldie Griffiths, Colonel of the 4th K.O.S.B. about 1908 and is worn by their pipers.

In 1951, the ROYAL SCOTS REGIMENTAL LOVAT was introduced and a length of the first web was presented to their Colonel-in-Chief, the Princess Royal. It is an attractive green Lovat overchecked at 1½ inches, with neat lines of red and yellow alternately, the overchecking colours of their tartan, the Hunting Stewart. The yellow is sided with the quiet green of the tartan ground.

We include THE THANE OF FIFE of doubtful parentage, but respectable age. It is a Glenurquhart very like the Mar in the ground, but overchecked with sixes of dark slate instead of green.

THE GLENISLA is used by the Earl of Airlie on his estates at Cortachy Castle near Kirriemuir in Angus. It is a small true Glenurquhart in off-white and dark brown one unit smaller than the Mar and without overcheck. The design is $2\frac{1}{8}$ inches overall.

These, then, are the principal examples of our District Checks. This somewhat pioneer effort is full of omissions, probably also of mistakes. It is necessarily somewhat disjointed and at times degenerates into language only understandable by the technical man. It was not easy to select points of interest and importance from so large an amount of unrelated detail. Some may think that its very modernity robs the subject of all claim to study. In fact, that in showing that our Scottish Districts Checks date only from last century, we have destroyed their interest and their romance. But the times and developments that brought them into being were times of vast social upheaval. A revolution, as is our wont, carried out without dust and bloodshed, but not less far-reaching for that; too near us yet to be completely pictured, too overcrowded with detail for us yet quite to grasp all its results and implications. Perhaps romance is to be found everywhere by the understanding mind, but however other places can make good their claim, there can be no doubt that amongst our mountains and glens he has lived since before the dawn of history and will live for ever...

> "...And all unseen
>   Romance brought up the nine-fifteen.
> Robed, crowned, and throned he wove his spell,
>   Where heart-blood beat, or hearth-smoke curled,
> With unconsidered miracle,
>   Hedged in a backward gazing world;
> Then taught his chosen bard to say:
>   'Our King was with us – yesterday!'"

Keep the Quality up!

The Shepherd Check

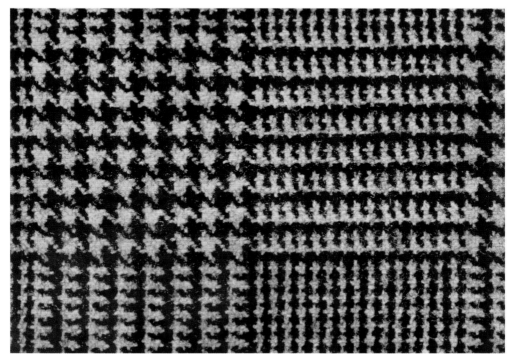

The Glenurquhart

The Mar

The Balmoral

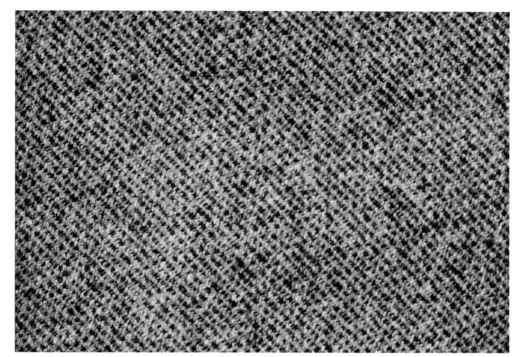

The Erchless

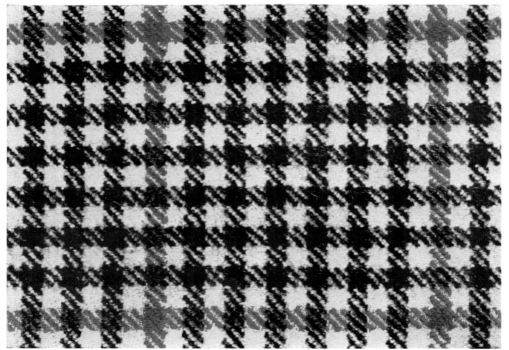

The Glenfeshie Mixture

The Scots Guards Check

The Coigach

TARTANS
PART II

THE name of General Wade must for ever be associated with the great highways and bridges, which opened up the Highlands in the earlier half of the eighteenth century.

"Had you seen those roads before they were made,
You would lift up your hands and bless General Wade."

He has, however, another claim to remembrance in connection with the Highlands, for it was, officially at least, through his initiative that the Highland soldier and the tartan were first introduced into the British Army. In 1724, Wade was sent to Scotland to reconnoitre the Highlands and observe their strength and resources. His report to the Government on the measures he considered necessary resulted in his being appointed Commander-in-Chief in Scotland.

In 1725, six independent Companies of Highlanders were raised for preserving the peace of the Highlands; each of these was commanded by a Highland gentleman of rank and position. The names of those commanders show that they were selected from clans that were considered well affected towards the Hanoverian Government. This experiment was very much on the principle of set a thief to catch a thief, but its ultimate result has been the addition of many glorious pages to British military history and a notable accession to the spectacular side of the Army.

One of the General's first orders to his new Companies reads thus: "Take care to provide a Plaid cloathing and Bonnets in the Highland Dress..., the Plaid of each Company to be as near as they can of the same sort and colour." The use of the word plaid when obviously meaning tartan is evidently due to a confusion of ideas which still persists in Sassenach minds and to which we have previously referred.

The colours eventually chosen were the black, blue and green, the familiar background of so many Highland tartans. It was, in fact, the ground of the Campbell (Chief), and the choice seems to have been dictated both by sentiment and reason: several of the Commanders were Campbells, and the subdued tone was more practicable than some of the more garish patterns. The rather sombre hue, as compared with the scarlet of the English troops, appears to have given the name of the Black Watch to these Companies, and when they were eventually absorbed in the British Army in 1739 and became the 42nd Regiment of the line, both the name and the tartan were retained. When this event took place, it is interesting to note that George II expressed a desire to inspect personally the uniform of his new regiment, and that on 15th January 1740, a "Serjeant and a Centinel" in Highland dress were duly presented to His Majesty, who set the seal of the Royal approval on the new uniform, and, we are glad to add, ordered the men "a handsome gratuity". We are sure a liquid refreshment would also have been greatly appreciated.

There are now five kilted regiments in the British Army. To give them their colloquial names, these are the Black Watch, the Argyll and Sutherlands, the Gordons, the Seaforths and the Camerons. In deciding the tartans for these regiments, the War Office seems to have followed the heraldic idea in using distinguishing overchecks on the same ground. The Argyll and Sutherlands wear the Black Watch or 42nd tartan, but whereas the older regiment put the blue bar out in the pleat, the Argylls show the green; this difference is accentuated in the case of the officers, as their green is of a lighter tone than the men's. This predilection for green is not without its significance: the Sutherland tartan, it may be explained, is practically the same as the Black Watch, but the green is brighter and gives the predominant tone. When the War Department committed the egregious blunder of linking the 91st Argyllshire and the 93rd Sutherlandshire – two regiments with no common traditions and territorially far apart – an effort appears to have been subsequently made to stress the Sutherland connection.

The Gordon tartan is simply the Black Watch with a yellow overcheck superimposed, and the Seaforths wear the Mackenzie, which has a red and two whites alternately. It is worthy of note that both these families have adopted these military tartans for their personal use. The Gordons, not being a Highland family, were formerly without one, but in the case of the Mackenzies, there seems no very obvious reason except, perhaps, personal preference.

Only in the case of the 79th Camerons has a different note been struck. This regiment was raised by Sir Alan Cameron of Erracht in 1798. The question of a tartan was difficult to decide, as the Cameron itself was too red to go with the regulation scarlet tunic. The problem was solved by the suggestion of old Mrs Cameron, Alan's mother, herself a Macdonald, to put the yellow overcheck of the Cameron on the Macdonald tartan; thus was produced the pattern known as the Erracht Cameron, on which a brave regiment has shed imperishable lustre.

The Lowland regiments, although not kilted, have each their distinctive tartans; these are worn as trousers by the men and as trews and riding breeches by the officers. The pipers in all regiments wear kilts. The difference between trews and trousers is that in the old Highland trews, in order to preserve the complete design of the tartan as far as possible, there is a seam only on the inner side of the leg, whereas, of course, in trousers, originally designed for plain colours or small patterns, there are seams on both the outside and inside of the legs.

The Royal Scots, the first regiment of the line, as becomes its Royal title, wears the Hunting Stuart – black, blue and green ground with intersecting overchecks of yellow and red. On the occasion of the 300th anniversary of the embodiment of the regiment, his present Majesty conferred on the pipers of the regiment the honour of wearing his personal tartan, the Royal Stuart. This is a privilege shared with the pipers of three other regiments, the Black Watch (Royal Highlanders), the King's Own Scottish Borderers and the Scots Guards.

The King's Own Scottish Borderers wear the Leslie tartan, a fact sufficiently explained by the old connection of that family with the regiment.

The Douglas tartan is worn by the Cameronians (Scottish Rifles). This has a territorial significance: the first Colonel was the Earl of Angus and the regiment is recruited in the Douglas Country.

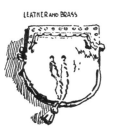

The Royal Scots Fusiliers wear the Black Watch, but their pipers are kilted with the Erskine. The only unkilted Highland regiment, the Highland Light Infantry, wear the Mackenzie tartan, but in a larger set than the version worn by the Seaforths.

Military tartans for the rank and file are nearly all made from Scottish wool, principally the native Cheviot. For officers' cloth, the finer Colonial Merino is used. The type of cloth called hard tartan is greatly in favour for civilian wear. This is made from Crossbred worsted. It is woven tight in the loom and is practically unmilled. It handles almost like canvas, but water runs off it as off a duck's back instead of soaking in, and it has excellent pleating qualities. These qualities would both appeal to the Highlander of the old days, and in the times before worsted could be imported into the Highlands, the same effect would be obtained by twining the woollen yarn very hard, weaving very tightly, and reducing the waulking or felting process to a minimum. Thus, we suppose, the old hard tartan was produced.

The military tartans are all woven in the Scottish mills. Originally, appropriately enough, the Bannockburn mills almost exclusively supplied the War Office, but later on the source of supply was broadened. During the Great War, the demand was increased a hundredfold, but the mills rose nobly to the occasion. Depleted of the best of their manhood, the old men, the women and the boys carried on at high pressure, working long hours to clothe the men in the field. Many a time, as the shuttles sped to and fro across the loom, must the weaver lassie's thoughts have gone to her own braw lad that her web was perhaps to clothe. Many a time must the mother – for many were called back from their homes to tend the looms – have thought of that "crumpled heap of bloody rags" that some day might hide all that was left of her son. In the early days of the war, the territorial basis of our army sometimes left a whole parish almost swept bare of its manhood after some disastrous action, and losses seldom came singly.

Early in the war, when we were being much pressed for khaki cloth, and even for horizon blue to clothe the French Army, Lochiel, who was then raising a battalion of his own Camerons, found it impossible to get any tartan from the Royal Army Clothing Department. He 'phoned a Border manufacturer and asked what could be done. It was the call of the blood, khaki and horizon blue might go hang – the answer came, "Damn the War Office, your men shall have their kilts."

It takes seven yards of cloth 27 inches wide to make a kilt. The cloth is woven 54 or 56 inches and is split up the middle, the outer selvedge always forming the lower edge of the kilt. In some cases, the pattern has to be turned in the middle for this purpose, as the lower edge of the kilt must always be at the same point or thread in the pattern – usually in an overchecked pattern about 3 or 4 inches from the overcheck. Similarly, in trews or trousers a particular line of the pattern must follow the crease.

A good weaver can turn out about 125 yards of "R. & F. thin" (as the kilting of the rank and file is called) in a week. In one small Border village, the united efforts of the weavers resulted in a weekly output of 15,000 yards (sufficient to clothe four battalions); this was maintained over many weeks. Dyeing, or rather the procuring of dyestuffs, also presented a problem, and it is to be feared that many of the dyes got by the Government from neutral sources were really of German origin.

We have dwelt perhaps rather long on the military aspect of our subject, but the Highlanders are a fighting race.

The tartan kilt was not making its first appearance on the battlefields of the Continent when the newly formed Black Watch made their debut with distinction at Fontenoy. Scottish soldiers had served in Continental armies for centuries before, and there is an old German print still extant depicting Highland warriors in their native garb. This dates from the Thirty Years War. As the drawing of the tartan is even more vague than that of the dress, it cannot be said to what clan they belong!

It is impossible in a written description to give any very adequate idea of a particular tartan. The most complete published collection is W. & A. K. Johnston's 2 vol. "Tartans of the Clans and Septs of Scotland", and their little handbook. There is a vast literature on the subject, and perhaps the most surprising thing about it all is the very small amount of definite information that research has unearthed. Nearly all Highland lore has existed by oral tradition, and even such a comparatively modern and definite subject as the design of the original tartan of the Black Watch is unknown. The cost, the names of the weavers, the yardage used, the modes of collection and conveyance are all recorded, but the design was known to everyone, so why say anything about it? And so the antiquarians are baffled and an entertaining problem is there for our amusement!

No proper classification of the tartans can be given, for their colour variations do not run on any special lines. There are two types the reader will often come across: Hunting and Dress. Where a tartan was in its ordinary form too brilliant for safety in the field or use on the hill, a quieter type of colour was used; sometimes quite a different design, like the Hunting Stuart, which in no way resembles the Royal Stuart, sometimes by the substitution of brown or other dark colour for scarlet, as in the Chisholm and the Fraser. In the Dress tartans, the opposite happens. When the regular tartan has seemed too sombre for ceremonial occasions, scarlet or white takes the place of some darker colour. But no very definite rule has ever been formulated for these changes and not all tartans show both varieties.

A distinctive tartan of interesting associations is the Rob Roy, with its large bases of black and red with the necessary twilled crossings; altogether there is not a very great number of individual colours, but the checks made from them are, as will be seen, extremely numerous and varied.

Generally speaking, in studying the individual clans and their branches, you will find a more or less definite plan in which slight changes of colour or design were introduced as marks of cadency while adhering to the general set of the original or Chieftain's tartan. Sometimes certain tartans are termed old, such as the Old Stewart, the Old MacCallum, the Old Sutherland and the Old Urquhart; these may either have been abandoned or the branch of the clan who wore them has ceased to exist as a separate entity.

There are, besides, black-and-white versions of several of the tartans, but the exact purpose they were intended to serve is not quite clear; amongst these are the Macleod, the Menzies and the Scott.

Altogether, it is a most fascinating study, and the interest is heightened by the degrees of uncertainty and the mists of controversy that surround almost every branch of the subject.

The Highland costume has been developed to a degree of barbaric splendour shown by few national costumes. It is particularly rich in accessories. These we have touched on in our little illustrations – some day we may find time to revert to this most absorbing side issue, now we can but touch on this rich theme. In "Scottish Woollens" No. 5, our illustration showed The MacNab in full regimentals. Here, we have illustrated four more forms of the purse or sporran. The dirk or dagger, sometimes worn in the stocking, sometimes hanging from the sword belt, was often very richly ornamented. Quite often, the scabbard contained also a small knife and fork. Then in head-dresses there is great variety: the Balmoral bonnet illustrated is worn by the young man who gazes from the Scottish-American War Memorial across the flowery valley of Princes Street Gardens up to the great rock of Edinburgh Castle. Then there are the shoulder brooches that held the plaids, often lovely examples of jewellers' work. The one we illustrate, worn almost smooth, just shows traces of the Thistle and the Rose, emblems of a strangely solid union of strangely diverse elements. Then there are kilt pins, shoe buckles, buttons, and hosts of other details, not to mention all the lovely work spent on shields and swords and guns and pistols and... and... and...

Note. Our military illustrations are from the magnificent new Scottish Regimental Museum in Edinburgh Castle, and our others from the Scottish National Museum of Antiquities, also in Edinburgh.

A DISSERTATION ON PATTERNS
PART I

E editors ought, as usual, to apologise for being late. Our irregularities have been worse than ever lately. Our secretary has had shoals of letters inquiring about our issues, and especially our last, which, after the article itself was printed, was unexpectedly delayed. It proved very difficult to find a suitable paper for our new supplementary plates. We had to find a paper to give a beautiful black and at the same time to give a fine texture for ordinary mechanical printing. We were seeking for something of the texture of hand-printed wood blocks in ordinary machine work, for our edition has now far exceeded all possibilities of handwork. To make up for our dilatoriness, we shall follow with Part II of our Dissertation in four weeks or so.

Our last few numbers have taken us into the borders of history, which was not altogether the programme we had arranged for ourselves. To judge by the correspondence they have produced, we seem to have been justified in dealing with tartans and District Checks, as our last four numbers have been surprisingly successful. There is a vast literature dealing with that most national type of design, the tartan, and there we had as our chief difficulty the summarising of a great mass of existing work. With the District Checks, the problem was somewhat different, for, as far as our investigations disclosed, nothing had been written on the subject apart from advertisements, which as a rule are more concerned in the picturesque than the truthful. Some day, we shall revert to other aspects of both our Checks and our tartans. Some of these days also we have promised ourselves to deal with the old native craft of weaving in Harris and the other parts of the Highlands, but here, again, there is remarkably little written that is more than the passing

49

impressions of tourists or the picturesque inventions of journalists.

The making of patterns is a much-debated subject in the Scottish Woollen Trade just now. In an essentially novelty trade like ours, the Pattern Department is in a way the most important in a mill. The money that the retail section of the trade spends on advertising, we spend on pattern making. Extravagant as the expenditure looks when it appears on the schedule of working costs, it seems as impossible to cut it down as it is for the great store to reduce its publicity and propaganda accounts. Admitted that there is a great deal of waste in pattern work: a great deal of inconsiderate use of patterns by the distributors – both in asking for needless patterns and thoughtlessly keeping patterns when making selections – and in the designing rooms, where useless ideas are often expensively developed. There is also a great wastage by theft of various degrees of directness – from the dealers who deliberately collect designs for sale, to the less-direct way of handing over designs to makers who did not invent them – for an idea, though intangible, may have cost a large sum to produce and is as certainly the property of its producer as his ox or his ass. But taking all things into account, it seems hardly possible for the Scottish manufacturers as a whole to reduce drastically their pattern costs if Scottish Woollens are to continue to lead in the fastidious and fashionable trade that they at present serve.

It is not altogether easy to explain technical matters to people not acquainted with the jargon of the trade. Everyday expressions to us are apt to be quite incomprehensible to others who have not been brought up inside a mill. For example, we are going to use the expression "overcheck" or "overplaid", which are English and American for the same thing. An overcheck, as the name suggests, is a check laid over some ground. The definite illustration we are going to use in our description of range making is the little black and white check worn by the shepherds of the Scottish Borders for the great shawls they carried to protect themselves in cold weather. It is illustrated in our District Checks supplement. In the Glenfeshie, the scarlet check is overlaid on this ground and is called an overcheck. The other word that perhaps needs explanation is "range", which is standard English, but is here used in a certain narrow technical sense, the explanation of which is one of the objects of our dissertation. It just means a series of patterns displayed in a particular manner, and becomes a sort of specialised noun not so very remote from its ordinary meaning.

Other technical terms, such as "warping" and various parts of looms, must await our paper on weaving for full explanation. Meanwhile, to be going on with, the "warp" is the series of threads fixed in the loom – the long way of the cloth, in fact – and the "weft" is the series carried across by the shuttle. The Old English word "woof" is now almost wholly a literary word, and is the old form of "weft".

We have always claimed that the undoubted lead we hold in the fancy woollen trade is not a matter of chance and not altogether a matter of harder work or more acute intelligence than is to be found elsewhere. That would be a claim too immodest even for us who are not famed for modesty. It is rather a national aptitude in the land, just as every country grows or produces something peculiarly its own.

It is not technical instruction that adds that final touch that makes a pattern range live. Always and everywhere, it is that intangible essence that transmutes our dross into gold. That sort of felicity that maketh an excellent thing in music. That part of the poet that is born not made. We in Scotland are well served by our circumstances. Nature in the long run is the fountain of such inspiration, the ultimate fountain of all life, as our city dwellers often forget. We have an incomparable variety of scenery – climate, geology, all our circumstances combine to give us endless variety of colour; a wealth of colour far more brilliant than elsewhere – in, as we might say, its everyday appearance. Did not Leonardo da Vinci when he came north from his native Italy, with its "grey repose of light", marvel at the exquisite blueness of the sky? Did not Linnaeus, that wonderful cataloguer of our plants and animals, fall on his knees and thank God for the spring glory of our gorse? Who that has seen them can forget the purple miles of our August moorlands, or the golden fairyland of our autumns of birch and bracken? It is not in Scotland but one fleeting moment, but every moment, so that men dispute which is the loveliest season of the year. More than that, we have a profound inherited love of Nature in all her aspects, as is witnessed by our great store of folk-songs, one of the finest in the world and showing everywhere a strange sensitiveness to landscape beauty. With such a heritage in the midst of such surroundings, how could we fail in inspiration?

That is something of the spirit. Let us now consider the form in which that spirit is embodied.

Pattern work at all its stages is extraordinarily wasteful in a weaving plant, chiefly owing to certain points in the arranging of a job for the loom. It must

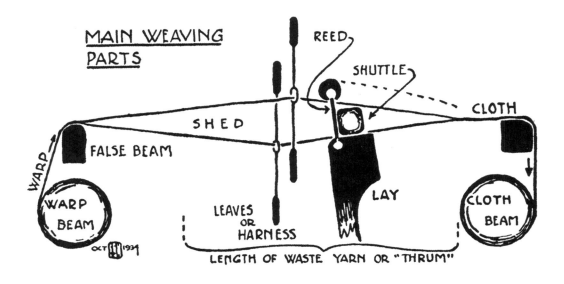

often have been a heart-break to the housewife in the old home-weaving days to see thrown away so many yards of the thread that had cost her laborious hours of skilled work to spin.

Let us follow in outline the history of a design from its start as a more or less indefinite idea in the brain of the designer to its arrival in the garment. Let us suppose it is to be developed in a cloth already established. From the available colourings of the yarns already in use for that cloth, the designer picks out a group of shades that seem most likely to give him the result he has imagined, and arranges them on a suitable weave. The necessary working instructions are written out and the warper collects the yarns specified and prepares a small length, let us say two yards long. This will yield nearly a yard of cloth, which the designer has concluded will give him enough scope for the development he requires. You will notice half the warp length will be wasted. This waste is the same for any length, and that is one reason for the high cost of weaving short lengths. This length of wasted yarn is called a "thrum", a word immortalised by Sir James Barrie in the title of his earliest and one of his greatest successes, "A Window in Thrums".

The warp is then rolled on the back beam of the loom and by hand each thread is drawn through a small eyelet in the weaving harness, whatever kind it may be. This process also is the same whatever length is being dealt with. It is illustrated in our Plate IV, which we send out as supplement to this number, although Plates II And III have not yet been issued.

A DISSERTATION ON PATTERNS
PART II

I N the weaving stage that follows, the work may be either carried out in a hand loom or in a modern power loom. In pattern making, the actual production part of the work is so trifling that it matters little to the speed whether the old-fashioned hand loom or the modern fast loom is used. In this way, the pattern rooms of the trade are the last refuges of the old hand methods that have been completely superseded in the general modern scheme of production.

The weaver ties his job into his loom and puts in the weft or shuttle threads for a few inches, and the "trial" is ready for the designer, who then proceeds to develop the idea. This is done by breaking off certain threads in the pattern and tying on to them threads of other colours. These are drawn back through the weaving harness and a few inches of the altered design woven. Let us say, for example, that the original ground chosen was a Shepherd Check in black and white, such as is illustrated in our District Checks supplement, and the designer wishes to develop his idea with overchecks or overplaids on the lines of the Glenfeshie. He breaks off a little group of the black yarn and on to each thread ties a scarlet thread. This little group is then drawn back through the harness and tied down so that it will not slip, and the weaver then with his shuttles follows the same arrangement of colours and so produces his new design, which we also illustrate. And so one after another, various developments of the original ground are tried out.

This trial we have imagined might yield a yard of cloth 18 inches wide – say three patterns in the width, for in the ordinary men's wear trade, 6 inches is a convenient size for the display of such sized designs as men's somewhat feeble nerves and very conservative tastes will endure. So we finish up with eighteen patterns all different. This bit of cloth like a patchwork mat is then passed through all the regular and complicated finishing processes given to full pieces of the cloth. This bit of cloth is called a "trial".

This preliminary work of trial making goes on for the most part in the gap that occurs between one showing season and the next – possibly a couple of months.

Next, the trials are assembled and looked over very carefully, and the most promising of the developments are chosen for range making.

Let us imagine that our Glenfeshie has been chosen for one idea. As things now stand, this is a childishly simple idea and would never be the subject of a trial in any ordinary cloth, for the days have long since passed when anyone connected with the trade has any doubt about what the Shepherd with a scarlet overcheck looks like. Yet

Mrs Ellice did not live so very long ago, and when her ingenuity devised this lovely pattern, it was a most original and outstanding novelty. We take it now as an easy illustration, so far have we moved.

Several methods of development are open to the designer. For example, he may consider the black and white as the base of the idea and develop black and white with different forms of overplaids, or he may consider the arrangement of the pattern chosen as his foundation. Let us suppose he decides on the latter scheme for his "range". This time, he will aim to produce a piece of cloth, say, 30 inches wide divided into five patterns 6 inches wide and, say, a yard long. His chosen pattern is, you will remember, black and white with a scarlet overcheck. He decides to arrange for a grey, a couple of browns and a dark green. The first 6 inches of his range will display his black-and-white ground; his second, grey and white, possibly with blue for the overcheck; his third, brown and white with orange; and so forth to the completion of his scheme. The sections of his warp will be separated by some special thread – possibly scarlet – to show where each pattern ends. The weaver then weaves,

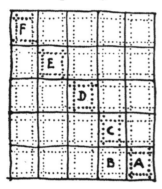

say, 7 inches of each. The result of all this activity is a piece of cloth 30 x 36 inches consisting of twenty-five squares of cloth of which five are "perfects" and twenty are various "cross effects", which may or may not be good according to the type of design that has been the base of the range. A piece of cloth of considerable cost and inconceivable utility! A glance at our sketch will at once show just what must happen. The first weaving is the black and white with scarlet overcheck A. These yarns carried by the shuttle must cross the cloth from side to side. The second pattern B is, therefore, grey and

white crossed with black and white, the overcheck blue crossed with red, and so forth over the whole range till F is reached with its green-and-white ground and possibly a gold overcheck. The "perfects" are obviously A, C, D, E and F.

As usual, when you make a statement of some kind, whole clouds of exceptions come humming out of the surrounding air. When we began French did we not all sadly wonder why we should bother to learn rules to which there were so many exceptions? Looking back, we see we have said "the yarns carried by the shuttle must cross. .They really don't need to. It is just a case of expediency. Bits may be put in by hand, and it is quite a common practice to make all the overplaids "perfect", for cross effects do not happen to be popular just now.

Next, this collection of "ranges" forms the season's "pattern set", and they are taken round the distributors to let them choose their styles – a privilege they often do not appreciate!

Let us suppose again our Glenfeshie is chosen. The distributor may decide to take three or four or more patterns, and chooses, let us say, A, the black and white; D and E, the browns; and F, the green and white. In the usual practice of the Scottish

Woollen Trade, this whole "style" or design becomes his exclusive property. It is not made again, and the remaining patterns on the range, although they may be quite as good as those chosen, go into the rag-bag. It has become a "confined" style. The distributor then orders for immediate delivery whatever length of cloth he needs for his travellers and a "piece", generally about 50 yards, 58 inches wide, for delivery in five or six months.

The pattern cloth might be anything from, say, half a yard up to 5 or 6 yards, 28 to 30 inches wide, in the ordinary wholesale merchanting trade or "model" lengths in the making-up trade.

The making of these lengths of pattern cloth finishes the manufacturer's part of the work. The tale is not yet ended. The distributor, if he is in the wholesale cloth trade, cuts his cloth up into bits of convenient size for his travellers to show to the tailors or the dressmakers who place their orders for the goods, which they in turn will later display to the connoisseur who requires a new suit. If the distributor is a maker-up of clothes, he makes a specimen coat or suit. Or if the cloth is destined for the fashion trade for ladies, its progress will be a little different and it will pass through the stage of the Paris or London dress shows and be displayed by carefully chosen mannequins before an audience as carefully fenced from gatecrashers as any society function. Thereafter, our Glenfeshie will appear worn by someone in the fullest confidence that being clad in Scottish Woollens he or she is safe from the slings and arrows of outrageous fortune. The life cycle is complete.

Besides this direct progression, there is the other modern development of sampling that has greatly increased the wastage of good cloth, and that is "bunching". In every tailor's shop hang pattern bunches, or for the ladies probably pattern books. To a greater and greater extent, this method is spreading, so that the tailor not only can show you a few lengths of cloth to choose from, but has countless bunched patterns from which you may make your choice, thus saving the tailor the capital involved in stocks, but in the long run adding to the cost of distribution. It is not easy to say which stage is most guilty of extravagance. Although the distributor pays full price to the manufacturer for the pattern cloth, this is but a small contribution towards the cost because of the exceeding wastefulness of making small quantities of cloth.

In this article, we shall not touch upon the sources of inspiration, or how the ingenious designer can reduce a lovely landscape or a beautiful picture or any charming scheme of colour he may see to the elements that constitute its attraction, and how out of these elements he can then build up a design for a suiting, or a scarf or a shawl. Just as in the studios of Hollywood, a scene full of colour is reduced to chemical and electrical symbols to be shown on the other side of the world as a picture in black and white accompanied by re-embodied voices, so can the accomplished designer reduce the riot of colour of the autumn woodlands or the calm beauty of a summer night to the ordered sequence of woollen threads to swathe the person of my lady or to clothe the lower limbs of her lord.

We are often asked what the designer does to instruct the maker of his cloth. Whether he paints a picture of his cloth or how he goes about his job. He does not paint, he does not do anything that looks even the least like cloth. He need be no artist in the everyday, immediate sense of the word. He makes a little plan symbolising the weave. We shall go on with the Glenfeshie. His plan looks like this. The crosses mean that the weaver arranges his loom to lift each thread twice and drop it twice when he is crossing his warp with his weft. We give a picture of the cloth much enlarged to illustrate the construction. Next, for the colour arrangement of the threads he writes: 6 of black and 6 of white for 78, and 6 of scarlet – according to the habit of the mill he may write this in many ways, but that is what it will amount to. He then gives a row of figures to show the width of the cloth; the size and quality of the threads, the number per inch; and all the rest, and the result no more resembles the brilliant Glenfeshie than the roll of film resembles what will later appear on the screen.

If you have followed this argument carefully, you will recognise that the inventing of a pattern begins a long time before it appears in the street. In fact, in the ordinary routine of pattern making, the interval is a little over a year. During winter, the Scotch manufacturer is making ranges for the next winter, and at the same time he is making the cloth for next summer.

You will also recognise that all this time the pattern department has been employed destroying good material. About half the yarn it obtains is wasted at once, and all the cloth it manages to weave goes to produce rags and nothing more excepting, with luck, orders. You will also appreciate the logical justice of the harsh American saying, "Nothing for nothing", and will understand that the world somehow, sometime, must pay for its patterns or do without them. Also that this pattern work has to be done by someone if we are to retain any high standard of beauty and novelty in our cloths. The mass producer is definitely not interested in novelty, for he can only run his plant on types that have already been accepted by the world, and have reached the stage of being required in bulk.

A WORD ON WEAVING

EAVING should have been outlined near the beginning of our series if we had followed a purely logical sequence. But in this bundling up of so many diverse things, as Montaigne puts it, we have not made any special logical rule, or rather have frequently designed a disciplined procession – horse, foot and guns – only to find our interests taking us down byways and into odd corners of history – a fine, mixed metaphor! Anyhow, in "Scottish Woollens", we are dealing with an Art not a Science, so perhaps fancy is a better leader than logic.

To tell the truth, we have been frightened of the subject. Tartans was a big subject that has filled a shelf or two of volumes from the most sumptuous folios down to quite humble small books, but weaving has filled whole libraries. It seems a hopeless job to deal with such a subject in four pages. In fact, we can only touch on a detail or two to suggest in a way the vastness of our spaces, the wonderful diverse lines of human activity, human invention, human effort that have gone to the evolution of the modern industry of weaving. Weaving is one of the great arts – world wide, set at the very gates of civilisation – uniting in a way all civilisations, all barbarisms, all people save those in the tropics, in that desperate struggle for life against the implacable destroyer and creator, Nature. It is always to these few universal arts that we must go for the history of the race. Building developed into architecture, and carries with it our only knowledge of man's earliest struggle for protection against man and beast and cold. This developing art gives us our only knowledge of races that have vanished like breath from a window pane. As difficulties were surmounted, the art blossomed into some of the loveliest flowerings of the human spirit, and mankind, freed from the bondage of necessity, lavished on his buildings the imagery of his dreams.

Weaving, in the same way, has developed from the purely primitive function of protection to a vehicle of thought and imagination. Weaving did more than steam, more than aircraft, to tell us of the world and other people. It was sails that brought the civilisation of the Mediterranean to our land, that brought the various ingredients together that made the Anglo-Saxon race, that joined the great continents of America to the outside world – Phoenicians, Venetians, Vikings, Conquistadores, Puritan fathers, French émigrés, Highlanders cleared from their native glens to make room for sheep. And as though the subject were too confined, the American expedition at present exploring the ancient sites of The Bible has just unearthed coarse linens evidently woven two or three thousand years before the Birth of Christ.

But this runs away with us. Our business is with Scottish Woollens and how the old craft developed into the great mechanical industry of today. The trade has kept  its old craft tradition in Scotland. The old, skilled craft evolved slowly in our old, poor country, much isolated by its poverty and, as things then were, by its remoteness from the centres of light in southern Europe. It is to this ancient and still well-remembered ancestry that our Scottish Woollen Trade owes its marked individuality.

In the construction of ordinary cloths, there are two sets of threads: the warp, running the long way of the web of cloth and for ordinary purposes of clothing from your head to your feet; and the crossthreads, the weft, or more anciently the "woof", a word only remembered nowadays by poets. In the simplest form of cloth construction, the first weft thread is passed under the first warp thread and over the second and so on right across; the second weft thread, which is really the same thread on its return journey, passes over the first warp thread and under the second, and this simple weave is called the "plain weave". But the great bulk of Scottish Woollens are made in a denser and more pliable weave, which we call the "common twill", but which has many other names elsewhere. It is over two and under two, moving one thread onwards each time. Apart from certain figuring threads used in decoration of cloths and certain threads forming pile effects such as carpets, tapestries and velvets, all woven cloths are constructed on these lines.

Perhaps the best way to deal with our job is to visit one of our Scottish mills, somewhere in the country amongst trees and fields and hills, probably employing about three hundred, possibly much less. We are not mass producers. No firm doing specialised novelty work can be big. To begin with, it would be beyond the wit of man to produce novelty in bulk. If bulk comes in at the door, novelty flies out of the window!

As we walk towards the Weaving Shed, a thin chattering fills the air, while somehow through it runs a rhythmic metallic clink, a sound that suggests thousands of typewriters all at work with the distant sound of a blacksmith at his anvil, overlaid on the chattering background of sound as the clear tones of the solo violin rise through the complex background of the orchestration.

As we open the door, an appalling clamour overwhelms us. A noise in which lecturing is impossible and even thought seems obliterated. Yet the girls and men seem to go about their business unaware of the pandemonium. It is very seldom that a worker fails to become completely accustomed to the outrageous noise or to be in the least deafened by it. Possibly the fact that outside the weaving shed the sound hardly carries means that the volume is not great, and so the ear after the first shock can endure the sound without injury.

As the yarn is brought in from the Spinning Room, it is fast wound on to various types of bobbins or, as we call them, pirns. Other machines are winding down hanks of coloured yarns that have been dyed in the yarn. For the warps, the yarn is usually wound on "cheeses" – solid cylinders of yarn with a wooden core possibly 6 inches long and 4 or five 5 in diameter – holding somewhere about three-quarters of a pound. Several ingenious types of machines are winding the weft on to long, narrow bobbins for the shuttles. The slick work of the girls who tend these machines is delightful to watch – as is all dexterity. True, the eye is easy to deceive, but no eye can

WARPERS' CHEESES AND
WEAVERS PIRNS FULL AND
EMPTY

follow the movement of the worker's fingers as she ties one thread to another – the dexterity of the conjurer applied to common jobs.

Next comes the warping, rows upon row of the cheeses are being built into the bank of the warping mill. A "bank" is a tall holder something like a bookcase, and in it, each on its steel spindle, the cheeses are arranged according to the pattern to be produced, just as the volumes in a bookcase follow some prearranged order. From there, these threads are drawn off on to the great sparred cylinder of the mill, where, by various devices, each thread is kept in its proper place. And as the cheeses whirl round, the bankboys watch the whole rushing spider's web to signal to the warper to stop his mill if a thread breaks or runs out. An elaborate and tricky job on complicated work such as our Scottish manufacturers make.

The bell rings to show the needed length has been warped, and then the contents of the mill cylinder are unwound on to the weaver's beam, a heavy, strong, wood-clad steel affair, say, nine feet long and eight or nine inches in diameter. It is shown in the diminutive pattern loom size in our plate of Drawing. "And the staff of his spear was like a weaver's beam", an ill weapon to fight with a sling and smooth stones from the brook!

Next comes the skilly job of Drawing. Every individual thread of the warp on the beam has to be drawn separately through a little eyelet in the weaving harness, again all according to a more or less elaborate scheme, rhythmic and balanced in its sequences like a verse of poetry, but often more elaborate in its scheme than any verse.

And all this time other preparations are going on. Some yarns are going through the doubling machines where two or three or more threads are being twisted together, sometimes at two or even three stages so as to produce some particular effect of colour blending, sometimes only to produce thicker or stronger threads. The twister spindles run invisibly at possibly two or three thousand revolutions per minute, putting on the turns per inch with mathematical precision according to whatever may have been decided. "Chains" are being put together by which the automatic action of the power loom changes the shuttle colours according to the pattern of the cloth, however intricate the design may be. Other chains are being made up by which the weaving mechanism is controlled and by means of which the actual construction of the cloth is decided, apart altogether from the colour scheme it may be carrying.

And so we arrive at the point where all these diverse activities converge in the power loom. The weaver's beam is lifted in and connected to the machinery. The weaving harness with its innumerable threads, each in its little eyelet, is tied up. The warp threads are attached to the cloth beam in front of the loom. The chains for the weaving and shuttle mechanisms are placed in position. The wheels governing the number of weft threads per inch are put on. The "reed" for beating up the weft threads put across the web by the shuttles is fixed in the "lay". The different colours for the shuttles are brought from the winding frames and put into their allotted shuttles. The shuttles are placed in their proper "boxes". The power-loom tuner in charge of the gang of looms weaves through a repeat or two of the pattern, examines the work carefully along with the standard for that pattern and sees that no thread has been wrongly placed. The man in charge of the work of the Power-loom Shed checks everything over again and sends for the weaver who looks after that loom. The weaver pulls over the starting handle and her machine adds its part to the infernal pandemonium.

A MODERN POWER LOOM

NOTE. Space does not allow us to reprint the diagrams from No. 1 illustrating weave constructions, nor from No. 10 showing the chief parts of the loom. The hand loom is from a sketch by the late James Riddel, A.R.S.A., R.S.W., of an old weaver at Kirriemuir, Barrie's Thrums.

SHETLAND WOOL

 HETLAND wool has long been famed for its very special qualities. It is a curious thing that the finest of British wools come from the two ends of the British Isles. South Downs from the rolling smooth hills that end in the cliffs of the English Channel, and the wools of Shetland – that windswept, treeless, rugged group of rocky islands that almost touch the region of the midnight sun. The Shetlands form a fairly compact group, about 70 miles from north to south, and about half that distance from east to west. Besides the main group, there is one detached island to the west – Foula – and then to the south the famous Fair Isle, which forms a sort of half-way house to the Orkneys, which, in turn, are only separated from the northernmost point of Scotland at John o' Groats by the narrow and dangerous waters of the Pentland Firth. It is a matter of opinion what constitutes an island. The inhabitants of Bermuda claim they have one for every day in the year. Some authorities might make out a like claim for the Shetlands: there are twenty-nine inhabited by people, about seventy more inhabited only by sheep, and unnumbered thousands inhabited by seals and cormorants and innumerable hosts of sea-fowl. There are also countless spiritual inhabitants – spirits of the dead and spirits of the deep, giants and trows, elves and fairies, mermaids, seal maidens, water-horses, finns, and ghosts and devils – who inhabit the wild precipices, caves, reefs and skerries that make up the group. It is a terrible sea in which the islands are set, where the Atlantic and the North Sea war together. It was not for nothing that Scapa Flow in the Orkneys was made the base of the British Fleet during the Great War.

As one writer says of Shetland: "It lies amidst boiling seas. Terrible tempests rage round its coasts. There is scarce a feal-thatched cottage within its bounds from which the cruel sea has not taken toll of its inmates." The shortest day is only five and a half hours, but the summers are almost nightless, and in summer calms its windswept bareness takes on that tender and wistful loveliness only to be found where life has a hard struggle to maintain itself against the elements. This northern outpost of Scotland was another of the parts of his native country discovered to the world by the genius of Sir Walter Scott, for before the appearance of "The Pirate", Shetland was indeed an unknown land. The climate is not cold. It is damp and mild. There is rarely either frost or snow, and this to a great extent accounts for the lovely softness of the native wool. In times not yet so very remote, the almost incredible ignorance about these islands can only be suggested by an anecdote. About 1810, the Commissioners of the Customs refused to pay the herring bounty on some winter herrings caught in the Shetland waters. The islands, they said, were surrounded by ice at that season of the year, and obviously no fish could possibly have been caught there! After all, the Shetlands are only between two and three hundred miles north of Edinburgh – reached in a short flight of the Highland Airways service from Inverness, or a little more from Aberdeen.

In early days, the Shetlands, like most of the islands off the Scottish coast, belonged to Norway, and the name is derived from the Scandinavian, meaning High-land – Hjaltland – Zetland – Shetland.

Up till the fifteenth century, Scotland had for long paid a sort of blackmail to Norway for the Hebrides, but various difficulties had been accumulating on the Scottish Crown, and in 1468 matters had come to such a pass that Parliament decided, like many a modem assembly, that something must be done. The Norway dues were long in arrears, and the "something" that emerged was the marriage of the young King James III with Princess Margaret, daughter of King Christian of Norway. In turn, King Christian found he could not pay his daughter's dowry, and gave the islands in pledge. Two years later, King James III bought them, and so another step was taken in the consolidation of the rising Kingdom of the Scots. The little Princess – only twelve years old when she was married at Holyrood Palace in Edinburgh with "unusual magnificence" – proved the most valuable part of the bargain, for, according to Hume Brown, "her prudence and virtuous living were to endear her to every class of her subjects". For a thousand years before, and some hundreds after, the history of the Shetlands was as rough and tempestuous as these wild seas – dim, unresting, only vaguely seen through mists. Under these ages of government, or ungovernment, the life of the islands went on pretty much unchanged, leaving its trace in land tenure, place names, the northern flavour of the dialect, and the clear influence of Norse blood in the people.

The preamble is not so irrelevant as may appear, for it is this isolation that has to so marked an extent preserved the characteristics of the Shetland sheep – little brisk beasts almost as ill to confine within fences as deer. Whether they are truly native, or whether they were original Norse, is seemingly still a matter of dispute. It is pretty definitely believed that the little Shetland ponies and the small, silky-haired cattle were introduced by the Vikings. In 1790, the Highland Society of Scotland – the ancestor of the chief agricultural organisation of Scotland, now popularly known as "The Royal" – appointed a Committee to report on Shetland wool and to suggest means of improving it. Their little old report lies on the table as we write. Printed at Edinburgh, "anno 1790", and sold by Burns's friend and first publisher, William Creech, amongst others. It is a beautifully printed clean old job with "f's" for w s's" in the old manner. We suppose it would be described as foolscap octavo.

To the eye, the chief characteristic of the true Shetland wool is a curious mixture of coarse and fine long and short fibres mixed all through the fleece. The general length of the wool is medium. Its touch is curiously soft and silky, reminiscent of fine Alpaca, or even of Chinese Cashmere – much softer than its appearance suggests. It felts well, and a quaint footnote in the report says "there can be no doubt of its answering for hats, which even the women in that part of the country might wear, with advantage to their looks and appearance". We wonder if the ladies "in that part of the country" really set more store on quality than on fashion in those days! We suspect it was the reporters, and not their wives, who put down that sentiment. Thereafter they tell how the Committee "directed to be purchased" in Edinburgh some stockings sold for about 5d. per pair! Had them "reduced again to wool", and got them made into hats "very obligingly by Mr Izet, the hatter." However, that development was never followed up – or, at any rate, no Highland hat industry ever came to life. They are on surer ground when they say: "it is certainly preferable to any other for stockings and probably for all light woollen manufactures, as shawls, waistcoats, etc." The hand knitting of most beautiful shawls has long been the pride of the Shetlanders. They still knit a great variety of articles, and the finest Shetland knitting is still unrivalled, but the industry is still almost as unorganised as when our report was printed.

"Shetland" is a description that has been sadly abused. As a lecturer at Barrett Street Trade School in London said the other day – he was describing the making of underwear – "This misrepresentation is to be deplored. Most of the so-called Shetland is woollen or shoddy mixture, and has no relationship to actual Shetland wool." One of the difficulties is that the total available is small. Our report suggests 100,000 as the probable number of sheep, and the very small fleece weight of 1½ pounds. This weight of 150,000 pounds is about the maximum probable amount at the present day, but, though the total weight of wool is still thought to be the same, the sheep now carry between 2 and 3 pounds of wool, so that the number of sheep is probably much under 100,000. Exact estimates are not possible, as the animals are sprinkled about amongst small peasant proprietors – crofters as we call them, udallers as they call themselves. Much of the wool is used up by the owners for their own requirements, or handspun for their knitted goods for sale. The probable clean weight of the wool would seem to be about 100,000 pounds, and the curious may start to calculate what yardage or how many articles that might yield, and if they would stretch from here to the moon if disentangled, or any of the other intelligent methods our journalists use in their efforts after vividness. Moreover, only a small proportion of that wool is really fine, for there has been much crossing of the sheep with coarser breeds.

In the finest of the gossamer lace shawls, the best of which are worth from £20 to £30 each, the handspun yarn runs from 30,000 to 50,000 yards of two ply to the pound. This may seem almost impossible to the mere manufacturer, but our reporters say that they exhibited "to the Society a specimen of the singularly fine woollen yarn spun by Miss Ann Ives of Spalding in Lincolnshire, which, although strong, is drawn to such a fineness that a pound weight of the yarn measures no less than 168,000 yards in length, which is equal to 95 miles". That same young lady says she thinks she could do still better with Shetland wool, and the reporters resolve that "it shall be sent".

Research suggests that Shetland wool for its weight gives 50 per cent greater warmth than any other wool, excepting such wools as Cashmere, which the purist might claim to be fur rather than wool. Such a figure must not be looked upon too critically, because there is great variation amongst the true wools, and there is no true standard on which a percentage may be based solidly, but there is no doubt at all about its quite remarkable warmth.

Shetland sheep are not all white, but the individual sheep are not dappled like the Alpaca and the Llama. There are wools of various shades of brown, fawn, grey, "moorit" or "murat," etymology unknown as the dictionary says, a sort of warm, middle-toned brown, and the so-called black, which is really a very dark brown. Most skilful use is made of these natural colours in the native knitted goods. The colours are not very fast to light, but they have a beautiful softness, not often attained by dyed shades of the same colours. Just wherein their superiority dwells is not easy to say. Probably the comparative unevenness of the shade has something to do with the subtle charm.

Nowadays, the larger flock-masters clip their sheep, but the crofters still pluck or "roo" theirs, driving them off the common lands or "out-runs" about once a fortnight to take off the wool that is ready to fall. This gives the crofters' sheep a most mangy and untidy look during the month or two – June and July – when the sheep are shedding their fleece, but it is not really a bad system so far as the wool is concerned – or the sheep – the fault is the time and labour wasted, and the obvious fact that the wool is less easy to classify when it comes to wool sorting.

And as a last word on our subject – the fine-woolled sheep go by the pleasant name of "kindly" sheep, a quaint name curiously suited to the chief properties of the lovely, warm, comforting garments that are made from their wool.

Note. It is very difficult to arrive at definite figures for the production of wool in Shetland, for the first and principal source of statistics, the wartime Wool Control, did not extend to the islands. The Department of Agriculture for Scotland suggests that the best we can do is to quote the Council of Industry's Report, paragraph 76: "On estimates generally current in Shetland, it is thought that the annual clip of wool of the pure Shetland breed is some 150,000 to 200,000 lb. The total clip from sheep of all breeds in Shetland is estimated at some 550,000 lb."

A WORD ON THE HISTORY OF THE SCOTTISH WOOLLEN TRADE

HE historian of the Scottish Woollen Trade does not need to go very far back in time to reach the beginnings of the era of organisation – the emergence of the old craft as an industry properly to be described as the Scottish Woollen Trade. Many of us can remember to have heard from our fathers' and grandfathers' personal reminiscences of the very early days – the days when the old, scattered craftsmen were beginning to find separate existence difficult, and when these disjointed particles were coming together and crystallising into these larger units that formed the beginnings of the firms that stand at the head of the industry today. Galashiels may claim to be the chief centre, although not the real fount and origin of the Scottish Woollen Trade, for its Weavers' Corporation dates back to 1666, and its Manufacturers' Corporation to 1777, handy dates to bear in mind. It must be remembered in discussing the early history of the trade that weaving was a craft universally disseminated throughout the length and breadth of Scotland, which accounts for the scattered distribution of the mills at the present time.

Not unnaturally before the age of railways, the craftsmen of the different parts of Scotland tended to travel along slightly different roads. Thus the west, taking advantage of the development of its connections with America, grew into the great Lanarkshire Cotton Trade. In this district, the making of very light cloths followed the development of the cotton trade. Silk and wool were added to the cotton, producing shirtings of all kinds, and the highest skill of the craftsman was ready for the introduction of the Paisley shawl. These beautiful shawls were originally copied from Indian shawls brought back from Kashmir by the Glasgow traders who had spread throughout the East and particularly through India, since the Union had turned the vast energies of the Lowlanders from war to trade, and for several generations a Paisley shawl was almost as indispensable to a bride as a wedding ring! Even now, in textile design, the influence of the East, which was introduced by this intricate and skilful trade, is still seen in the "Pine" motive, and in the richness of the use of abstract colour.

Before the end of the eighteenth century, the industrialising of the west was well developed. John Galt, in the "Annals of the Parish", gives a sympathetic and very realistic impression of the cotton workers both in prosperity and in depression. Lord Cockburn in his "Journal", writing as a lawyer rather than a literary man, describes the terrible state of Paisley in 1843: "Indeed, what answer can be made to 10,000 people who violate no law, but simply stand on the street and say truly – We have no work!... This is an entirely new element in the population and the prospects it conjures up are terrible. ...I see no ground for expecting that so long as we are a nation of manufacturers we can ever be uncursed by these heart-rending visitations."

The northern side of the Forth, the Hillfoots, following one trend of the west country, developed its old serge trade almost solely into the shawl and knitting yarn trade, and later into linings, tartans and fancy materials generally. So by natural growth, it became the chief home of the Scottish part of the ladies' trade, which in general tended to be too unsubstantial for Scotland.

"Blyth Aberdeen" took the old Lindsey Woolsey – a linen warp crossed with wool – evolved a great industry in that thriftiest of cloths, the Aberdeen Wincey, and formed, as it were, a sort of link with the great old Linen Weaving Trade of the east coast, which was always specially concentrated in the Kingdom of Fife. Down the east coast, this developed under another side of the Indian influence into the Jute Trade of Dundee and Angus.

The detached north developed an exotic trade in Chinese, Persian and South American wools. It is interesting to follow the lines of these developments of the Scottish Woollen Trade. It is in these high-roads and by-roads of commerce that we can trace our local and national history more truly than by the study of the larger and more striking happenings of politics. When our young men went over all the world seeking adventures and fortunes, they never seemed to forget the possibilities of grafting new branches on the old stock. The Moray coast traded largely with the Pacific coast of North and South America. The early nineteenth century saw a fleet of little schooners, manned by eight to twelve men, sailing from such villages as Garmouth, at the mouth of the Spey. Round the Horn they went, right up the coast as far as the Columbia River, where Portland in Oregon now stands. As one modern steamship owner said: "The Lord was kind to little boats in these days." So these young men brought back bales of Vicunas, Alpacas, Llamas, and other strange wools for the mills at home.

All this time, the Highlanders and the Islanders continued on their way as craftsmen, the men weaving, the women spinning, dyeing the wool and finishing the cloth in the intervals of extracting a difficult and insufficient livelihood from their crofts and from the sea – much the same today as a hundred or two hundred years ago. Immovably immersed in the old ways, the Highlands and Islands have shown a strange resistance to change. It is perhaps good for the State to be reminded now and then that material prosperity is not the only object of life, that the chief end of man is to glorify God and enjoy Him forever, and that the appeal of money just does not exist for some people. This was discovered in a peaceful way by our hard-headed Lancastrian, Lord Leverhulme, in the failure of his far-reaching plans for the development of Lewis and the betterment of the islanders.

A hundred years earlier, the north passed through the long and painful conversion to sheep and cultivation, culminating in the first decade of the nineteenth century in the great Sutherland Clearances, one of the most pitiful stages in the long history of our country, a piece of history so clouded by the agony of broken hearts that even to this day the truth is not to be discerned. As out of strength comes sweetness, so out of these tribulations, the Empire and the world have been enriched by the development of many remote lands. In Canada, in Australia, in the United States, in New Zealand, the ruthlessly transplanted Highland stock has flourished and has brought forth fruit.

The Scottish Borders, with Galashiels as centre, plodded steadily along the road of solid common sense, producing the solidest of everyday cloths – Gala Tweels and Gala Greys, and, later, with the Government's help under the Act of Union, Blues, such as have ever since formed the staple wear of our sea-going men, and it was really from this Border trade that the modern Scottish Woollen Trade most directly developed. The country of the Scottish Borders is a true sheep country developed from the earliest civilised times by the monks of the great Abbeys, and so logically the proper foundation of the Scottish Woollen Trade. As far as the Borders are concerned, Galashiels is the obvious centre, and it is there the Scottish Woollen Technical College was built in 1909, leaving Hawick to supply the teaching for the knitting side of the Woollen Trade. Galashiels is on one of the main lines from Scotland to London. It is the junction for the Tweed Valley group, Peebles, Innerleithen and Walkerburn. Selkirk is but 6 miles away. Hawick and Langholm are not far, and even the scattered centres to the east, St Boswells, Earlston, Kelso and Duns, are not very remote.

The other concentrated area is the district with the homely name – the Hillfoots – that rich, narrow, alluvial plain between the precipitous Ochils and the Firth of Forth. Stirling, where Bannockburns unknown of Bruce came from; Alloa, famed for knitting yarns; Dollar, Alva, Menstrie, Tillicoultry. For the rest, there are mills scattered all over Scotland – large and small, founded on the local needs of long ago, sometimes developed into large concerns, sometimes remaining as little country businesses serving the needs of the farmers round their doors. In fact, our Scottish Woollen Trade is truly National and truly Native, and even now is truly on a Craft Basis.

Now this brings us to a very important point that can hardly be overstressed, for on it is based our claim to far more fame and attention than we are entitled to from our size. We claim no less than that our products are absolutely essential to the traders in the finest clothing throughout the world. Our Scottish designers are to be found throughout England and North America, New Zealand and Australia, and we submit that there is an inherent reason for this, just as seed potatoes of the best also come from Scotland by virtue of the soil and climate. All design of form or colour, and especially of colour, is based on Nature. By its soil, its climate, its very bones as one might call its geological structure, our land is the most brilliantly and variously coloured land in Europe – possibly in the world. When Leonardo da Vinci went to France, he was struck with the intensity of the blue of the sky, and no observing traveller from the south can in like manner fail to be struck with the transparent brilliance of the sky in the north of Scotland. Spring, summer, autumn and winter show a wonderful and greatly changing procession of delicate and endless harmonies of colour from which the colourist can always refresh his mind and replenish his store. Moreover, the love of Nature is deeply embedded in our Scottish character, as witness our folk songs. Finally, our mills are not segregated in great industrialised areas where Nature is but a pale ghost of her vigorous self, but are sprinkled up and down the land in little villages or small towns, so that in many places the designer has but to lift his eyes from his desk to be refreshed and stimulated by the sight of hill and moor and stream.

Nor does this superlative excellence depend solely on the aristocracy of the trade, as one might call the masters and the designers. They are rather leaders than aristocrats, and are the product of the country, too, for both masters and men have come of one of the most conservative stocks in the world, skilled for generations in the working of wool, and there are few masters in the Scottish trade today who have not been brought up in their mills, and few workers who are not the sons and daughters of craftsmen and craftswomen. There is thus, as a foundation for the trade, a great mass of inherited and traditional skill. One very happy result has been a close understanding between the masters and the men – for when men have been brought up to work side by side, learning their jobs together, reverencing the same traditions, it is not surprising that amongst them there has never arisen any labour trouble.

The Scottish mills are small. Mass production is not the habit of the Scottish trade. The Scottish manufacturers do not compete in cloths the sale of which depends purely on price. This is because of the large sums spent every year on designing and other experimental work, and because of the expenses involved in any high-class and varied type of manufacture. It does not mean that for value given or for the services rendered to mankind a high price is exacted. Nor in honesty does it mean that the Scottish manufacturers have a soul above large orders and vast business, and never cast envious eyes on the simple types of work that were required for the clothing of all the Allied Armies during the Great War.

The fundamental sources of efficiency vary greatly in different trades. These are determined by the incidence of the cost of raw materials, capital, labour and all the varying items that in combination make up the selling cost of the product. In some trades, small units have no chance against large concerns. In woollen manufacturing, the effective production unit is surprisingly small, so that even a little country mill with one set of carding machines can put up a good fight against the largest plant. The Scottish Woollen Trade has shown complete resistance to large-scale amalgamations and trusts, such as have formed in nearly all the great industries of the modern world. This could only be due to some such fundamental economic reason, coupled with another almost as important that enables even the small price handicap to be overcome. The process of manufacture must be capable of infinite variation of the product in the manipulation and combination of raw materials so as to give full scope to individual ingenuity and skill, without imposing too serious an addition to the costs of production. History shows to what a wonderful extent this is true of the Scottish Woollen Trade. And so with soil and climate combining to give us incomparable natural colouring, with a national character saturated with love of beauty, with a national energy always ready to seek new outlets for its power, above all, with such a splendid and ancient craft founded solidly on the soundest economics, how could our Scottish Woollen Trade fail to be in the very forefront, not of Scottish or even of British industries, but of the industries of the world?

ABOUT CHEVIOT SHEEP

"Day set on Norham's castled steep,
And Tweed's fair river, broad and deep,
And Cheviot's mountains lone."

 AS the car breasts the summit of the Carter Bar, after the long pull up from Catcleugh, and begins to glide smoothly down the steep descent to Jedburgh, the occupant suddenly becomes aware that he is entering a new land. The hills, it is true, do not differ in character from those he has just left behind, but instead of closing in on him, they are spread before him in an endless vista, range upon range, rolling or conical, dark brown or green, showing where heather or grass predominate. Hills, hills, nothing but hills, this is Scotland, and surely by no other gate could the entry be more impressive. He may or may not know, but he is gazing over Teviotdale, Liddesdale, Eskdale, Ettrickdale, Yarrow and Tweeddale, for far in the distant west, the giant Laws of Peeblesshire close in the view and leave to the imagination, what is true in fact, a vision of more and still more hills. To left and right runs the long line of the Cheviots, the traditional boundary between England and Scotland, Carter Fell, Peel Fell and Larriston Fells stretch towards the Solway, while The Cheviot and Yeavering Bell lead the eye to the low lands that border the North Sea.

In few places in the British Isles can we get such a sense of space or a greater feeling of being alone with Nature. Only down in the wooded depths by Jedburgh or in the rich lands of the Merse that bound our northern horizon does there seem to be any evidence of human habitation. As we swing round the first bend of the zig-zag descent, the huge bulk of the Cheviot comes more directly into our ken – this is the hill – there are no mountains so-called in the Borderland – that for the moment holds our interest, for on its broad slopes have grazed from time immemorial a breed of sheep that bears its name. This is the very home of the breed, and all the hills within our view, nay many in the far Highlands and beyond the seas, are its by conquest.

We have used the word immemorial, but we have no intention of delving too deeply into the origin or evolution of the breed. It is stated on several authorities to have been introduced into Scotland about the year 1372, but

THE EILDONS FROM THE NORTH

our interest in it really awakens towards the latter half of the eighteenth century.

At the beginning of that century, agriculture in Scotland was in a very backward state: methods were primitive to the verge of barbarism, cultivators were poor, and to say that they were unenterprising and showed the greatest aversion to new ideas is possibly to understate the case; but owing to various reasons, political, economic and social, this state of affairs underwent a complete transformation during the progress of the next hundred years. The emergence from what was practically a crofting system to one of large farms tenanted by men of some means, of wider vision and more open to new ideas would naturally lead to an awakened interest in sheep breeding, thus we find in the year 1760 attention being turned to the improvement of the Long or Whiteface sheep, for by these two names the Cheviot sheep was then known.

The Cheviot is classed as a Mountain sheep, a name that is self-explanatory and distinguishes it from the lustrous or long-woolled sheep, such as the Leicester, the Lincoln or the Border Leicester that graze on the lower and arable lands. It shares the hills of Scotland with another Mountain breed, best known as the Scotch Blackface. Both these breeds are said to have originally come from the north of England and have completely ousted an older, if not primitive, sheep known as the Tanface.

The Tanface are but a memory, although a trace of their blood may linger in the stock of the Whiteface invaders.

The Blackface and Cheviot, now unchallenged, share the pasture of the Scottish hills and mountains, and a long battle – if one may apply the word to anything so peaceful and pastoral – has ended in a draw.

The Blackface were first in the field, and had penetrated far into the Highlands, while the Cheviots were still grazing only on the hills of that name. In Ettrick Forest up till after the middle of the eighteenth century, the Blackface, variously known as the Heath, Linton, Forest or Short sheep, reigned supreme. It was about 1760 that in the Borders the long controversy as to the merits of the two

KEEP THE QUALITY UP! KEEP THE QUALITY UP!!

breeds first arose. It is here perhaps necessary to explain that in the production of wool, the aims of the manufacturer and the farmer are by no means identical. The manufacturer has one constant wish: the production of a good standardised wool that will suit his requirements, either for combing or for carding. He wishes the breeds to be kept separate, so that in blending he knows where he is. Naturally, he wishes them to be brought up to the best possible standard within themselves and, even by a certain amount of crossing, to be improved. The farmer, on the other hand, is torn by conflicting emotions, so it is a wonder that, like Sir Brian de Bois-Guilbert, he does not die of them. He has to consider in the first place the question of profit. Wool may be cheap or dear, and according to that the question of the manufacturer bulks in his view as of less or more importance.

A larger and heavier fleece may not mean more money. A fine fleece may mean more delicate sheep and the consequent risk of loss by death in a hard winter.

He has also to consider the butcher and if the price of mutton is high, the importance of the manufacturer recedes. Also he has to consider the market price of the sheep itself.

As none of these values are constant, he has difficult decisions to make and, being human, he does not always make the right one.

The Blackface fleece is coarse, long and open. It contains a considerable proportion of kemp or short dead hairs, due to the poverty of the feeding on much of the mountain land. The wool is only fit for carpet yarns, or, when not too coarse, for the rougher sort of homespun cloths. The mutton, on the other hand, is very fine.

The Cheviot fleece is relatively much shorter and finer, it is crimpy, clean and dense, and the finest is almost free from kemp. The bulk sort is very regular and eminently suitable for Scotch tweeds, in the production of which it has played a great and distinguished part. The mutton is also very good.

Another element enters into the controversy and the hill farmer's calculations, an important one in our climate of widely varying winters: the relative hardiness of the two breeds. Here also opinions are divided, and while it is generally conceded that the Blackface will do better on extreme altitudes, the Cheviot will go into the mossy and marshy hollows where the other breed will not follow. To generalise, the former will do relatively better on heather and the latter on grass. The Cheviot, let it be said to its eternal credit, is a contented sheep – that is, it will readily adapt

KEEP THE QUALITY UP ! KEEP THE QUALITY UP !!

itself to circumstances, and by keeping its mind easy will thrive under adverse conditions – a lesson to humanity.

The peaceful penetration of the Southern Uplands of Scotland by the Cheviot breed appears to have begun about the date we have mentioned, 1760. The Scottish farmer gradually came to recognise that here was a breed that was possibly as hardy as his Heath sheep, and probably a great deal more profitable. In 1776, when the battle was fully joined, we find that: "Mr Thos. Scott on Carter Fell, a mountain 1600 feet high, exchanged with Mr Walter Hog, in Ettrick Forest, five white-faced for as many black-faced rams, but had every reason to regret the experiment, which was far from being the case with Mr Hog." Writing about 1790, Sir John Sinclair remarks: "So much convinced are the farmers of Ettrick Forest, of Tweeddale and Liddesdale of their superior excellence that they are now converting their flocks as quickly as possible into the Cheviot breed." Ten years later, the argument is still raging, for in the summer of 1801 we find Sir Walter (then Mr) Scott on a hunting expedition in Ettrick Forest, not as the Scottish kings of old for deer or game, but for Border ballads, met at Ramsay-cleugh for a social evening with the neighbouring farmers, including the Ettrick Shepherd himself. The conversation, instead of running on the legendary poetic lore of the district, which was uppermost at the time in the Border Minstrel's mind, kept interminably to the everlasting question of the Long and the Short sheep. Scott was frankly bored. Perhaps the story is best told in Hogg's own words: "So at length putting on his most serious calculating face he turned to Mr Walter Brydon (his host) and said, ' I am rather at a loss regarding the merits of this very important question. How long must a sheep actually measure to come under the denomination of a long sheep?' Mr Brydon, who, in the simplicity of his heart, neither perceived the quiz nor the reproof, fell to answer with great sincerity, 'It's the woo', sir; it's the woo' that mak's the difference, the lang sheep hae the short woo' and the short sheep hae the lang thing, an' these are just kind o' names we gie them, ye see.' Laidlaw got up a great guffaw, on which Scott could not preserve his face of strict calculation any longer, it went gradually awry, and a hearty laugh followed." Hogg adds, "When I saw the very same words repeated near the beginning of 'The 'Black Dwarf', how could I be mistaken of the author? "

In "The Forest" at least the Long sheep eventually won, for Lord Napier, in his evidence before the House of Lords in 1828, says of Selkirkshire (Ettrick Forest), "...the black-faced sheep have all been driven out of that part of the country and substituted by Cheviots."

Captain Tom Elliot, a name of world-wide fame in Cheviot sheep breeding, to whom we are indebted for a good deal of our information, furnishes a simple explanation of the terms "Long" and "Short". As a matter of fact, there is no difference in the actual length of the sheep of the two breeds, but if a man is dressed in a shaggy overcoat he will naturally look shorter than a man of the same height wearing a closefitting Chesterfield, so the Blackface sheep, with his coarse, open, wide-spreading coat looks shorter than the Cheviot, with his compact, close fleece.

We have referred to Sir John Sinclair, and he deserves honourable mention, for not only is he the godfather of the Cheviot sheep, but it was he who first introduced it to Caithness, the most northerly County of Scotland, in the year 1791. From there, it rapidly spread to the neighbouring County of Sutherland, and has given us the famous Sutherland wool, which has been used in producing many of the choicest tweeds. Here, again, the conflict of ideas regarding the relative merits of the breeds was renewed, but ended in a substantial part of the county's acreage being absorbed by the sheep from the lowland hills.

Patrick Sellar remarks that "...from 1805 to 1820, from a few hundred Cheviot sheep that the County (Sutherland) then contained, their number had so increased that 100,000 fleeces were sent annually to the manufacturer." In 1837, we read further that "...the contest is still carried on between these valuable breeds, but decidedly in favour of the Cheviots." Evidently, like "The Gael", the Blackface "...maintain'd unequal war". Experience has, however, more or less solved the question, and it can now be said that, as a rule, the flocks of one breed or the other occupy the pastures that are best suited to their different natures.

An interesting echo of this migration from south to north is referred to in the reminiscences of a Highland lady, writing of Wester Ross in the late eighties of last century. We believe the practice that she refers to still persists, but is gradually dying out:

"Talking of shepherds, it had never struck me how little imagination they displayed in naming their collie dogs. In our part, the prevailing names were Tweed and Yarrow. Later I was told that those were a survival of the time when Cheviot sheep were first introduced into the North. The dogs, owned by the shepherds who drove them up from the Borders, were usually called after their own rivers, and so the names clung to our district. And it never, until later, struck me as curious that all our shepherds, who, in those days, could not speak a word of English, always delivered their instruction in that language to their collies. 'Gome in to ma fut here' was a usual expression. Again, I am told, this has been handed down by the Border shepherds who, of course, addressed their 'dogs' in English – or rather Scots."

When Sir John Sinclair introduced these sheep to the far north, they had never been known by any other name than the "Long" or "Whiteface" sheep, names that had little meaning where other breeds could be so described. He therefore christened them Cheviots, and by that name they have been known ever since, a name that has extended itself to a large class of fabrics woven in Scottish mills. It may interest our English and overseas readers to know that the proper pronunciation is Cheviot as in "cheese", and not Cheviot as in "level", or Sheviot as sometimes pronounced by our friends across the Atlantic.

SMAILHOLM TOWER

While the sheep were undergoing these introductions to pastures new, the question of the breed's improvement was also receiving considerable attention.

It is to be assumed that in the unsettled state of Scotland during the preceding 400 years, little heed would be paid to this matter, although earlier than that, while Berwick was still a Scottish seaport, there is a tradition that a Spanish (Merino) strain was introduced. It is also possible that some of the qualities that attracted the improvers of the late eighteenth century may have been derived from this source. Berwick, in 1318 and the succeeding years, was the chief connecting link between Scotland and the whole of the Continent of Europe, and its exports of wool and imports of sheep were considerable.

In the Borders, the idea seems to have been more towards the strengthening of the frame and increasing the size of the carcase, and with that object Lincoln or Leicester blood was introduced.

In the north, the inclination tended towards a fine fleece, and crosses with both Merino and Down sheep have been tried. The Southdown sheep is derived in part from the Merino. Speaking broadly, these two divergent ideas have accounted for some of the differences still observable between the Sutherland and the Border Cheviot. Both, if carried very far, were open to serious objections. Increasing the size of the sheep could only be done at the expense of losing to a great extent those qualities for which the wool was justly prized; a certain softness of constitution would also manifest itself, and breeding for fineness alone would endanger the stamina of the sheep in a climate that, although generally mild, is subject to occasional winters of great severity, and, especially on the high ground, to violent climatic changes.

Thus after many experiments, the farmers seem to have accepted the idea that the best improvement can be carried out by selective breeding within the breed itself.

A curious difference in the habits of the Merino and Cheviot sheep is worth noting. In a flock of Cheviots, you find that the sheep range apart in twos and threes, but the Merinos keep together like a drove passing through the country. They form a sort of camp at night, and nothing will induce them to "lie abroad", as the shepherds call sleeping on their own particular bit of ground, like other mountain breeds. The second of these traits manifests itself in the cross, but curiously enough not the first. So you find a Cheviot sheep with a strong strain of Merino in it feeding apart during the day, but returning at night to camp with its fellows. It can easily be appreciated that on a large hirsel of several thousand acres, an individual sheep that has chosen the outlying ground has a considerable journey to make both morning and evening.

But the breed has wandered far since their immemorial ancestors first looked out from the lofty slopes of their native hill over the wide Borderland and grey North Sea. In New Zealand, in Punta Arenas, and the Falkland Islands, on lonelier mountains and by more turbulent waters, their descendants may now be found peacefully grazing.

Wherever Scottish farmers have penetrated and wherever climatic conditions suit, they have introduced this hardy breed, as honest and as sound as the fleece they annually yield to the shearer and as the cloth into which it is ultimately woven. A "contented" sheep.

OUR ILLUSTRATIONS

Both our illustrations and decorations are by W. B. Lawson, whom we may almost claim as "Our Mr Lawson". The initial letter shows a typical Cheviot ewe with her lamb. Our little frieze just shows how all Nature vies with Scottish Woollens in Keeping the Quality Up. The two landscapes are true Border landscapes, both deep in history. The great hill of the Eildons was cut into three by the Devil as one of the jobs given to him by the wizard, Michael Scott – strange it should always be virtuous to cheat the Devil! Trimontium, the great Roman Camp that guarded the Central Marches, lay on the banks of Tweed below these hills. The great landmark of their trisected mass most naturally gave the name to the camp. [The Editors hereby disclaim all responsibility for any anachronism that may be implied in the above report.]

Smailholm is one of the chain of Border keeps built to defend the Marches from our Southern neighbours, the English. It was here that much of Sir Walter Scott's early boyhood was spent.

SPINNING

"And all the women that were wise hearted did spin with their hands."

PINNING is one of the oldest industries in the world and, in its various forms and materials, one of the most useful to mankind. Textiles of all sorts, woven or knitted, from fine woollens to hairy homespuns, from silk to sackcloth, from linen or cotton to fireproof asbestos, all are made from spun yarns. Spinning is also responsible for twines for fishing and tying up parcels, and for hawsers for mooring transatlantic liners to the quay. In short, it has innumerable uses.

The theory of spinning is simply that fibres, arranged longitudinally and then twisted, will give a long, continuous thread, which will be as strong as the material used will allow.

In primitive times, the fibres had to be teased out by hand to a well-mixed mass, which was put on a stick or distaff, usually attached to the waistband or tucked under the left arm, and from this a few fibres or hairs were drawn off and twisted into yarn. Until a century and three-quarters ago, it was entirely a hand process. Even to the present day, hand-spinning lingers in the Highlands and Islands of Scotland, and in many parts of the world the machine has not displaced the wise-hearted women who worked at the curtains for Solomon's Temple.

As twisting the end of a thread in the fingers was very laborious, some other means had to be found. The earliest of these was the spindle. This was a stick from 8 to 30 inches in length, weighted with a whorl near one end to help it to spin, and with a notch at the other. This is illustrated in Fig. 1, in which c is the wool fibres from the distaff, b the whorl or weight that gives force to the spindle a. To this, the yarn was attached, and it was twirled in the fingers or between the right thigh and the palm of the hand, and allowed to fall towards the ground, suspended by the yarn that was being spun. When this became too long, a length was wound round the spindle, caught in the notch, and another length begun.

The whorl was usually of stone or metal, but ancient spinsters were not particular, for any balanced solid little weight can serve to keep the spindle twirling. In the Scottish Antiquarian Museum in Edinburgh, there are two examples, one made of peat and the other of a potato.

At a later date, probably about the fourteenth century in Europe – although three thousand years ago in India – this spindle was placed in a bearing, and rotated by a band passing over a groove in the circumference of the whorl and round a large wheel which was turned by hand. This was known as the "muckle wheel" in Scotland, and is illustrated by our second drawing, drawn like the spindle from an example in the Scottish Antiquarian Museum.

The next difficulty to be overcome was the winding up of the yarn on the spindle as it was spun, and it is interesting to note that on a modern spinning mule, this still gives more trouble than the actual spinning.

To the simple spindle was added a flyer, which rotated on it and was driven by a second band from the same large wheel, but which had a whorl of a slightly different size, causing it to rotate at a slightly different speed. The difference in speed of rotation, or the amount by which the one overtook the other, wound the yarn on the spindle, and thus turned the spinning into a continuous process. This more complicated arrangement is illustrated in our third figure. Here a is the spun yarn on its bobbin, which is rotated by the right-hand pulley, and b is the flyer that winds the yarn on to the bobbin. The series of little hooks enables the winding to be controlled by hooking the yarn successively into one after the other and so spreading it along the bobbin, c represents the fibres from the distaff or whatever arrangement has been used to hold the oiled and carded wool. It passes through the hollow spindle by which means the twist is controlled.

Fig.2

A modern spinning mule is an adaptation of the simple spindle, whilst a spinning frame is an adaptation of the spindle and flyer.

Having reached the modern mill, we must begin with the raw wool and follow it through the processes preparatory to the actual spinning. These are many and, under present-day conditions, very exacting. One cannot mix up white and natural brown wool and sell the resultant mixture, whatever it may turn out to be. A shade has to be matched exactly, and may consist of one colour to form a solid shade, or several, with or without white, to form a mixture.

Colour itself has been written about elsewhere in this series, and this article is only concerned with it indirectly.

Blending wools is a very important feature of good spinning, and it varies widely, depending upon the desired result. Certain costume cloths presently in vogue require blends that might turn an orthodox wool foreman's hair grey. Some of these queer blends mix fine, short Merino with long, coarse wools more suitable for carpets, or ostrich feathers and shredded cellophane – or almost any fantastic fibres – but apart from freaks such as these, great skill and knowledge of the characteristics of wools from different countries and of sheep, as well as of cloth-finishing, are required to make a blend that will give a strong, level yarn and the desired handle, whether soft, crisp or leathery.

Once the wool blend is settled, and has been mixed and dyed, the colours must be carefully weighed out in their proportions and again mixed, which is not such a simple process as might be imagined. It is essential that the colour of the whole making of yarn be level from beginning to end. For instance, without the greatest care in the work, too much white might show in the second half of the batch.

To illustrate this, let us say that a quantity of a certain mixture is required – say, one thousand pounds altogether. Suppose this needs, to produce the correct shade, seven hundred of dark brown, two hundred of fawn, and one hundred of white. The method employed to avoid shading is to spread on the floor of the blending room layers of dark brown and white alternately, using perhaps 150 pounds of the dark brown and all the white, then, taking an armful from top to bottom of the pile, as one might cut a many layered sandwich cake in order to get equal amounts of each flavour, this is put through a mixing machine. A second layout is made, this time of the whole batch, in layers of brown, the brown and the white we have already mixed, brown again, fawn, brown, brown and white, and so on until all the colours are used up. Again slicing from top to bottom, this is put through the mixing machine, and the result should be a level shade.

To ensure fast dyeing, the natural fat and all other dirt must be washed out of the wool, but as oil of some sort helps wool to card and spin and counteracts the electricity in dry wool, a special oil is added, usually while the mixture is travelling in a thin layer along the feed-board of the mixing willey. This having been done, the wool – blended, matched as near as possible for colour, opened, mixed and oiled – is ready for carding.

We are now faced with another problem. The yarn to be produced must be of a uniform weight throughout. To this end, each portion of the wool fed to the carding machine is automatically weighed and the correct amount fed – so many ounces per minute. From this point onwards a careful check must be kept on the weight.

Carding wool consists of passing the oiled wool between finely adjusted rollers, covered with innumerable small sharp wire teeth called card clothing. These pluck each lock as it comes along, until every individual fibre has been pulled out and rearranged. This card clothing is like a fine wire brush, about as long as the bristles of a toothbrush.

Another article in the series deals with the difference between carding and combing and the respective woollen and worsted cloths that result.

At this point, the colour is finally checked very carefully and any necessary correction made. In the batch we have been following, a few pounds more of fawn might be required, or perhaps, if the brown dyeing were too yellow, the addition of a small quantity of a redder-brown would be necessary to bring it to the exact shade of the standard.

The wool must next be "condensed" – that is, formed into thin ribands or "slivers", which, when twisted, form the yarn. There are several ways of doing this, the most common in Scotland being to use a roller covered with the ordinary card clothing from which the wires have been cut away in rings right round it, to form gaps of, say, ¼ inch in every inch. This roller is the last on the machine. It is called the doffer – a nice old English word with a flavour of bygone days lingering about it – and is probably about 30 inches in diameter. As it revolves, it only picks up wool on its clothed ¾-inch rings, and the ribands of wool from these are removed and rubbed between oscillating leather rubbers to form thin regular slivers, like threads without any twist, and these are wound on spools.

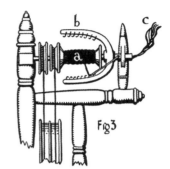

Fig 3

The scene now moves from the carding to the spinning shed. What is now called the self-acting spinning mule is an elaboration of Hargreave's Spinning Jenny, invented in 1764, which was able to spin eight threads simultaneously. It has been improved by Crompton and others, until to spin between four and five hundred threads at the same time is now quite common in the woollen industry.

A drawing of a modern mule was given in Plate II, and by contrast Plate VIII. Sent out with this number illustrates the old simple method of the distaff and spindle.

The spools of condensed sliver are laid on the delivery drums of the mule, and each end is passed between rollers and given a turn round the spindles, which are on a movable carriage. When the mule is set in motion, these spindles revolve, giving twist to the sliver. At the same time, the rollers deliver more sliver and the carriage moves away, keeping the yarn taut. When about two-thirds of the way out, the delivery rollers stop, but the carriage continues to the end of its two-yard travel, and the yarn is reduced to its correct weight by stretch, the fibres, lubricated by the oil on them, slipping alongside one another till they are finally bound by the correct amount of twist.

If an uneven piece of sliver is twisted, the twist all runs into the thin places. If the yarn is now stretched, the stretching will all take place where there is least twist – that is to say, at the thick bits – and will thin them down and automatically level the thread. This happens from the time the rollers cease to deliver sliver until the carriage stops in its farthest-out position. Additional twist is now added, the amount depending upon the purpose and required strength of the yarn. Practically speaking, the less twist the softer the handle – the more twist the greater the strength.

The carriage now moves in again to the delivery rollers, winding up the spun yarn as it goes, and then the whole process is repeated. The whole complicated action of spinning and winding is automatically controlled. The boys and girls who tend the machine have nothing to do but mend threads that break and empty the machine when its bobbins are full. This is by far the most complex and wonderful of all the machines of the textile trade and its official name is the "self-acting mule".

Many of the best cloths are made of two-fold, three-fold, or other fancy yarns that require additional processes, but with that exception, the yarn, when wound on to suitable bobbins, is ready to be woven into cloth.

VICUNA

ICUNA has become an almost fabulous word. A few years ago, round about the beginnings of the Great War, it looked as though the beast itself would soon be a fabulous animal. The word itself has become, like many other words, deflected by trade use – or truly by trade abuse – so far from its proper and immediate meaning that without the adjectives "pure" or "real" it means something quite different from what it should. The Woollen Trade is perhaps no worse than many another great trade in thus misusing our native language, but it has a very long list of black marks against it. A number devoted to Woollen Abuses would be interesting and would cover a surprisingly wide field of human activity. Most of these words have passed through a stage of doubtful honesty, some to emerge in respectability: "His honour rooted in dishonour stood." Homespuns no longer remember they ever had a home. Harris had to be reminded by Government that it originated in the Western Isles of Scotland. In the market-place, Vicuna occupied a midway position. It is a real material of so exquisite a fineness that it is capable of imparting the most beautiful smoothness, softness and closeness to fine black coatings. During the whole of the nineteenth century, and especially in the days of Queen Victoria, such coatings and such coats were the necessary badge of respectability in all the professions and for all business men throughout most of Western civilisation. In this way, it came about that to have a black Vicuna coat was the last word in respectability. There never was more than a most infinitesimal quantity of Vicuna wool available, so it became the habit of the West End tailors of London to describe all fine black smooth-finished "broad cloths" as Vicuna; and then less-fine cloths; and, finally, the name sank past the levels of respectability and finished its rake's progress as a blend of shoddy and cotton. In this dégringolade, the old reprobate retained but one memory of the ancestral halls from which evil living had banished him – the cloth was still black and still close in finish.

The Vicuna is one of the camel tribe. Its scientific name is *Vicugna vicugna*. It is a native of Southern Peru, and the present geographical distribution of the animal is surprisingly narrow considering that it is not difficult to keep it alive and healthy in zoological gardens in many parts of the world. Its natural home is the high uplands of the Andes, between Lake Titicaca and the coast. These lands lie about 10,000 to 13,000 feet above the sea, and even there attempts at regular domestication seem to have failed completely.

The Vicuna is a graceful, swift little animal, slim and neat like a small antelope. Verrill, in "Under Peruvian Skys", describes how he has seen them on the Sumbay Pampas where "they easily outrun the trains and vanish in the distance ahead", even when the trains are running at 45 miles an hour. They wander about in small groups consisting of one male with three or four females. They are by nature shy and timid, but unfortunately are most inquisitive and can always be lured to their destruction by any unusual sight, such as a rag or a bit of bright cloth, and our same authority narrates the curious ease with which they can be guided anywhere by a string, which they will not try to cross. The natives used to herd them by hundreds for slaughter into corrals by the simple method of stretching converging lines across the Pampas. So keen was the demand for the wool, the skin and the meat of the Vicuna, and so easy its wholesale slaughter that thirty years ago its total extinction seemed almost certain. After several unsuccessful experiments, the Government of Peru has prohibited the killing of Vicunas excepting under strict control. The wool is only exported under licence, which is supposed to cover the natural casualties in the herds; and besides the export duty, the Government collects one-half the export price of the wool. Of course, in so sparsely peopled and difficult country some doubtless gets out through Bolivia and otherwise. There is no part of the world where bootlegging is not a popular trade, but the result is that no statistics are available! One guess is as good as another – our guess is about 10,000 to 12,000 pounds of raw wool in a year, yielding about 7000 to 8000 pounds of yarn. This shows what a tiny affair this whole trade is now. "A cloth for Emperors" indeed.

The wool is the finest that exists. Its fibres measure about 2500 to the inch, about half the thickness of the finest Merino sheep's wools. It is a dark tobacco colour, remarkably unvarying and remarkably fast considering the low standard of fastness in the colouring of animals. As is usual, the outer part of the coat is paler, so that the general aspect of the animals is a warm tawny brown that blends perfectly with the bare country in which it lives. The coarser parts – the "britch" – and some old animals are paler, but, broadly speaking, this dark natural ground limits the colours available quite definitely to very dark shades – even blacks are apt to be rusty and navy blues peacock in tone. But the outstanding glory of the wool is its incomparable touch – possibly equalled by some of the softer furs and by the delicious feeling of a small kitten, but otherwise by no means to be imitated. The even rarer but much less valuable wool of its relative, the Guanaco – or Huanaco as Prescott spells it – at its best is nearer than anything else. Fine Chinese Cashmere is a good second, but although very lovely it is different in character – perhaps we might say as the finest Claret is different from the finest Port: different and a little inferior!

In these little monographs, it is not always easy to steer between Scylla and Charybdis; between indefiniteness and advertisement of some particular firm. But it may be allowable to say that we – who must otherwise remain nameless – have now been working Vicuna since 1847. Possibly that was its first introduction to Scotland, although not to manufacturing Europe. But by many centuries that was not the beginning of its use. In that strange old communistic empire of the Incas, it was reserved for the Royal House. They knew how to spin it to the finest yarns, and to this day the finest native work cannot be excelled in quality by our own machinery.

According to Prescott's authorities, it was made into curtains and carpets – which seems inherently improbable unless in the limited sense of fine mats – clothing and, in particular, ponchos. The poncho is the almost universal outer garment of South and Central America. It is simply a straight piece of cloth – a blanket, in fact – with a slot in the middle through which passes the wearer's head. It is very practical and very primitive. On horseback especially it shelters horse and rider from sun and rain, and like a large cavalry cloak, it covers the saddle, the knees and the reins. Like a blanket, it varies through all degrees of workmanship, from the coarsest material to the most beautiful and elaborate examples of weaving and embroidering. We have examined both ancient and modern ponchos ornamented both with woven silk and added embroidery that we could not excel – so fine and so close as to be almost waterproof. Where we moderns excel is in our elaborate surface finishes by which – at the sacrifice of a good deal of thriftiness in wear we must admit – we can to a far greater degree than the native craftsman bring out and exhibit the beautiful softness of the wool.

Is Vicuna a wool or a fur? According to the late Professor Cossar Ewart of Edinburgh University, no line can be drawn. In his day, Professor Cossar Ewart was the greatest authority on certain aspects of animal breeding and especially in regard to fleeces and all matters connected with wools and hairs. He said that parts of the Vicuna fleece could not microscopically or by composition be distinguished from such a hard straight wool as Leicester. Vicuna mills or felts quite freely like a sheep's wool – better than many types. It dyes alike, although more reluctantly as it were, and takes more dye to produce a corresponding shade. It is curiously warm, but whether this is a direct result of its fineness or that it actually has higher insulating properties in its composition we cannot say. Certainly, weight for weight it is the warmest clothing of all the wools.

It is not an easy material to deal with if the best results are to be got. It requires very careful sorting. The individual fleeces are small, from ¾ to 1½ pounds, and contain at least as great a variety of qualities as the fleece of the sheep. In common with all wools verging on furs, the fleece of the Vicuna consists of two sets of hairs – a fine set grown on the outer skin and a longer and stronger set grown on the underskin. In many species of animal, the strong hair is developed into a close and shiny surface capable of throwing off heavy rain, and the fine, soft under-fleece provides warmth – an arrangement beautifully illustrated in our domestic cat. For fine cloth-making the long, coarse hairs must be removed. The natives do this by hand plucking, and the first lots in this country were likewise hand plucked. That has long passed the limits of practicability and the hair is now removed by special types of carding machines, such as we have described in our numbers dealing with "Woollens versus Worsted" and "Carding and Spinning". It is a very slow and consequently dear process.

It is a small affair this trade in Vicuna. It would still be small if all that the natives of Peru use in their handicrafts were added to all that reaches the mills of Europe and America. But it is a trade without which we would be poorer, for it is one of the most exquisite luxuries that the craft of man has evolved out of his surroundings, and it is one of the few threads that carry us back to possibly the oldest civilisation in the world, the Empire of the Incas of Peru.

It is always difficult to know where to stop in writing a "Scottish Woollens" number. It is like wandering through a picturesque and beautiful country. In admiring the lovely views of mountain and lake, pausing to watch a bird or a moth, to examine a flower or an unfamiliar tree, to appreciate the comely art of a cottage or a roadside church, in admiring all these and a thousand other things of interest one forgets that night falls and that a bed must be reached! So in our subjects, we are led to countless interests of life and art and economics into which it is tempting to turn aside. It is tempting to quote Prescott's fascinating "History of the Conquest of Peru", the preface dated Boston, 1847 – not up to date perhaps, but still the classic authority – to follow his accounts of the four Peruvian "sheep": the Alpaca, the Llama, the Huanaco and the Vicuna: how they live on the ychu grass that does not come north of the Line and so limits these beasts to the Southern Andes; how in the days of the ancient Empire of the Incas great roundings up of the countryside took place every season, but never oftener in one place than every fourth year – sometimes a hundred thousand men being used in one of these great battues; how the wild beasts were killed and the "sheep" shorn and the wools stored in the Government store-houses; how the Vicuna wool was reserved for the worship of the Sun and for the ceremonial chaplet and clothing of the Royal Prince at his inaugural ceremony. And thence all the history of the Conquistadores, of Drake and his raids, of the later peaceful raids of the little ships built of good Scotch pine along the shores of the Moray Firth and manned by eight or ten men who brought the Vicuna wool to our shores: of trade amongst the ruins of the Spanish Empire – "round the Horn and back again" – so interestingly told in Dana's "Two Years before the Mast". But we have reached our limit and, like Pepys, must close our book "and so to bed".

OUR MAP

APS are a joy and a delight to every boy and to every man in whose heart the fires of adventure still burn.

Our Map started out with the simple idea of giving our Overseas friends some idea of the position of the land of Scottish Woollens and some idea of whereabouts the various members of our National Association dwelt. It was only to be a small supplement to "Scottish Woollens". Then we thought, why not make it an attractive little map with some flavour of romance about it? Let's have it not penny plain, but tuppence coloured. Let's throw our Scottish economy to the winds and have three colours – our National colours – the colours of freedom, of the three great democracies. We are sorry that in this volume we have had to cut away the borders of the original map – a design composed of Stars and Stripes enlivened with Maple Leaves. And the idea kept on growing as all lively ideas grow. We would add our distances are from London. (Just a whisper in your ear: quite a lot of people in London think of us as living either at the North Pole or just outside the reach of their buses, so, perhaps, these figures might help our fellow countrymen too.)

Then we thought we would outline two or three short tours for friends who might find themselves with a couple of days to spare here and there.

Then we thought our Map looked so attractive that we would print a few on fine vellum for anyone who wished to frame it as a souvenir or a forecast of a visit to our land.

Our Map requires some explanation. First of all, the homes of our members are marked in capitals. As the Association includes almost every firm, these towns and villages illustrate very completely the distribution of the Scottish Woollen Trade up and down the old sheep districts in which the trade originated long before the days of the great industrial revolution. At a few key points the distance from London by road, which does not differ much from the distance by railway, is marked in black.

For the general good of the Map we have also marked a few places on which Scottish Woollens do not shed their light: Dumfries, for the memory of Burns; the Cromarty Firth, the base of the U.S.A. Navy during the Great War; Balmoral and the Castle of Mey as the Scottish Homes of our Royal Family; Stornoway, the centre for Harris Tweed, and so forth.

We have such untold myriad of lochs and rivers that we have only put in a few that fit into our narrative: Loch Lomond, for the sake of Scott; Loch Maree, for its own sake, one of the loveliest expanses of land and water in the whole world; Loch

Ness for its Monster, and because, with its neighbours and a long groove extending far into the North Sea at one end and into the Atlantic at the other, it forms one of the two great rift valleys of the world (the other is the great chasm of the Dead Sea, which cuts down through almost the whole length of Africa). There are parts of the north-west so full of lakes that there is almost as much water as land on the Map, and everywhere in Scotland is so inter-mixed with the sea that no point can anywhere be found 40 miles from salt water.

On general principles, we have marked in red the main railways, and lastly, also in red, we have marked our selected tours.

By this Map we hope also to impress on our friends that beautiful as are Scottish Woollens, we produce something even more beautiful in Scottish scenery.

Our argument always has been that our Scottish Woollens owe much of their outstanding excellence to the country itself and its influence on the people of Scotland. Their independence has been maintained against powerful neighbours because of the mountainous and rugged nature of most of the country. Its unsuitability for agriculture has made it less attractive to colonising invaders, and so has left the stock more characteristic and, as we might say, more native. The wonderful and unrivalled variety of our landscape is, and always has been, the outstanding influence behind our designers, and suggests a fundamental reason why our leading position in the trade of making fancy woollens should continue as long as the national energy remains to take full advantage of these initial advantages.

Scotland is quite a small country, and in the compass of a day's motoring, the traveller can pass through a variety of scenery such as exists nowhere else in the world in the same space. For example, starting not so very early in the Border Country of Sir Walter Scott, the traveller passes amongst the gentle, rounded green hills of the Tweed Valley, most magnificent sheep country and the original country of the Cheviot sheep. He passes by Edinburgh, through the plains of the Lothians, the most densely populated area in Europe, famous not only for its coal and iron, but for the oatmeal that has helped to make Scotland famous. Far ahead, behind the fertile foreground, rises the rugged skyline of the Highlands. About lunch time, beyond Perth or Crieff, he enters the Highlands and passes the afternoon amongst the almost uninhabited mountains of the Grampians. In the late afternoon, he comes down through the desolate and heather-clad moors into the wide cultivated strip of coast lands and sees across the shining waters of the Moray Firth the countless mountain tops of Sutherland against the sunset. The journey is only a little over 200 miles. We have no ranges as vast as the Rockies or the Alps; our most barren places have not the soul-oppressing desolateness of the Arizona desert; our deepest gorges are tiny compared with the fantastic depths of the canyons of Colorado; our plains are not to be compared with the plains of Lombardy for fertility and magnificence. But the whole country is of a size more easily understood by man, more friendly and repays intimate acquaintance most wonderfully.

Our climate is a good climate to live with. Warmed by the Gulf Stream, it is far warmer than its latitude would suggest. It is not very wet, although the even distribution of the rainfall leaves our summers less reliable than holiday-makers would like. It varies from the dry parts of the east coast with about 24 inches, to about 60 or even 80 on the west coast, and that is one of the items in making up the wonderful variety of our scenery. It also leaves our atmosphere in perfect state for the perfect production and manufacture of wool. Inside a modern factory, of course, any kind of atmosphere can be kept up indefinitely, but the country is beyond our control, and in Scotland we stand about 10 per cent moister than most of North America. Moreover, the much smaller range of temperature gives us an advantage more reliable and everlasting than any protective tariff. We have a real advantage in producing wool and woollen clothes and our rivals just cannot help it.

Beneath all this wonderful variety of climate and scenery lies the structure of the country.

A marked feature of our Map is the great difference between the East and West coasts, and here our geological history comes in. Those long arms of the sea that stretch inland and give the tourist the plague of ferry crossing, besides wonderful beauty and variety of landscape, are really submerged land valleys. We have not submergence on the overwhelming scale shown by the submarine canyons discovered by the U.S.A. Coast survey – there is a scale model of the New England canyons in the Museum of Science in Chicago – but what happened with Scotland was that on an axis running more or less along the west coast, the country gently turned, sinking the mountains to the west into islands and raising the sandy bottom of the sea on the other side into the level coast lands of the east.

We have always tried to demonstrate in these small monographs how completely everything in the world is interlocked, tied together by invisible and unknown bonds of intimacy, so that to imagine that we can stand alone is one of the ultimate imbecilities. We heard a quaint illustration the other day. A lot of our cured fish is sold locally by the fishermen themselves: they catch the fish and "smoke" them at home, so that there are differences between the fish smoked, not only in different districts, but by different fishers. This arises partly out of the particular wood used for the smoking. Our friend suggested that the fish were not as good as usual, to which she got this reply, "Weel, ye see, Mem, wi' this revolution and disturbance in China, oor mill is no makin' silk bobbins for the Chinese and a canna get birch chips to smoke the fish." A story to recommend to all politicians for study.

Tours throughout the south are so easily found from Edinburgh or Glasgow that we have not mentioned all sorts of long and short excursions through the Scott and Burns countries – these parts are too well known. But for the longer journeys in the north, some guidance is necessary if the best is to be seen in the shortest time. On mileage, all can be done in a day, but all would be better in two days, for Highland roads even yet are in parts narrow, rough and steep. Even apart from the fact that the traveller should be there to admire the scenery, safety requires speeds down to 20 miles an hour, and there are considerable lengths of road where cars can only pass at the prepared passing places.

Tour No. 1 (222 miles), from Inverness, goes along the shores of the Beauly Firth due west and turns north through Beauly and Dingwall. About eight miles further north take the hill road to Bonar Bridge, from which one of the finest views in the north opens before you. Thence to Lairg and straight north to Tongue, about 40 miles, by the Crask, across one of the most desolate and almost uninhabited districts in Scotland. All along the north coast till near Thurso the road winds up and down amongst rocky scenery through the country of the deeply-cursed Clearances, which emptied the Highlands and peopled Canada. Thence through strangely different country of flagstone fences to John o' Groats, the furthest point of mainland Scotland. The road home is right down the edge of the sea, here and there commanding glorious views of sea and land, and testing the driver's nerve with steep hills and sharp corners. The road is excellent all down to Inverness.

Our second tour (120 miles) takes the great new Glen Albyn road up Loch Ness, where good luck may give you a glimpse of the famous, some say fabulous, Monster. Twenty-eight miles up the loch take the Glenmoriston-Skye road to Cluanie. This takes you through some of the finest mountain country. The steep and narrow hill road from the little Cluanie Inn takes you back to Fort Augustus by Glengarry. Fort Augustus is the site of one of the chain of forts built early in the eighteenth century to subdue the Highlands. From Fort Augustus it is most interesting to return by the precipitous Glendoe road by Whitebridge and Daviot to Inverness.

Tour No. 3 (174 miles) takes you through the finest of the easily accessible scenery of the west coast. Inverness by Beauly once more; at Muir of Ord, leave the main road and pick your way by a maze of small and lovely roads to Garve and Achnasheen. For a few days' hill climbing, Kinlochewe and Loch Maree are ideal, and Gairloch for bathing and boating is ill to beat. Thence the return journey is by Dundonell. The road is steep and winding and for many miles passing is not easy, and the theatrical descent at Gruinard Bay leaves you wondering what the hill was like before it was "improved". On the way back, the road can be varied by passing Strathpeffer Spa, the hospital headquarters of the American Army in the Great War, and the little old Cathedral of Dornoch.

No. 4 (160 miles) starts from Perth – or, if you like, from Edinburgh or Glasgow – just as straight as the crow flies north to Braemar. The road passes through the rich, small-fruit growing country of Blairgowrie and over the abrupt old military road by the Devil's Elbow, no longer a terror to high-power modern cars, but one of the old hill test routes. The road goes right down Strathdee to Aberdeen past the Royal Estate of Balmoral, beloved of Queen Victoria. It is more interesting not to go all the way to Aberdeen, but turn south at Banchory by the Cairn o' Mounthe road. A view of surprising extent is seen from the top. The summit is the very edge of the mountain area, and the land falls away north, south and east over the foot-hills to richly cultivated country and the sea. There is a good choice of roads back to Perth

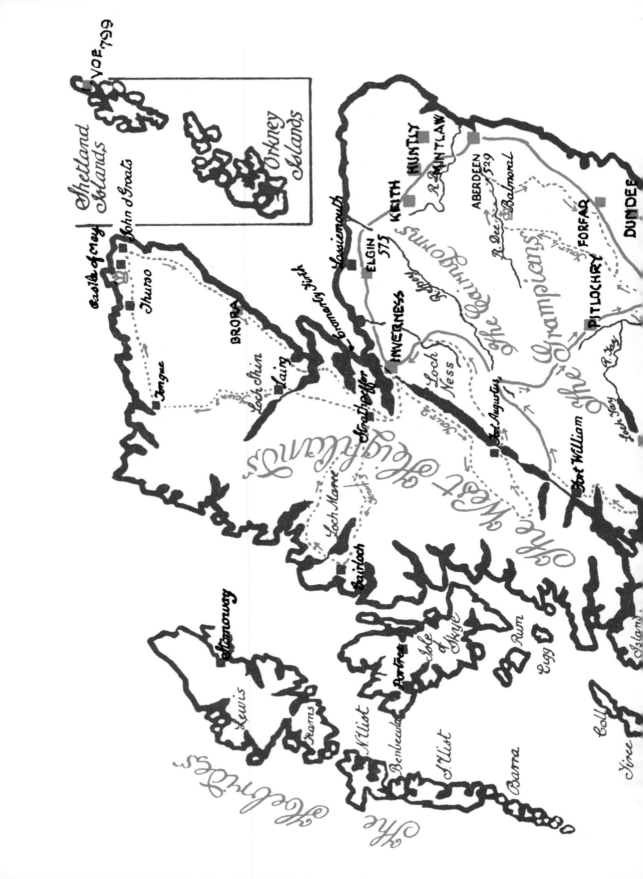

MAP DRAWN BY ROBERT BURNS, R.S.A., IN 1937.

Brought up to date January 1956.

Members' towns are marked with red squares and are in capitals. Names only of general interest are marked in italics.

The numbers sprinkled here and there are the miles by road from London.

The Tours are shown by Dotted Lines and a few of the Railways are shown in red.

through Barrie's "Thrums" (Kirriemuir) and Strathmore, past the home of the parents of the Queen Mother at Glamis, one of the oldest inhabited houses in Scotland.

Route 5 (289 miles) starts from Glasgow right north past the far-famed Loch Lomond, and through the desolate Moor of Rannoch, well known to readers of R. L. Stevenson's "Kidnapped". Through the savage Glencoe to Fort William, beneath Ben Nevis, the highest mountain in Great Britain. We propose the return journey by Laggan and the Great North Road to Dunkeld, and thence home by the Sma' Glen, Crieff, St Fillans, Callander, the Trossachs and Aberfoyle for the memory of Scott's "Lady of the Lake" and "Rob Roy".

We are overwhelmed by the mass of interesting material suggested by our Map, but we must not finish without a word about guides. The outstanding book of general interest is H. V. Morton's "In Search of Scotland". For guide-books proper: "Blue Guide to Scotland," edited by Findlay Muirhead, published by Ernest Benn, 1932, 12s. 6d.; Ward Lock's "Complete Scotland," 7s. 6d. For maps, as a broad, general indicator, the Dunlop Touring Maps of the British Isles, published by Burrow & Co., London, at 3s.; for more particular, purposes the Ordnance Survey (Government) ¼ inch, or Bartholomew's of the same scale. For local purposes and walkers, there is nothing to be compared to the Ordnance 1 inch to the mile, and for climbers and walkers, there are no district guides as complete as the Scottish Mountaineering Club Guides, published by Douglas & Foulis, Edinburgh. Finally, the best authority on roads and hotels is the Automobile Association, Fanum House, London. And, ladies and gentlemen, within the compass of our space, that is all we can say.

BIRTH-PLACE OF HARRIS TWEED

N amateur in most trades is at a disadvantage in competition with a professional, and so, as we are amateur editors, we generally discover our mistakes only when our kind readers write and point them out. "Our Map" has had an extraordinary success, which has fortunately obscured faults in No. 17, which kept it company. We have three mistakes pointed out to us. No prize is offered for their discovery. We have now corrected them! And so we come to our present subject.

A foreign buyer to whom patterns of Harris Tweed had been submitted is traditionally reputed to have inquired innocently as to who Mr Harris might be, and on being told that no such person existed and that the cloth shown was a native product of the Outer Hebrides of Scotland exclaimed, "Ah, that so desolate part in the far North where the people are still savages!"

Thirty miles from the Scottish mainland, in the very maw of the Atlantic, lie the Outer Hebrides: swept in winter by gale and tempest, but enjoying a summer of calm and beauty. The remoteness of the islands and the difficulties of communication have discouraged the ordinary traveller, and until recent years, with the exception of occasional sportsmen who came up to fish for salmon and stalk deer, visitors were few and far between. The extravagant and ill-informed reports of superficial observers have greatly misrepresented the life and habits of the islanders, whose generous and intimate hospitality was often ignorantly abused. The islanders' innate distrust of strangers and a propensity for "telling the tale" have misled many too-gullible inquirers whose extraordinary reports have been widely circulated.

The physical characteristics of the islands present a glorious combination of moorland, loch, mountain and sea. Wide stretches of peat moor studded with myriads of small freshwater lochs and deeply indented with winding tentacles of the sea sweep down from the north to the rugged hills of the south. There are several small rivers and innumerable streams abounding with salmon and trout. As becomes a fishing community, the villages are almost all on the coast, and there also the small patches of cultivated land are to be found. Outside the Port of Stornoway roads are few and in most cases of poor condition as until recent times mere tracks across the moor sufficed. One main road runs from north to south of the island connecting Lewis and Harris, and linking up with many of the larger villages.

Although today through the Port of Stornoway a not inconsiderable traffic in all kinds of merchandise is done with the islanders, the day is not so far past when the community was self-supporting. Of necessity, the people were then dependent

WIDE STRETCHES OF PEAT MOOR

on the produce of sea and land. They grew their own crops of barley, oats and rye, reared their stock of cows, horses, sheep and goats, built their own boats and houses, and made both linen and homespun woollen cloth. The islander must have been a handy man, for at varying times he was farmer, fisherman, mason, carpenter, shipwright and weaver. To a lesser extent, this is still true today, for he continues to cultivate the land and pursue the fishing, builds his own house and weaves cloth in his home. He grows crops, although nowadays mainly for the feeding of his stock, which consists of cows, sheep and an occasional horse – goats and hogs having almost disappeared.

The historical and traditional aspects of the island present a wealth of study of amazing interest. Geologists agree that the Western Isles and parts of the West Coast of the mainland opposite are the oldest land surface in the world. This was dry land before the Alps were pushed up from the bottom of the sea, before the mighty ranges of the Rockies were formed. As one would expect, there are many relics from bygone ages, of which perhaps the most famous is the Stone Circle at Callanish, which "was old when Rome was yet unborn". Not far away on a hilltop overlooking the sea is a splendid example of an ancient Hebridean fort, or broch, and throughout the islands there are numerous remains of stone circles, beehive huts, burial places and underground chambers, while the peat bogs continually yield fresh treasures of antiquity. There is no written record of these remains to tell us of the peoples who brought them into being, and we can merely speculate as to their origin and purpose. As one authority puts it, "the evidence of these silent witnesses seems to point to the presence, in remote times, of well ordered communities who certainly possessed a knowledge of leverage; possibly some acquaintance with the science of astronomy; obviously distinctive burial customs; and in all likelihood a religious cult concerning which we know nothing; and who have left behind nothing but their monuments."

In the Norse Sagas of the Viking period, one finds the earliest references

CALLANISH STONES—KNOWN IN THE GAELIC AS
THE FALSE MEN

to the Western Isles, as from the eighth to the thirteenth century the islands were in the hands of the Norsemen who intermarried with the ancient native race and the Celtic element that came over from Ireland. The islands were ceded to Scotland after the Battle of Largs and in succession passed through the hands of the Macleods, the Mackenzies and the Mathesons. To this day, the Norse type persists in parts of the islands, especially in Ness, and both place-names and customs bear witness to their influence. From the thirteenth to the seventeenth centuries, the islands bore their own part in the making of history as far as Scotland is concerned, and their internal history is similar to that of the Highlands under the Clan system.

In 1703 one of our earliest travel books was published, "A Description of the Western Islands of Scotland: by Martin Martin, Gent". It had the imprint – London printed for Andrew Bell at the Cross-Keys and Bible in Cornhil, near Stocks-Market, 1703. When a boy, the great Dr Johnson was given a copy of Martin's book by his father and it was this that set the venturesome old man touring with his assiduous Boswell round these little-known and remote regions in 1773 in a kind of royal progress. The actual volume given to him by his father travelled with the two adventurers and is now in the Scottish National Library in Edinburgh. The volume was reprinted by Eneas Mackay in Stirling in 1934. In Johnson's days, such a tour was considered as hazardous as a journey to the Far East. "The Outer Isles were roadless and storm-swept and for the long sea journey only open boats of no great size were available".

He found "the natives are generally ingenious and quick of apprehension: they have a mechanical genius and ... a gift of poesy, and are able to form a satire or panegyric extempore, without the assistance of any stronger liquor than water to raise their fancy. They are great lovers of music; ... they are still very hospitable, but the late years of scarcity brought them very low, and many of the poor people have died of famine."

He mentions several peculiar remedies for illness, such as, "The jaundice they cure two ways – the first is by laying the patient on his face and pretending to look upon his backbones, they presently pour a pail-full of cold water on his bare back; and this proves successful. The second cure they perform by taking the tongs and making them red hot in the fire; then pulling off the clothes from the patient's back, he who holds the tongs gently touches the patient on the vertebrae upwards of the back, which makes him furiously run out of doors, still supposing the hot iron is on his back, till the pain be abated, which happens very speedily and the patient recovers soon after."

Wherever he went, Martin was hospitably received and was accustomed to receive gifts with such addresses as "Traveller, we are sensible of the favour you have done us by coming so far with a design to instruct us in our way to happiness, and at the same time to venture yourself on the great ocean: pray be pleased to accept this small present, which we humbly offer as an expression of our sincere love to you."

The simplicity of the people, especially of those in the smaller isles of the Hebrides, made their happiness apparent.

"They have cows, sheep, barley and oats, and live a harmless life, being perfectly ignorant of most of those vices that abound in the world. They know nothing of money or gold, having no occasion for either; they neither buy nor sell, but only barter for such little things as they want: they covet no wealth, being fully content and satisfied with food and raiment; though at the same time they are very precise in the matter of property among themselves: they have an agreeable and hospitable temper for all strangers. Their houses are built of stone and thatched with straw, which is kept down with ropes of the same, poised with stones."

Such was Martin Martin's experience in the Outer Isles, and even today the stranger will find many of the old customs still intact, although famine no longer takes its toll and medicine has changed its ways of combating disease. The islanders still lift their voices in song at work and at play, and there is still a ready welcome for the stranger.

CARLOWAY DUN: ONE OF THE FINEST BROCHS IN SCOTLAND

With the decay of the Clan system after the Jacobite Rebellion of 1745 and the succession of bad years on the land, emigration on a large scale to the Colonies took many of the islanders from their homes. The lack of security of tenure and the extortionate landlordism of these times drove the people from Highlands and Islands, and the dreadful "Clearances", which sent families and whole villages from their ancient homes to distant lands, were the means of bringing into being the Crofters Act of 1886, which made it possible for the people to dwell again in peace and security.

In the nineteenth century, education penetrated to the Outer Isles, and schools controlled and run by the churches were planted throughout the various districts. The standard of education was high and the zeal and merit of the pupils was such that many made their mark at home and abroad. The spread of education brought with it an expansion of trade in the islands. Fishing, an industry which

TOLSTA CHAOLAIS: "MYRIADS OF SMALL FRESHWATER LOCHS"

the Dutch had commercialised in the island waters as early as the seventeenth century, became of great importance. Herring and white fish, such as cod and ling, were cured and exported to all parts at home and abroad. Ship-building was a flourishing business in the Port of Stornoway until the advent of steam. The Congested District Board, which was appointed to deal with the special problems of the islands and similar districts, introduced blood stock to improve the breeding of cows and sheep. They also sent up to the islands a skilled craftsman to improve the methods of making cloth, which previous to that were very primitive.

In the days when cloth was made only for the islanders' own use, the wool was entirely carded and spun by hand, was dyed in yarn and warped, woven and finished in the most primitive way. Owing to the methods used, the cloth was full of imperfections, and the work involved was exceedingly tedious and laborious. The carding and spinning was done by the women during the long winter evenings at the fireside, while the men repaired their nets, and the stories and songs of olden times helped to lighten the burden of the work. The warping was done working with two threads and took almost two days to warp a length of tweed, while the weaving on the rudimentary loom with the shuttle thrown by hand was incredibly slow.

When the Duchess of Sutherland of that day took an interest in the islanders' tweed and persuaded the Congested District Board to send someone to help to improve the methods of tweed making, many of the old ways were changed. Small carding, and later on spinning plants, were introduced; dyeing pots of a fair size were distributed to the various districts so that the wool could be dyed instead of yarn; warping stakes were provided and the warpers taught to work with thirty-six threads instead of two, and fly shuttle hand-looms greatly extended the scope of the weaving. The finishing of the tweed was also improved. Formerly, the shrinking of the cloth was accomplished by tramping the tweed in small tubs with the feet; but now the women were made to sit opposite each other in rows while the tweed was spread on a long plank between them and was thumped, squeezed and slapped to the merry rhythm of the "Waulking Songs", until shrunk to the desired width.

In 1911, the Harris Tweed Trade Mark was first registered by the Harris Tweed Association Limited, and the mark required that all processes with the exception of carding should be carried out by hand, and the output was thus of necessity very limited. The name Harris Tweed was officially adopted, as it was in the Harris portion of the Long Island that the cloth was first made.

As time went on and the tweed became known and established in popular favour, it was found necessary to develop and organise the industry so that the growing demand could be met. More and improved looms were introduced and special dyed shades and special finishes required by world-wide trade were obtained on the mainland. The expansion during the war led to the importation of yarn on a gradually increasing scale from mainland mills, and latterly the quality of such imported yarns made to a price was greatly detrimental to the traditional reputation of the cloth. After the war, the industry suffered from competition of cheap imitation tweed made on the mainland, and even on the Continent and in Japan, which was sold as genuine Harris Tweed. The situation became steadily worse, and at last the Board of Trade was approached and a revision of the original Trade Mark secured, which was in keeping with the development of the industry and which confined the entire process of production of Harris Tweed to the Outer Hebrides.

A NORTH UIST LANDSCAPE

A HIGHLAND CROFT

The definition set forth was as follows:

"'Harris Tweed' means a tweed made from pure virgin wool produced in Scotland, spun, dyed and finished in the Outer Hebrides and hand-woven by the islanders at their own homes in the Islands of Lewis, Harris, Uist, Barra and their several purtenances, and all known as the Outer Hebrides."

It was further provided that "wherever the Harris Tweed Trade Mark is used, there shall be added in legible characters to the Harris Tweed Trade Mark the words 'Woven in Harris' or 'Woven in Lewis' or 'Woven in Uist' or 'Woven in Barra', as the case may be, and for the purpose of distinction there shall also be added the word 'Handspun' in the case of tweeds made entirely from handspun yarns."

Small finishing and dyeing plants have since been erected in the islands to undertake the special work that formerly went to the mainland. Today, the making of tweed provides a livelihood for hundreds of men and women in the islands, and the failure of the herring fishing in several successive seasons has turned many more of the younger generation to the making of "Clò Mór" – the "Big Cloth" – as it is called in the Gaelic.

Although the majority of the island folk are bilingual, the language of hearth and home is still Gaelic.

In Stornoway itself, where most of the incomers have congregated and settled down, English and Gaelic go side by side, but in the landward parts of the island, one is at a definite disadvantage without Gaelic, because many of the older people have very little English; some of them have none whatever and all of them are much more at ease in the native tongue. Both languages are taught in the schools, and Gaelic ranks along with French, German and Latin in the final examinations.

The Gaelic accent of the isles is softer and more melodious than that of the mainland, and environment and tradition have established certain peculiarities of pronunciation and idiom that cannot but captivate the fancy. It is interesting to find that the English of these Gaelic speakers is more than usually free from accent and from slang, owing to the fact that it is first acquired in school and is learned really as a foreign language.

The haunting melodies of the islands with their essential undercurrent of sadness are known to lovers of folk-songs throughout the world. Labour lilts, lullabies, love songs, dance tunes, and beautiful descriptive eulogies of mountain, glen and sea, handed down from time immemorial, link the present with the past and preserve the true spirit of the Gaelteachd. Several musicians, including the late Mrs Kennedy Fraser, have published arrangements of these songs with English words. An Comunn Gaidhealach, the Gaelic Society whose headquarters are at West Regent Street, Glasgow, can give authoritative direction to anyone interested in Gaelic songs and publications.

Some of these days we hope to come back to the subject of this ancient and primitive cloth industry, and should we be spared long enough, we promise that we shall devote a "Scottish Woollens" to the whole art and process of making Harris Tweed, which is such an interesting contrast to the highly mechanised and intricate business of making Scottish tweeds.

A BLACK HOUSE

HARRIS TWEED

This is the Harris Tweed Trade Mark. It is controlled by the Harris Tweed Association. The mark is affixed by the Association's Inspectors only to cloth that undoubtedly complies with the strict definition laid down by the Government.

CASHMERE

HRISTMAS has just passed and the Editor and the Author – that is, us or we – had been reading "Gulliver's Travels". Not that Gulliver is particularly a Christmas book, but because we were on holiday and could read what we liked. We had just come to the place where he sails to Luggnagg and we rebelled flatly against the bleak and despairing view of life in the story of these Strulbrugs who were born to live for ever. These immortals were marked from birth, and the future held for them no prospect but misery. Their powers decayed as did those of other men. They outlived their interests and their friendships. They became a burden on the community and were hated from the beginning. This image or simile or allegory, or whatever you like to call it, is not true, we agreed. Another idea was borne in upon us. It has to do with the immortality of Scottish Woollens; also it was a cheerful idea and so we pass it on. We discussed our own feelings and experiences, and they were not at all like the experiences of Swift's old men. It is true our combined ages did not amount to an important contribution to eternity, but they were a start. We found that we had never been any younger and were certainly not any older than we ever had been. We examined different parts of our lives. We found we had always lived just our life-time – neither more nor less. The only difference between our childhood's days and our grown-up days was that when we were children it was an almost interminable age to look forward to next Christmas – today it seemed almost time to be thinking of presents again. There could be no doubt that in two or three hundred years we could look forward to living for ever in the genial, friendly, warm atmosphere of Christmas.

This was a much more satisfactory conclusion than Swift's dismal illogic. So we took a piece of chalk and, in spite of quotas and currency restrictions and duties and politicians, we followed Buster Brown's example and wrote up, "Resolved: We Will Live Forever."

In the intervals of reading Gulliver, we had been discussing the war in China and wondering how we were to write a "Scottish Woollens" on Cashmere, and how long it might be before there would be a proper supply, and if there were any chance that the Japanese would manage to kill all the goats in China. We thought not.

All Cashmere comes from Central Asia, from China from the mountains up towards Thibet and away across the back of the Himalayas to Bokhara. The finest comes from the Eastern end of this great tract of half-explored mountains and finds its way down to Tientsin, where it is classified and packed for the Western markets. It still travels as it travelled long before Polo explored the Great Silk Road in the thirteenth century. It comes down to the Hoad in countless little loads by every means of transport – on the backs of men, of yaks, of camels, of horses, on rafts buoyed up with inflated skins, on boats down the interminable water-ways of China. A slow journey, probably more than a year long, down to Tientsin, whence modern transport whisks it swiftly to Europe and America. Thinking of the map, we are apt to wonder why the Cashmere should go all across the vast continent of Asia instead of reaching some port of India. Then we remember the stories of the still unconquered Everest and we have the answer. Across the vast barrier of the Himalaya there are no routes. There is nothing for it but to go round. Anyhow, what does time matter? Time was made for slaves.

Thus it happens that of Cashmere nothing but the name comes from India. That name itself brings before us a most romantic interlude – the History of the Paisley shawl. We have promised ourselves some day to add this story to our "Scottish Woollens". It is a story most intimately connected with Scotland: the East India Company – the ever-wandering Scots with their strong memory of home – Pashmina shawls; Paisley and its beautiful adaptations of the work of the weavers of Cashmere. Paisley shawls became almost a necessity to the Early Victorian bride. R. L. Stevenson in that incomparable fragment, "Weir of Hermiston", writes of "her best India shawl in a pattern of radiant dyes". And have we not with us at this moment a charming ghost of these old splendours evoked by Laurence Housman, Helen Hayes, Pamela Stanley and Anna Neagle?

All this is only remotely and by derivation connected with Cashmere, the raw material. The finest of these cloths from Cashmere were made up from the carefully picked tit-bits of the wools of goats, sheep and yak; and their curiously soft and slippery touch gave the name to the even finer product of the Chinese uplands and mountains. Goats' Hair was not a suitable name, for it applied equally to the very coarse material used by the Arabs for their black tents and other very rough wools.

To sum up, the finest Cashmere is Chinese, and it comes from a comparatively small district west of Pekin. It is followed by Manchurian. The coarser qualities come down on to the Persian Gulf and are known as East Indian or Gulf Cashmeres. They run almost into Mohair in character, and lack almost entirely the exquisite silky texture of the Chinese wools.

In Chinese Cashmeres, the three principal colours are white, which is the least common, grey, and brown. These are beautifully soft shades of stone colour, the warm shades known as "brown," although they are not really dark enough or definite enough to be brown in ordinary parlance. Now and then, there are darker shades, say half-way between black and white in depth.

The Gulf Cashmeres are also of three leading shades – white and fawn, which, unlike the Chinese wools, form the bulk; and brown, a much darker shade than "brown" Chinese. Of course, all these shades vary greatly, and those who buy "natural" colours, in the correct sense of undyed, need not expect the standard of matching exacted for ordinary colours. Small quantities of very fine material come from Northern India under the name Pashmina, and also small quantities of dark wool from Turkey of a markedly inferior type (probably partly Ibex).

In all these many types of Cashmere the bulk of the wool is not white, and so, when pastel shades are in fashion, white rises to an utterly disproportionate price.

The Angora goat that produces Mohair followed the Dutch settlers to the U.S.A., the Cape and Tasmania. Seemingly, no effort has ever been made to acclimatise goats of the Thibetan type beyond their native hills. Cashmere wools are thus entirely Asiatic.

Before the Great War the very finest Cashmere came from Russia, but, as far as we can learn, this Russian Cashmere was grown in the Caucasus and Turkestan. It was like the Chinese wool in character, and is in fact equalled by occasional lots of the best from Tientsin. We have not been able to find out anything about these Russian wools – whether the various "Plans" run by the U.S.S.R. have exterminated the goats or whether these wools are absorbed by Russia for their home trade; but they never appear in the Sales now.

In telling the story of Vicuna, we told how many of these rarer wools form a sort of double coat for the animals – a strong outer coat growing from the under skin as a protection from the weather and a fine fleece of the softest hair growing from the upper skin to keep the beast warm. Cashmere is like that and has to go through a slow and expensive mechanical preparation to remove the coarse hairs. The difference between the two lots of hair is most remarkable. The fine wool is finer than even the finest Australian Merino; the coarse hair often as coarse as the coarsest Cheviot. Cashmeres, during preparation, may lose from about one-quarter of their weight up to three-quarters or even more.

The quantity of Chinese Cashmere coming into the London Sales varies from two thousand to four thousand bales a year. Possibly double that quantity would represent the whole produce for the service of the world. Each bale might yield, say, 200 pounds of prepared wool, so that in a good year there might be about 1,200,000 pounds and about half that quantity in a bad year. The quantity of Cashmere varies greatly from year to year – far more than ordinary wool. Possibly in a season of poor prices, each one of the innumerable owners of a few goats just keeps his wool. The fine shades of scientific management cut no ice in Thibet. So we have no very proper figures to go on, and must, just like Evarra, lay down the law for ourselves. "Thus Gods are made and whoso makes them otherwise shall die." It is about a quarter of the quantity of fine Eastern Camel, and although it is a vast quantity compared with Vicuna, it is a very small flea-bite compared with sheep's wools.

From Persia, the total runs to about five thousand bales. The chief collecting centres are Meshed and Kerman. About two thousand bales of the best come from Kerman. East Indian wools, like Russian, have ceased to appear. It may be that the native trade uses more than formerly, or it is quite likely that the new disinfecting regulations in Britain have deflected them into Persia. Persian Cashmere has never been popular in the London Sales and only appeared spasmodically. Some years it all goes to Russia. Some years Germany takes a considerable quantity. The wool is now classified and packed in bales. Until a few years ago, it was exported as it came down from the mountains, "roped" – that is, twisted into a rope-like form. As one of the principal people handling these wools says, "The strong hairs that were typically goat were rolled inside and a liberal amount of sand was added."

Now a word about the uses of Cashmere. Its chief feature is its exquisite softness and warmth – partly real, from its excellent non-conducting properties; partly imaginary, from the satisfying sense of luxury and comfort that its use induces. It is so fine that it can be spun to very small yarns. Its most unrivalled use is for garments that give warmth without weight. No one with knowledge dare dogmatise on this, but we may venture a very cautious opinion that probably a fifth or even a quarter less weight is needed as compared with other wools. This is a point little appreciated by buyers who insist on their Cashmere cloths being of the same weights as the more proletarian cloths of sheep's wool. Thus they kill two birds with one stone: they add to the price they have to pay, and they destroy one of the chief delights for the wearer. The wool is expensive enough for the extra weight to make a marked difference to the cost.

In China, one of its most valued uses is in making "wind hats". Again, readers of Everest books will remember the constant and terrible winds that seem to blow for ever in these desolate regions. In Europe, a lot of fine Cashmere was used in making the finest Austrian felts for both men's hats and women's. It makes a material smooth, pliable, lustrous, wind-proof and almost water-proof.

But perhaps the most beautiful feature of Cashmere is its lustre. This feature is most marked in Chinese. Under wet brushing or raising, it develops a beautiful, shining, rippled surface. It is true this lovely effect cannot be fixed and that it tends to disappear as the cloth ruffles under wear, but it is a delight to look at, and to a certain extent revives again if it is lightly brushed in the direction of the pile while it is wet on the surface with a shower of rain.

From the trader's point of view, Cashmere, like all limited materials, has a drawback. It fluctuates enormously in price. Not many years ago, the sudden and remarkable success of a ladies' material made in France under the trade name of "Kasha," and containing only a percentage of Cashmere, sent Cashmere prices whizzing upwards like a rocket. White rose to prices rivalling – nay, exceeding – Vicuna. It is quite independent of wool, and may be climbing steeply upwards while wool is slithering downwards into a morass of slump conditions.

This beautiful wool has another drawback, which it shares with all the wools not grown on sheep. It is very inelastic. One of the most valuable features of sheep's wool is its resilience, so that in closely cut garments, it returns to its shape after being stretched. Skirts continue to hang straight. Trousers do not bag at the knees. This lack of spring is certainly a disadvantage in many ways. It causes quite a lot of difficulties in manufacturing, but it has a compensating advantage in its perfect draping qualities in such uses as shawls, scarves, knitted garments, and fine dress goods.

Cashmere is dear – no, rather let us say expensive – but it costs no more to make up than the cheapest cloths. As it approaches the wearer costs accumulate upon it as upon everything else – transport, manufacturing, making-up, and possibly much the highest of all, distribution. None of these can be entirely avoided, but the inevitable result is that the finest and most expensive materials show the highest proportion of intrinsic value when they reach the wearer. To a greater or a less degree, this applies to all our cloths, and it is one of the greatest and most real of the many advantages of wearing Scottish Woollens.

CHEVIOT WOOL

 HE two home-grown wools that are of the most interest to the Scottish manufacturer are Cheviot and English Downs. Both breeds are named after their native hills – the Cheviot from the range of that name which forms the traditional boundary between England and Scotland, and the Downs from the chalky ridge that stretches from the Kentish border to the extreme west of Wiltshire; but while the latter sheep are still mainly to be found on their historic pastures, the Cheviots have invaded the whole of Scotland and Northumberland.

Down wool forms an important ingredient in the blend for many Scottish yarns, but we propose to deal with it in a future number.

Cheviot is the most essentially Scottish of all wools; it is grown at its best in Scotland and the great bulk of the clip is manufactured in Scotland. It gives its name to a type of cloth that is characteristically Scottish, and recognised as such over all the world, so much so that it is inclined to overshadow the other products of our mills.

The wool would seem almost to have taken on the character of the true native Scot, in that, under a slightly rough exterior, it is sound and honest at heart. It is in every respect a sound wool, strong and wear-resisting, and possessing that indefinable quality of "bone", which gives it life and strength without harshness.

Technically, the wool can be described as regular, crimpy, lofty, clean and dense. Off good grassy pastures, it is a snowy white, but on mossy ground it is apt to become stained; but always it maintains its inherent brightness, and when dyed this adds lustre to the colour.

In a previous number, we dealt with the history of the sheep; it might interest the reader to hear the annually recurring story of the wool, the clipping, the marketing and its final transformation into cloth.

The shearing of the sheep – or "the clipping" as it is always called – takes place towards the end of June or the beginning of July, according to climatic and seasonal conditions. The exact date at any farm is usually fixed by arrangement with neighbouring farmers, as the shepherds of each may assist the other at this function, which indeed is the most important of the year in a pastoral district.

It is a day of strenuous work for all, not without its festive side; the bleating of sheep mingles with the barking of dogs, and above the din the occasional cry of a shepherd. There are alarms and excursions as when a sheep bolts or a dispute arises amongst the dogs, of whom there are probably about four pairs present; in the latter case, their masters' attention is diverted from their immediate task and the matter settled with sticks and shouts.

Although the work starts at an early hour, the sun is usually low on the horizon before the last sheep is shorn and the last fleece packed. There have, it is true, been breaks for necessary refreshment, and the interpretation of "necessary" depends on the host's hospitable nature and his ideas of what is necessary and fitting; and on this, too, depends the trim in which, after a cheery parting, the neighbouring shepherds finally call off their dogs and start on the long tramp home.

A fine set of men these Scottish "herds", and their intelligence is matched by the wonderful dogs they have trained to assist them in their work. To see these dogs working at their daily round or at sheep dog trials is a revelation. Their wonderful patience with a refractory, frightened or stupid sheep is a marvel of skill and restraint – an object lesson to humanity.

To return to our wool: this is already packed, unless its ultimate destination is still undecided, in which case it will be built into a neat pile in a shed or barn, each fleece carefully rolled up with the clipped side exposed.

Home-grown wool is almost invariably packed into sheets of a more or less standard size, say, 9 feet by 5 feet, except where there are difficulties in transport, such as in the Highlands and Islands, where it has sometimes to be conveyed in rowing boats to the waiting steamer; under these conditions, it is packed in long bags of approximately half the size of a sheet.

Packing is all done by hand, or to be more correct, by hand and foot. The sheet is suspended by ropes from a crossbar or hooks. One or more men throw the fleeces into the sheet, while another standing in it tramps them down. There is a certain art in this, and a well-packed sheet gladdens the eye of an expert. Dominion or Overseas wool is usually packed in square-ended bales under hydraulic or other pressure, and therefore occupies less space, weight for weight – an important matter in sea transport.

The ordinary farmer's clip of Cheviot wool contains a proportion of about a fifth of hogs, or yearling sheep, shorn for the first time. This wool runs a little finer than that of the older sheep, and, if sold separately, brings a slightly higher price. If the clip is sold as a whole, the proportion of hogs is an element in adjusting the price.

A large proportion of the Cheviot wool is clipped in the washed state – that is to say, about a week or ten days before shearing, the sheep are put through a pond or dammed-up burn, and thereby most of the natural grease and grit that adheres to the wool are removed. When this is not done, the wool is sold as unwashed or greasy at a correspondingly lower price level.

The mention of price brings us to the subject of marketing. To the pastoral farmer, the sale of his wool is an all-important matter. It is often said that the wool pays the rent, but whether it yields a surplus or leaves a deficit depends on the market level of the commodity. To indicate how much the price factor may affect the wool grower, it is only necessary to quote a few figures that illustrate the violent fluctuations that have taken place since the war period. In 1920, most farmers would get about 42d. per pound for their Washed Cheviot; in the following year, they were lucky if they got 9½d.; in 1924, it was up at 27d. and fell to 8d. again in 1931. Actually, we know of a farmer who received £1500 for his Cheviot clip in 1920, and for a similar clip £350 in the following year. It means that a man for the same outlay and effort and risk of capital may get in one year a return of only one-quarter as compared with another.

There is, of course, an economic price at which the wool can be grown, and if it falls below that no one appears to benefit, and even the ultimate wearer of the cloth pays the same price for his suit.

Generally speaking, the farmer has three main outlets: he can send his wool to a broker to be sold at auction; he can entrust it to a wool merchant or dealer, who will either buy it outright or act as an intermediary; or he can make his own bargain with a manufacturer. This last-mentioned method, common enough

in those happier pre-war days, has gradually been abandoned, and we must confess to a certain sentimental regret, because, before the speeding days of motor cars, these private purchases often involved long and pleasant excursions into the glens and calls at many friendly farmhouses. To the writer, the mere sight of a Cheviot sheep, the handle or smell of a fleece, will call up memories of forty or fifty years ago – of glorious June days spent in Yarrow or Ettrick, of long cracks (talks) in farm kitchens – the usual reception room except on state occasions – kitchens where the Border Minstrel or the Ettrick Shepherd had or may have sat; the very names of the farms, Altrieve, Eldinhope, Tushielaw, Deloraine, etc., summon up the "ballad notes" of which the air is full. Or if the guidman was outby, we might follow him on to the hill. In memory, we can "still feel the breeze down Ettrick break". Are the June days ever so fine as they used to be? The hills seem to have grown steeper.

The farmer certainly knew the purpose of our call, but the subject was not broached with any indecent haste; not till the weather and current topics were exhausted was the subject of wool mentioned. The approach would as a rule be casual. By a time-honoured custom, the purchaser of the clip in the previous year had the first refusal. If you happened to be in that position, there was really nothing to do but settle the price, but both parties knew full well that the price would not be settled that day: wool was not bought and sold in that way. The conversation would drift on about the state of trade, the merits or demerits of the particular clip or the price of Colonial wool; the bull points would be stressed by the vendor while the would-be purchaser adopted an unqualifiedly pessimistic outlook. The final words were almost always "Well, we'll be seeing you at Hawick," perhaps coupled with instructions to send over your wool sheets. This meant that the bargain was practically concluded and the price would be amicably adjusted at Hawick Fair a few weeks hence.

Hawick Fair – now, alas, no more – was held on the Tower Knowe in that town on the third or fourth Thursday of July each year, where for the day would be gathered most of the Border sheep farmers, the wool brokers and dealers, and other buyers. Here would be fixed the prices that would more or less rule for months to come. The arguments were long and apt to be tautological, lasting often into the late afternoon, till some hardy spirit would break the ice, a bargain would be struck, the news passed round in a flash, and then there was a scramble to sell or to secure the wool. Within the grey walls of the rather mediaeval hostelry that overlooked the busy scene, many bargains were clinched with the customary rites.

Hawick Fair was held for the last time in 1915.

While Hawick was always the principal Fair for pure-bred Cheviots, there were others in the Borders of greater general importance and earlier date at which much wool changed hands.

St James's Fair, held at Kelso, dates back at least to the days of David I in the twelfth century. It used to last eight days, but has now dwindled to one. Its proximity to England rendered it popular with the people from across the Border, and to this day much of the wool there is sold to English buyers. In the days before our union with England, quarrels frequently arose between the patrons from the two nations. A feud of more recent date was apt also to disturb the serenity of the Fair – that was between the Magistrates of Jedburgh, the County town, and those of Kelso. Jedburgh claimed the right to collect the market dues, a claim resisted unsuccessfully by Kelso, but not until many broken heads and minor injuries had been incurred. This feud lasted over many years, but presumably is now settled or at any rate abandoned.

It is to be noted that in the Proclamation of the Fair, all old and new feuds are prohibited; this prohibition, however, would not weigh much with the hot-headed Borderers. The Fair is held on St James's Green, a haugh between the rivers Tweed and Teviot, surely one of the most beautiful spots in Scotland. The ghosts looking down from the mouldering ruins of Roxburgh Castle, the site of which dominates the scene, must sometimes have been reminded of

"Old unhappy far-off things
And battles long ago."

The Fair was originally "cried" on the fifth day of August, the festival of St James the Apostle, the Patron Saint of the Parish. It is now held on the first Monday in August.

Another Fair is St Boswells. Its importance, at least in former days, is at once put in its proper perspective by the story about James Hogg, the Ettrick Shepherd. His friend, Sir Walter Scott, had with considerable difficulty secured a much coveted invitation to the Coronation of George IV. This Hogg regretfully declined as it would have interfered with his attendance at the Fair. John Lang in mentioning the circumstance adds: "My sympathies are with the Shepherd." This was at one time a great horse, sheep and wool fair, but much of its glory has departed. It is held on St Boswells' Green on the eighteenth day of July in each year, or, should that fall on a Sunday, on "the next lawful day". Naturally, being partly a horse fair, the gipsies are always there in force. When it was held on a Saturday or Monday, their arrival or departure disturbed the Sabbath calm of the rural parish, a fact lamented by the Ministers in both "Statistical Accounts of Scotland". The countryside is more accustomed nowadays to having the peace of their Sundays broken.

The wool sold here is mostly half-bred. St Boswells, incidentally, fixed the dates of Hawick and Bellingham Fairs, the first being held on the Thursday immediately following and Bellingham on the Saturday after Hawick. Bellingham is in Northumberland, and some of the best Northumbrian Cheviot clips are disposed of there.

Much more could be said or written about these Fairs. Their story is much interwoven with the domestic and national development of Scotland and particularly with the development of the Scottish Woollen Trade, but it is rather beyond our present purpose to go more deeply into the subject.

No mention of Fairs, however, would be complete without reference to the Inverness Fair. Here, the produce of the large flocks of Caithness, Sutherland, Ross and Inverness are still disposed of by private bargain. Much of the wool is the finest Cheviot in the country. The Fair, which lasts two or three days, is also something of a social function, and in days gone by was the great annual outing of the sheep farmers from the counties we have mentioned.

Most of the wool now goes to auction, where it finds its relative price level; and the farmer who improves his breed and gets up his wool in good condition is encouraged, and he who neglects these things is not. The trouble in the old days was that each farmer, apart from his expressed conviction that his wool was the best in the "Watergate" (valley), always expected and usually got exactly the same price as his neighbour irrespective of merit.

The principal auctions for Cheviot wool are held in Edinburgh, Leith and Hawick. The wool is exposed in the brokers' warehouses for one or two days before the sale takes place. As there are hundreds of lots to value, they are fatiguing days for the valuers, who are in some cases wonderfully expert, and, with the assistance of a few brief notes on their catalogues, can retain a sort of mental picture of each particular lot amongst the many that they have to value. The atmosphere of the sale-room is excited or depressed according to the state of trade; the lots are knocked down rapidly, probably at the rate of five a minute in a good market, but at other times the sale drags and the buyers simulate an indifference that they may or may not feel.

The sale over and the lots claimed, the buyers hurry off in their motor cars, and there are few opportunities for the social intercourse that we used to enjoy in the long waits for the infrequent trains of bygone days.

In a few days, the warehouses will be emptied of most of their contents, and the wool will have departed on what is probably its last journey in the raw state.

Received at the mill, the wool, after being weighed in, will remain for a longer or shorter time in the wool store, but it will eventually appear at the sorter's table. The sorter takes out each fleece from the sheet separately and spreads them, one at a time, on the table with the exterior upwards. He then proceeds to take from the different parts of the fleece the various qualities and throws each sort into the baskets or boxes that surround him. These qualities may run to six or eight, or even more in number, according to the purpose for which they are being sorted. The fleeces may vary a good deal, but a good fleece will yield a large proportion of the bulk sort and proportionately less of the lower sorts, which may have to be sold or disposed of in another manner from the manufacturer's main purpose. According to the percentage yield of the bulk sort, taking other factors into account, the buyer's judgment will be confirmed or otherwise, and he be satisfied or the reverse with his purchase. At any rate, a lot or clip may "sort up" well or badly, and the matter is noted for future reference.

At the sorter's table we say good-bye to the Cheviot wool as a raw material; its transformation into Cheviot cloth will be referred to at some later date.

OUR ILLUSTRATIONS

OUR illustrations are by Mr Robert Burns. The first is a typical scene of the arrival of the wool from the farm at one of the Border Mills. It shows the type of cart still largely used and the way the Cheviot wool is packed.

The little initial letter is also a bit of Border scenery with the small black-and-white collie dogs now mostly used by our shepherds.

The wool sorter is typical of what may be seen in any modern Scottish mill.

The sheep is really a portrait "painted from life". It is a fine Cheviot ram of the Leaston flock belonging to Mr Charles Stodart and bred by Captain Spence.

The small landscape is the Shepherd's cottage at Damhead of Traquair, where Mr Robert Beatie grazes an excellent flock of Cheviot sheep. This is very typical of the smooth, steep hills of the Border sheep country.

FREEDOM

"WITH A GREAT SUM OBTAINED I THIS FREEDOM."
Today it is well to remember the price our forefathers paid for our freedom before we say today's price is too high. We have been born free. No new growth this love of freedom. The history of our people shows how in each generation no price was thought too high. No matter what our form of government might be – kingdom or commonwealth – there is no rank in our race that has not contended for it, there is no rank today that does not possess freedom. To illustrate this old craving for liberty, we have chosen five quotations. Not just quotations from the poets dealing with more or less imaginary situations, but words of stress from times of great crises in the race. We have chosen two Scottish, two English and one American. Of Scotland, a Parliament and a Poet. Of England, a Queen and a Statesman. Of America, the union of our two races, a great Leader of the People.

* * *

"Ah! Freedom is a noble thing!
Freedom makes man to have liking:
Freedom all solace to man gives:
He lives at ease that freely lives.
A noble heart may have no ease
Nor anything else that may him please,
If Freedom fails: "

* * *

"For, so long as a hundred remain alive, we never will in any degree be subject to the dominion of the English. Since not for glory, riches, or honour we fight, but for liberty alone which no good man loses but with his life."

"As for the King of Spain, I do not fear all his threatenings; his great preparations and mighty forces do not stir me. For though he come against me with a greater power than ever was his Invincible Navy, I doubt not but, God assisting me upon whom I always trust, I shall be able to defeat him and overthrow him. For my cause is just."

"My Lords, if I were an American as I am an Englishman, while a foreign troop was landed in my country I never would lay down my arms – never – never – never!"

FOURSCORE and seven years ago our fathers brought forth upon this continent a new nation, conceived in liberty and dedicated to the proposition that all men are created equal. Now we are engaged in a great civil war, testing whether that nation, or any nation so conceived and so dedicated, can long endure. We, are met on a great battle-field of that war. We have come to dedicate a portion of that field as a final resting-place of those who here gave their lives that that nation might live. It is altogether fitting and proper that we should do this. But in a larger sense we cannot dedicate, we cannot consecrate, we cannot hallow this ground. The brave men, living and dead, who struggled here, have consecrated it far above our power to add or detract. The world will little note, nor long remember, what we say here, but it can never forget what they did here. It is for us, the living, rather to be dedicated here to the unfinished work they have thus far so nobly advanced. It is rather for us to be here dedicated to the great task remaining before us, that from these honoured dead we take increased devotion to that cause for which they here gave the last full measure of devotion; that we here highly resolve that the dead shall not have died in vain, that the nation shall, under God, have a new birth of freedom, and that the government of the people, by the people, and for the people, shall not perish from the earth."

Our first is from Barbour's "The Bruce", written about 1350, modernised a little in its spelling for the old Scots is difficult for any but a student. The word "liking" means joy or pleasure and has quite gone out in modern Scots.

Our second is from a letter from the Assembly of Barons – the nearest thing we had then to a Parliament – to Pope John XXII protesting against the excommunication of Scotland for not admitting the sovereignty of England in 1320. The original is in Latin and we quote the translation in "Facsimiles of National Manuscripts of Scotland," Pt. II.

Our third is from an address to Parliament by Queen Elizabeth in 1593.

Our fourth is the peroration of a speech on the American War delivered in the House of Lords by William Pitt, Earl of Chatham, on 20th November 1777. He was near the end of his life, but to the very end, his burning love of freedom never cooled.

Lastly, Lincoln's oration delivered at the dedication of Gettysburg Cemetery on 19th November 1863, to an audience bitterly disappointed and ashamed. Strange that contemporary opinion should have so misjudged one of the great speeches in the long history of man. "The stone which the builders rejected, the same is become the head of the corner."

APOLOGIA

THE Scottish Woollen Trade has been built up on export. So small a country as ours never could use all we can produce. We have specialised in novelty work of fine quality. Now the production of work of individuality necessarily means small manufacturing units and comparatively high prices. These are inevitable accompaniments of such work, no matter what it may be – pottery, glass, iron work – right up to the purely individual work of the painter or sculptor. This obviously means that our trade is not organised for mass production, and, consequently, that Government contract work is not the staple trade of Scotland.

It is a fact usually ignored, but very obvious when pointed out, that a sudden great increase in the National output of any trade can only be obtained by the organisation of the small units. In a country like ours, so permeated with industrialism, the possibilities of expansion are quite magical. In a complicated and highly skilled trade like the Scottish Woollen Trade, any sudden increase in the staffs is impossible. Numbers of skilled workers simply do not exist over and above those steadily employed. In general, big businesses are run so that no great expansion of their output is possible, but in the countless little leisurely mills, output goes up and up under National stress IF every individual is convinced that he is working for a Cause and not merely for a Business. The adaptability of the Scottish Woollen Trade has always been its most outstanding feature, and the quantity of war work that the trade has been able to do has been a very useful addition to the fighting strength of our country.

In 1914 our circumstances were very difficult. Almost on the outbreak of war, the Belgian and French woollen manufacturing districts were wiped out. Our own little army was complete and splendidly equipped, but it had to be multiplied by ten or twelve. We were a totally unmilitary nation, utterly unprepared for war on the scale of 1914. Later, we had to clothe our Allies, completely deprived of all their own mills. Gradually the organisation of the Woollen Trade was built up by the Trade itself, and Scotland was left as a self-contained unit to manage its own affairs under the wing of the Central Control in Yorkshire. Mills that never had tried a night shift managed somehow to extemporise. Every possible man had volunteered for active service and every factory was short handed. All limitations went overboard – women worked all night, older men did jobs they had forgotten about since they were apprentices. This was typical of all Scotland, and doubtless it was equally true of England. The people at home were as willing as the men in the trenches – they only needed to be told what to do.

Now in 1939 circumstances are different. The importance of war work remains paramount and obviously must take precedence over everything else at all costs. It does not appear that anything like the strain will be put upon the industry that was put upon it during the Great War. This time, one of our chief duties is to maintain exports so as to keep the balance of trade manageable under the flood of war materials pouring into France and Britain. For such a purpose Scottish Woollens are an amazingly valuable cargo, probably averaging £1500 per ton, rarely less than £1000, and sometimes, in extreme cases, exceeding £4000. As far as can be seen at present, supplies of wool will be available. The risk is that panic buying may rush up prices to dangerous levels, to be followed inevitably by the dire results that followed the great boom after the last war.

To our overseas friends we say – Wear our Scottish Woollens. Not only will you do yourselves good service in satisfaction and value, but you will contribute notably to the great Cause of Justice and Freedom.

SCOTTISH WOOLLEN MILL IN WAR TIME

AR is with us again and the lads are all away, gone as their fathers went just twenty-five and a half years ago. Quietly they departed; there was none of the pomp and circumstance of war, no blazing beacons as of yore called them to saddle and ride, but the call was answered. The gaps in the factory ranks have for the present been filled, but the further call on our manhood will surely come, and then the women will step into the breach and the old men will emerge from their retirement as they did before. The ranks will be closed, history will repeat itself, no doubt with variations, but the spirit is still the same.

Our towns and villages are full of khaki-clad figures and the mechanism of war; even portions of our mills are occupied, not by our own men, but by those who will be their comrades in the struggle that lies ahead, and who are for a few fleeting weeks or months our guests, until they move on – to what?

The women are feverishly knitting the comforts that are so urgently needed, and women and the able-bodied older men are busy perfecting themselves in all the manifold branches of A.R.P., Hospital and Red Cross work; but these are spare-time jobs, and their trade, the manufacturing of the essential material for clothing the Forces, must be carried on at full pressure.

Inside the mills themselves, there is no very evident change, at least to the occasional visitor. He may note a certain quickening of the tempo, an absence of those signs of slackness that have been all too frequent during the years of depression. Work and seeming prosperity have come, but for the most unwished-for reasons. The pay envelopes are heavier, but the cost of living has risen; the anxiety that blends itself with courage, hope and determination is there.

Let us enter the weaving shed, for in other parts of the mill there is little outward and visible change, except perhaps a vaguely sensed feeling of urgency. As we enter, our ears are assailed by a roar and clatter – that is the music of the looms, for it is music to those who have seen them silent and impotent against the rising force of so-called national self-sufficiency and the ebbing tide of export trade. All is now stir and movement, conversation practically impossible, but to another sense, that of the eye, there is also a difference. Glance along row after row of busy looms – where are the bright colours and varied designs of other days? Nothing but khaki, khaki, its neutral shade fading into the distance. Here and there, however, the monotony may be broken by a patch of Air Force blue or a spot of colour indicative of what is now familiarly called "civilian work", which must be put through as time and material permit.

We have said that history repeats itself, but to those of us who remember the last war, there is a change. There is, for instance, none of the blue and white all-woollen flannel to relieve the eye – it is now made of wool and cotton mixed and is, therefore, taboo in the Scottish mills; but more than all do we miss the bright colours of the Highland tartans. The War Office has decreed, and with reasons that appear unanswerable and must be accepted, that the Scottish Regiments should wear the new khaki battle dress on active service. Few will doubt the necessity and wisdom of this edict, but there seems no adequate reason why kilts and tartan trews should not be issued for walking-out dress. Shortage of material is alleged, but the Scottish mills could easily cope with this as they did during the last war. Although we are assured that it is only "for the duration", gloomier spirits maintain that the death-knell of tartans as far as the Army is concerned has been sounded. We do not agree, as we hardly think, quite apart from sentiment, that the powers that be will lose sight of the great recruiting value of our historic tartans and the kilt. Incidentally, it may be mentioned that this cloth is a monopoly of the Scottish mills, and that it is now practically the only one we are permitted to supply in peace time.

From the looms and their contents let us turn to the weavers themselves.

Assiduously and imperturbably amidst the deafening noise, they go about their work. From a leisurely three days a week or a spell of a week or two with an occasional holiday, they have suddenly been stirred into the greatest activity; their numbers have been increased by older women who had already retired, and by many married women who, with their men away on service, have relegated their household duties to what would otherwise have been their leisure hours and have come back to their old jobs.

The ordinary work of the weaver is often very complicated and requires great attention and skill. The Government work is much more simple, but still it is constant and exacting. There is also the added strain of exceptional winter conditions and the somewhat depressing effect of the "black-out" arrangements, which affect even the daylight hours. All the same there is an air of cheerfulness about, which the company and the movement help to maintain.

We have started with the weaving, but let us now turn back to the beginning and have a look at the Wool Store, where we hope to find wool arriving in large quantities and the foreman cheerfully checking it in. But, alas, there are other alternatives. We may find no wool arriving at all, or it may be someone else's wool. So the foreman may be sunk in gloom and his remarks about the Wool Control will be quite unprintable.

At their tables, the sorters, depleted in numbers, are busy, mostly on Government work, which although greater in volume is much simpler than the civilian. This remark applies also to the batchers, who revel in a succession of big batches all of the same kind and find even the increased manual labour makes easy going compared with their normal task with its much greater variety.

"BUT THE SPIRIT IS STILL THE SAME"

The adaptability that has been shown by the Scottish mills in turning over at short notice to mass production is indeed remarkable, when we consider that it is a highly specialised trade and deals mainly in relatively small quantities, very fancy designs, and cloths requiring many different yarns even for one pattern. With the bulk orders the machinery output efficiency is enormously increased, and, incidentally, the labour and number of hands required reduced. It is found possible also to combine this with a not inconsiderable production for ordinary civilian trade.

We now continue our journey through the Wool Scouring House to the Dye House, where we find all steam and stir. Here, again, the work, although increased in volume, is considerably simplified. The dyer's tale of woe principally concerns difficulty in obtaining special dyestuffs and also the rising prices of those that are obtainable. But he cannot point to any lack in the supply of the essential dyes for National purposes. A relevant thought strikes us as we pass through the Drying-room to the Willey House, where the wool is mixed, oiled and teased prior to

119

carding; oil may become difficult to get.

In the Carding Room and Spinning Flats, the same tale may be told of the comparative ease of dealing with large quantities, and we hasten on lest the foreman, who we can see is pondering the subject, should raise some matter for a grumble; indeed, we can almost see a probable cause as we note that the shaft is going a bit slowly – the peak load of the day is now on. Every department is busy and the engines evidently all out. We now cross over to the Yarn Store, the ante-room of the Weaving Shed, and in passing note another war-time change: the bulk of the yarn, instead of being carefully built into boxes, a laborious process, is hurried away straight from the spinners' baskets to the yarn winders.

We will step aside for a moment into the adjacent Pattern Shop, as the Pattern-weaving Department is called to distinguish it from the Pattern Office, where patterns and orders are dealt with. Here we see the only apparently derelict part of the mill, a row of empty looms, or perhaps one or two running. These are, of course, narrow looms and cannot produce ordinary full-width pieces. Most of the usual weavers are away or have been absorbed into other jobs. The head designer is in his office, but he is working with a skeleton staff. The work of pattern-making is reduced to a minimum, but the export trade at least must go on, and possibly the customers will find that a smaller and less-bewildering set of patterns is not altogether disadvantageous.

We pass through the Weaving Shed a second time and come to the Mending Department. Here we see the large rolls of khaki cloth passing quickly over the birlers' tables and the darners' perches. Knots and other little blemishes are removed. Threads broken in the weaving are replaced, but there are no fancy threads here or elaborate decoration to take up the darners' time; indeed, if it were not for a certain proportion of ordinary goods, the usual staff would be too big.

At the Mill House, our next stopping place, we are brought face to face with a major problem that the Scottish manufacturers have had to tackle in this war. The Royal Army Clothing Department has concentrated its demand from the Scottish mills chiefly on the Army greatcoating. It is a heavy and very well-milled cloth; relatively it is easily and quickly woven, but takes a great deal more time in the mill than an ordinary piece. Milling, we might explain, is the felting or fulling of a cloth to thicken it by means of soap, hot water and friction, thereby reducing the width and length in the case of this particular cloth by about 25 per cent, and greatly increasing the weight per yard. This naturally improves both the wearing and weather-resisting qualities. As the time occupied in treating this cloth is three to four times more than is usual for Scottish cloths, it naturally upsets the balance of production as between this department and the weaving. The Mill House, therefore, forms a bottle-neck, which can only be overcome by longer hours or added machinery. The milling of the greatcoating cloth is a very heavy job, both for the men and for the machines, construction of which is relatively light, being intended to meet only the needs of the ordinary trade. Many, therefore, are the breakages and small and large repairs that have to be executed, with consequent loss of time and production, and the head millman's job is more harassing than his colleagues' work in other departments. The problems have, however, been tackled and overcome, and Scotland is pulling its full weight in producing the necessary goods. The cloth has also to be waterproofed, a process presenting new problems to some of the manufacturers.

Little need be said of the Finishing Department, where the Government cloths are easily handled, and so the pieces eventually arrive in the Warehouse, where they are passed and measured over a table and checked by machine, and then laid aside for the Government inspector when he pays his weekly or bi-weekly visits. This war-time inspection of the goods at the mill is a great advantage from many points of view. The normal peace-time procedure is to send the consignments to the Government stores, where they are passed and afterwards distributed.

No account of the war-time changes in our mills would be complete without a reference to the "black-out" and the onus it has put upon us. This is not, of course, peculiar to our trade, but an ordinary woollen textile mill has hundreds of windows and acres of glass roof. The windows present no particular problem except a financial one; but the roofs are a very different proposition, and also from our point of view a novel one. Painting, although we were advised to do so at first, has proved unsatisfactory; it chiefly excludes the light through the day and does not keep it in at night. Most of this work has had to be undone and curtains substituted – a costly proceeding, indeed it runs into hundreds of pounds even in a moderate-sized factory. To work constantly in a half light would have had a depressing effect on the workpeople – the very thing we wish to avoid – and would not have helped efficiency.

It might be asked, how, under existing circumstances, do we hope to carry on our export trade, which has always been the backbone of the Scottish industry and which in common prudence we should try to preserve in unbroken continuity. Our ability to do so depends on certain factors, the chief of which are the availability of machinery and of raw material, and, of course, the command of the seas. Owing to a certain amount of foresight on the part of the Government, it would appear that they will overtake their military requirements without commandeering all the textile machinery, and a fair proportion should be available for normal purposes, and especially for making goods for export.

The ample supply of raw material depends to a large extent on the third factor, which we must leave to the British Navy.

Other difficulties can and will be overcome.

Again, after an interval of less than twenty-two years, we are asked to beat our ploughshares into swords and our pruning-hooks into spears. We do not complain, we only "trust that somehow good will be the final goal of ill".

Twice in less than a generation we have seen our sons go forth to war. Again we see the structure of our trade trembling, rebuilt after the devastation of the Great War with so much patience and enterprise. There is no grumbling at these sacrifices.

The spirit of our workpeople is that of the Crusaders of old. No doubts exist in our minds as to the righteousness of our cause or the final issue of the conflict. The work of two decades falls in ruins, but we will rebuild in a better world.

"Say not the struggle nought availeth,
    The labour and the wounds are vain,
The enemy faints not, nor faileth,
    And as things have been they remain.

*   *   *   *   *   *   *   *

"For while the tired waves, vainly breaking,
    Seem here no painful inch to gain,
Far back, through creeks and inlets making,
    Comes silent, flooding in, the main.

"And not by eastern windows only,
    When daylight comes, comes in the light;
In front, the sun climbs slow, how slowly!
    But westward, look! the land is bright."

? ? ? WHY ? ? ?

WHY should we have started the Wool Control? In "Scottish Woollens", we have always shunned figures. They are not interesting to most. They have to be read very slowly and very carefully, and nowadays we are so desperately scientific that statistic stalking has become the chief sport of journalists. As we say in Scotland, we are fair deaved wi' figures – plagued, deafened, stupefied, stunned! But once in a while, we may be forgiven a few.

Why then have WE started to control Wool? Wool is so widespread in its sources and so universal in its use that it is only by Government action that its control is possible. The British Empire produces nearly half the world's supply. Ours is thus the only Government, or rather group of Governments, able to undertake this duty with any hope of success. A universal slump in wool would ruin farmers in every quarter of the globe – a rocket rise would deal harshly with every wearer of woollen materials. The depression bound to follow a panic would ruin industrialists in every land. Thus the Wool Control, although we all curse it most heartily, is a benevolent organisation, even if it is founded on necessity and the hope of plunder.

The next "Why" is, why should the needs of the fighting men put up prices so vastly? After all, they have to be clad anyway. The answer is, war is unbelievably wasteful – wasteful of wool as well as of everything else. Utterly and hopelessly wasteful; a tale told by an idiot full of sound and fury. Now, the world's supply of such a commodity as wool does not vary much from year to year. It has slowly risen over several generations as its use has spread. But the world stock of sheep cannot in a moment be increased by working double shifts or any such device. There never is any great margin, and a run of prosperity, or a period of depression, is quite enough to cause great fluctuations in price.

Now for our figures. They are given in greasy pounds. Seemingly, no one has so far been rash enough to calculate the effect of such a gigantic washing. Wool comes off the sheep's back in various states of dirtiness. Some sheep are washed a couple of weeks before clipping. This wool is almost clean. Some of the finest Merinos have in them so much grease and yolk as to lose up to 80 per cent. Some wools from dusty regions like Peru may contain half their weight in sand. It is easy to understand why no one has calculated the weight of clean wool available. Last year, 1938/1939, the world produced 3991 millions of pounds – the highest total in ten years, which is the whole time for which figures are before us. In that time, the lowest year was 1934/1935 with 3628 millions. Our Empire produces 1848 million pounds, leaving for the rest of the world 2143. Far the largest unit is Australia, always round about 1000 million; its lowest figure, last year's 985 million. The

United States produces 458, South America about 600.

Our own small island produces quite a quantity, 107, of which our Scottish contribution was 27 millions. Four per cent covers the Scottish variation.

France, and her African possessions, grew 117 millions, so that the Allies possess all but half the wool total of the world. We have not included Turkey, whose production would put us well over half, and, against this grand total of just on 2000 million pounds, the enemy can only command 45 millions.

THAT IS WHY WE NEEDED THE WOOL CONTROL.

THE WOOL CONTROL

THE Wool Control has been modelled on the organisation set up during the Great War. When the Great War burst on a surprised Europe, chaos reigned for a while. No one knew what to do. The immediate effect was a general stoppage of trade, with the great hardships and suffering that at once follow under modern conditions. Belgium and North France were engulfed in the abominable flood. Helpless crowds of the people choked all the roads and crowded every boat, fleeing before the barbarous invasion of the armies of Germany. The principal woollen districts of Europe ceased to be, and a terrible strain was put upon the British Woollen Trade to supply clothing to all the Allied Armies of Europe, as well as to our own rapidly growing forces. Prices collapsed and then began to rise utterly out of control, and so out of two years of disorder the Wool Control was born.

The opinion was universally held that a trade so intricate as the Woollen Trade could only be worked by those engaged in the trade itself. The result completely justified the argument and, under the guidance of these purely voluntary committees, order soon reappeared. Scotland had its own control committees. The Wool Section, which distributed the raw material, worked on its own system of allocating wool according to type or description, instead of by actual lots, which is the usual custom of the trade. This was an ingenious device to overcome the difficulties of the day. No one could tell where any particular ship might dock. The Admiralty directed ships to any port from Caithness to Land's End. A certain lot of bales might be landed at a little place in the North of Scotland or at one of the great ports – Leith, or the Clyde, or Liverpool or Plymouth – and it might take many weeks for any particular lot of wool to find its way to any particular mill. This was overcome in Scotland by giving manufacturers wool of the required quality that might be most conveniently situated. We believe it was a fact that no Scottish manufacturer ever lost an hour's work for want of wool, in which we were much better off than our more particular neighbours.

The next step was the Cloth Control, which arranged for the supplies needed by the various Government services. Every member was chosen from the trade by the trade. They knew the capacity of each individual mill. They regulated the supply of labour and they allocated the work to be done. The system worked smoothly and well, and the output they organised was a surprise to everyone concerned. Certain prices for work on each cloth were arranged, and these "conversion" costs, as they were called, reduced estimating and contract-placing to a very simple business. There were two "conversions", from the wool to the yarn, and from the yarn to the cloth. We all thought there would be considerable local differences in costs of manufacturing. The Government agreed that any manufacturer or district finding the arranged costs too low could apply for special rates. In actual fact, no one did apply, which just showed how difficult it is even for an "expert" to form a sound judgment under new circumstances.

Great Britain has always been the most important centre of the Woollen Trade, which is the obvious reason why the British Empire is so much concerned with wool today. It is only to be expected that Colonists should tend to develop the enterprises in which they have been brought up at home. So we may claim the British Empire as the chief source of wool, without ignoring the pioneer work of the Spaniard in South America, the Dutch at the Cape and in Tasmania, or the Spaniards, the South Germans and the French in the breeding of the finest fibred wools – such names as Merino and Saxony at once proclaim their origin. Thus it is both a duty and a necessity that we should control wool supplies.

It is obvious, of course, that the main purpose of the Wool Control is to help on the war. The Woollen Trade can quite well look after itself, except for its overseas supplies. It follows, therefore, that no more control need be instituted than is required for the immediate National purposes of our Allies and ourselves. Thus the more useless wools – from the Service clothing point of view, be it understood – were at once excluded, such as camels' wools, Cashmeres, Alpacas, and Shetland wool; also all wastes and by-products of every kind excepting the two principal combing wastes, laps and noils. Fine Merinos are not needed for Army clothing (except to a limited extent for Officers' use), but they constitute an immensely valuable export. We have something very near a monopoly in these wools, for we have bought the entire production of Australia and New Zealand, and a considerable quantity from the Cape. As long as we can keep the seas, there will be wool enough for everything required for the export trade. There never is a world surplus of wool. War is dreadfully wasteful, and supplies therefore must be a little short. To prevent this shortage causing a panic rise in price, the Wool Control, with its purchases and rationing methods, has completely stopped speculation in wool.

The method of working is shortly this. The great colonial clips were bought at 30 per cent above last season's prices. All wools in the hands of merchants in this country were taken over at agreed or valued prices, and thus our Government owns all wools in this country, except the excluded classes we have mentioned.

Every manufacturer is expected to devote a considerable part of his machinery to National work. There is no compulsion, nor is any special proportion asked.

National service requirements, then, have the first call on supplies of wool.

For civil work, every manufacturer is given a ration based on the size of his mills, share and share alike of the wools available and not needed for National work. Now this sounds very easy and very simple. It is not simple at all, for there

are scores or hundreds, nay, thousands of kinds of wool, and one man's food is another man's poison. To control the needs of the Woollen Trade is a problem of the utmost complexity and almost inconceivable difficulty – a problem far beyond any ordinary Government department to extemporise – so once more volunteers from the industry are working the machine. The machine creaks and groans a bit, but it does forge ahead and it will improve.

The ration is arranged for four months at a time, and prices for that period are fixed.

These rations are divided into three parts: one for raw material, one for Scotch spun yarns – woollen yarn this is – and the third for English worsteds, and it is just another indication of the difficulties of the job that it has been found necessary to divide the ration in this way.

Our offices now look like the brood combs of a bee-hive decorated with varied colours of pollen. We spend laborious days and blacked-out nights filling up light-blue forms for wool, brighter-blue for woollen yarns, orange forms for worsted, pink forms for export, yellow forms for wood to repair our floors, white forms for dyes and chemicals, and so forth, and so on, but we do get the goods!

The next business to be looked after by the Wool Control is Exportation. The Woollen Trade, and more particularly the Scottish Trade, has always been predominantly export. In the men's trade, we have been the pioneers and leaders. The wild scramble for national self-sufficiency that has swept the world since the

Great War has dealt very heavily with Scottish Woollens. The Treasury is now conscious of the fact that, without exports, it will not be easy for us to pay for our needed imports of all sorts of munitions and raw materials. So export is helped in every possible way, and our slogan, "Keep the Quality up", is as binding a command as ever.

Thus the second claim on the available wool is for export orders. It is surprisingly difficult to arrange this preference. At present, it is based on past exports with 25 per cent, added, but in a fancy trade like that of Scottish Woollens the fluctuation might be far more than 25 per cent. Also, in anything so fickle as the sale of fancy woollens, no one has the least idea of whether or not he can repeat any performance he may have been able to put up. However, with goodwill, knowledge and ingenuity, this will be overcome.

Lastly, there is the Home Trade. The Home Trade must just put up with what is left. The lucky ones are those who wear Scottish Woollens. Long after everyone else is reduced to rags, they will parade the streets looking fresh, fashionable and prosperous.

THE WAR GOES ON

"The nations not so blest as thee
Must, in their turn, to tyrants fail;
Whilst thou shall flourish, great and free,
The dread and envy of them all."

 THE war goes on. Eighteen months have passed since that September Sunday morning when we heard our Prime Minister announcing over the radio that we were at war. It is to most of us an unforgettable memory. We recall the voice, now forever silent, we recall the sorrow and disappointment that were blended with the courage of his words. We remember perhaps our own reactions.

The Nation heard with grim determination. How much grimmer that determination has since become. It is as well we cannot foresee the future. "Sufficient unto the day is the evil thereof."

Another Prime Minister has promised us blood and toil, sweat and tears on the road to victory; that it will be victory few of us doubt.

There is much more to be done than what is metaphorically known as "wielding the sword". In no war of the past has the part to be played by the civil population been so important and their exposure to danger so great. The toil is welcome. "They also serve who only stand and wait."

Our Trade, while contributing and continuing to contribute its quota of men and women to the Services, has two functions of great importance to perform. Firstly, we have to help to the utmost of our capacity to clothe the Forces, and, secondly, and of almost equal necessity, we have to try to sustain the economic position of our country by getting and fulfilling in spite of all difficulties as many export orders as we can.

Since last we wrote about our mills under war-time conditions, many and great changes have taken place. We have had to adapt ourselves to these.

Almost our first preoccupation was to find the extra supply of skilled labour. The changes in trade, mostly bad, during the inter-war period, the uncertainties and lack of confidence caused by Hitlerian activities during the last phase have had their attenuating effect on the available numbers of our craftsmen, and of our women too.

The task has not been easy, the inevitable drain on our man-power, caused by the demands of the Services, has not helped. The training cannot be accomplished overnight. Fortunately, we have a great tradition for good work behind us, and the inherited skill of the workers makes it easy for the young people to learn their job. Truly one might say it is in the blood. The old people, too, have responded nobly.

Our younger men continue to depart, but in a more ordered sequence than we were accustomed to in our 1914–1918 experience, and this allows us to plan ahead. The main thing is that the output keeps up, and the Scottish mills have so far answered to all the calls that have been made upon them.

The Wool Control, to which we devoted our last number, appears to be functioning adequately and efficiently in spite of occasional grumbles. Wool, coal, oil and other essential commodities come to hand in time – sometimes in the nick of time!

The Ministry of Supplies, greatly helped by our own Scottish Rationing Committee, places its contracts at the right time, and in the right quarter, thus securing that continuity so essential to full production.

The Luftwaffe has not so far paid much attention to the Scottish woollen mills. We touch wood as we write! Our turn may be coming, but production up till now has not been interfered with. The small size and scattered situation of our mills in their little country villages have probably given us a measure of protection, for individually they are not worth troubling about.

So much for our essential duty of clothing the troops. We turn now to the almost equally important subject of Export trade.

Since early April of last year, the problem of Export has become not only more complex, but the field more restricted. "The Nations not so blest" as ours have in their turn fallen to the tyrants, and in their fall not only have they closed their doors to us, but they have rendered the task of the U-Boat and the enemy bombing aircraft more simple.

It is now on the Western Hemisphere only that we must rely for the bulk of our Export trade. Thousands of miles of ocean lie between us and our markets, and it is there that our enemy has his greatest chance of destroying our commerce. We look to our Navy, and not in vain, for the protection of our sea-borne trade, and to their gallant comrades of the Merchant Service, to whom to offer praise is almost banal, for the working of our trading ships. They must guard and carry the supply of wool on which we depend, and the goods into which it will be ultimately converted.

What a heartening sight it is to see a large convoy arriving safely at its destination. Such a memory comes back to us of an August forenoon when we stood on the strangely deserted golf course at North Berwick and gazed out on the sunlit Forth. The long line of a convoy was slowly m a k i n g its way up the Firth, stretching from behind the Bass Rock and as far as the eye could see towards Inchkeith. How much longer it was we could only guess. From what quarters of the globe had this heterogeneous collection of ships been gathered? Through what perilous seas had they been safely shepherded?

Through none perhaps so perilous as those that wash our own shores, but the thought uppermost in our minds was one of thankfulness that they and their cargoes were safely home, and of pride in our Navy who had brought them.

Before us on the beach, the barbed-wire entanglements were a grim reminder that invasion was a very real threat.

Our Government is doing all it can to encourage and assist the Export Trade. Facilities are given for obtaining the necessary wool, and precedence where desired is given over Army contracts. Our chief object is to prove to our customers that we can accept their orders and execute them without undue limitations or delay. It is impossible to pretend that there is not a war on, or that accidents due to enemy action will not occasionally occur, but our desire is to inspire confidence that orders will be fulfilled, and that dates of delivery will be kept. To help us in our endeavours, a Committee under the title of "The Scottish Woollen Export Council" has been set up and is rendering valuable assistance in oiling the departmental wheels. The Mills of God grind slowly, and Government departments are inclined to arrogate to themselves some divine attributes!

131

This Council is not an ephemeral thing, but will continue after the war. It looks beyond the immediate present to a future when trade may be freed from some of the shackles that intense Nationalism has imposed upon it in the period since 1918. Most of us are inclined to agree that our war aims are summed up in three words, "Winning the War", and that our peace aims may very well be left to look after themselves. Still if "There'll always be an England", there possibly will not always be a war, and in our less occupied moments we have occasionally time to think what we will do under these circumstances. This is one of the functions of the Council. It is thinking ahead and planning for what we hope will be a better and more sensible world.

Meanwhile, the home trade must be satisfied with the crumbs that fall from the table – or, in other words, take what it can get. We must be content with our old clothes until they wear out, and, if the cloth is of Scottish manufacture, that will be a very long time.

Let us now turn to the mills themselves. The war goes on. What changes have the passing months brought? Nothing that is very obvious to the eye. The all-predominant colour is still khaki. The workers may be fewer, but there is seldom any idle machinery. The constant drive for the fullest production puts a strain on it that calls for frequent repairs, great and small. The few mechanics that are left are kept busy coping with them. In that far-off day that we look forward to, a great overhaul will be necessary, but for the present we must get on with the job.

In our lives, too, as the sternness of the conflict has impressed itself more and more on our minds, the changes have been gradual. The so-called Hours of Leisure, when we are not actively engaged on productive work, have been filled with other duties. The services of protection and defence make many calls on our civil population, calls that sometimes compete in their demands for helpers. Few indeed of our workers can say that when their normal work has ceased, their day's toil is over. Satan's job is temporarily lightened. There are not many spare moments for idle hands.

The A.R.P. Services, with their occasionally overlapping requirements, absorb most of our remaining able-bodied manhood, and even a good many of our women who can undertake the lighter part of fire fighting. Such of them, that is, who are not engaged in Red Cross and V.A.D. work.

The events of last spring and early summer have called into existence another body no less essential, with the threat of invasion always a potential and very real danger. We refer, of course, to the Home Guard. The veterans of another war, and our young lads who are thirsting to get a rifle into their hands and to fight for their country, have gladly embraced this opportunity of possibly "having a crack at Jerry". We feel, and rightly feel, that if we could only meet our enemy face to face instead of 30,000 feet up in the air or a few feet under the water, there would be little doubt as to the result.

We are fighting for all we hold dear, for all we deem essential in a life that would be worth living. We are fighting because we must. We are fighting almost alone, with all due acknowledgment to the brave remnants of our Allies. We are fighting, we think, with the sympathy of the vast majority of mankind. Unmeasured blood and treasure are being poured out in the struggle, but so far the blood and treasure have been mostly ours.

The war goes on. The end is not in sight.

Between civilisation as we have known it and the most brutal tyranny the world has ever seen stands, at the moment, only the unconquered and unconquerable spirit of the British people.

> "Still more majestic shalt thou rise,
>   More dreadful from each foreign stroke:
> As the loud blast that tears the skies
>   Serves but to root thy native Oak."

DAWN
JAN 1941

WHY DOES WOOL SHRINK?
PART I

HIS is a chronicle of ignorance. We start with a very common question and we cannot answer it: "Why does wool shrink?" In spite of ancient knowledge of the fact, we can as yet answer but half the Why. This shrinkage is a very curious and important fact, and like so many other wonderful everyday happenings – sunrises and wind and such like marvels – we just take it for granted and don't wonder at it very much. For hundreds of years, this curious fact of shrinkage has been known to wool craftsmen. It has been amply utilised in making clothing of all sorts. Its benefits have been thoroughly appreciated and its drawbacks thoroughly cursed for countless generations. More than that, the processes by which it can be brought about and controlled are thoroughly well known – and yet no one knows just how or why one aspect of it exists.

There always were inquisitive folk in this world, but they are much more common than they used to be. There always were seekers after knowledge, but they were few in ancient times. It always was these curious ones who made progress possible beyond very primitive stages, but modern education has elevated curiosity into a cardinal virtue, and modern industry has endowed it with limitless riches, countless temples, innumerable high priests and lesser ministers. Modern education has also endowed it with a more impressive name: Research. Research has almost run away with us.

> "O, I wad like to ken – to the beggar-wife says I—
> The reason o' the cause an' the wherefore o' the why,
> Wi' mony anither riddle brings the tear into my e'e,
> – It's *gey an' easy spierin'*, says the beggar-wife to me."

It is doubtful manners to quote French – it is certainly bad manners to translate your quotation. Scots is perhaps rarer and certainly less understood, so we may be pardoned for translating the beggar-wife – "'Tis fine and easy to ask."

There are really two completely unconnected happenings included somewhat loosely in the term "shrinking". The Woollen Trade considers "shrinking" as applied only to the final processes by which cloth is brought to its most stable and perfect condition. People generally, and our women-folk in particular, look upon "shrinking" as that very disagreeable and unhappy phenomenon that steadily diminishes the size of a woollen garment as it goes back and forward to the laundry.

These two ideas of the meaning of shrinking actually refer to completely different phenomena. They have no connection whatever, in spite of the fact that they seem to happen in the same way to the same garments. In fact, within limits, they actually do happen to the same garments. We shall consider the two meanings separately and we shall first consider the trade meaning of shrinking.

About this part of our subject quite a lot is known. It is so important in the story of cloth making that a whole specialised craft has grown up around it, and cloth working, or shrinking, is quite a large and important branch of woollen manufacturing. This branch of the trade has a separate existence, partly for physical and partly for moral reasons: physical because of the highly specialised skill and elaborate machinery involved in delivering woollen cloth to the tailor in the most perfect condition; moral because the shrinker discovers and exposes faults and frauds on the part of the woollen manufacturer. Even in Scottish woollens there is no harm in having some sort of check on the condition of the goods, and the clothworker can cure certain kinds of faults that may develop and be undiscoverable in the final stages of making woollen cloth.

Consider what happens to wool during the many processes that we have from time to time described in "Scottish Woollens". As it passes through these many processes and these complicated machines, wool is treated with considerable if respectful violence. Under several of these processes wool becomes almost a semi-plastic. In the washing, it is soaked in hot alkaline solutions to remove dirt

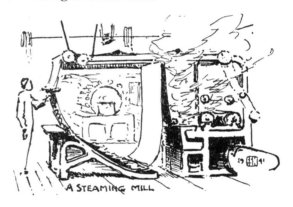

A STEAMING MILL

and natural greases, and in this process wool comes perceptibly near the melting point when it might turn into jelly. Then it goes through the ordeal of dyeing – boiling in many chemical solutions. Next, it is oiled and passed through the teeth of the teasing and mixing machines, followed by the violence of the carding and the contortion of the spinning machinery. Then the various preparations for the weaving, and finally through the most violent actions of all, the felting, cropping, finishing, and final drying, steaming and pressing, and all the other pullings, pushings, and stretchings involved therein.

However carefully and skilfully these processes are carried out, certain stresses and tensions are created both in the individual fibres and in their combination in the growing fabric of the cloth. Time and Nature little by little release these stresses, and the fibres and the fabrics settle down to a stable condition. The curly fibre that has been straightened gradually returns to something like its original shape. It has been flattened and thinned down by the removal of its natural water and by heat and tension in the drying, and it slowly swells back to its natural form. It has become sharp and bristly in the surface shearing of the cloth: it resumes its softness as it loses its sharp edges. The cloth itself has become distorted in the drying and pressing, necessarily made longer and wider and thinner by the action of the processes. More or less all these processes are carried out under heat and wet, and so once more the wool becomes perceptibly nearer melting. All these processes are necessary for the creation of a good, solid cloth, but there are left in the cloth what may be called excess tensions, which are harmful to the stability, the softness and the suppleness of the cloth. The trade of the clothworker is to study these matters and to help and hasten Nature in correcting them.

Like all ancient processes this clothworking is fundamentally simple, although, like gardening, it calls for skill and judgment in carrying it out. England was the chief modern home of woollen cloth in the final stages of its development, and so it is not unfitting that the trade of clothworking should be centred in London – "dear, damn'd, distracting town" – and that the principal and most perfect conditioning process should be called "London Shrunk", and that the London clothworkers are even yet the principal exponents of the craft. So well known has the term "London Shrunk" become that, like "Homespun" and many other terms, it has almost passed into trade language, and the London clothworkers have altered their mark to "Shrunk in London" ever since 1931.

We do not pretend to be able to give directions for London Shrinking, for each firm has its own carefully guarded secrets. Moreover, it is probable that these details could hardly be put on paper, but consist rather of many small touches that only long experience can impart. The Scottish Woollen Trade is full of such little unimpartible "secrets," and that is largely what gives individuality to the products of the Scottish Mills. As of Chaucer's Miller, it might be said of the good clothworker, "He hadde a thombe of gold, pardee."

A BATTERY OF PRESSES

This, then, is an outline of the treatment. The cloth as delivered by the Scottish mill is, let us say, 59 inches wide or even 60. It is intended that when used this should be a good 58. It is usually sold on the old Scottish yard of 38 inches, and should come out eventually at 36 inches good measure.

Most of the clothworkers use damping sheets, usually made of worsted. These are soaked in cold water. The web of cloth is then folded into this damping sheet, or it may be that the web is steamed with moist steam or possibly actually sprayed. Anyhow, by one of several means, the cloth is thoroughly damped and warmed. It is left in this state for one or two days, and is then unrolled and the web is hung up over sticks to dry slowly and gently by natural air. This takes say a further forty-eight hours.

When it is judged ready, it is taken down and folded for pressing in the hydraulic presses. Between each layer of cloth is inserted a sheet of highly glazed and very fine hard cardboard, known as a press paper. If the piece is to be hot pressed with a high glaze the papers have been heated in an oven, and special heavy cast-iron plates also heated, possibly electrically, are placed between each web. If the piece is to be cold pressed, the papers are not heated. Each press holds ten or fifteen pieces, and it is then pumped up to whatever pressure the clothworker considers best for the particular job. Pressures generally range from 30 cwt. to 3 tons per square inch.

After possibly twenty-four hours, the press is released, the webs are taken out, and the papers changed. If hot pressing is being done, new hot papers are used; if cold, the position of the papers is just altered a few inches so that the marks caused by the edges of the papers are removed by the second pressing. Again, the pumps apply the pressure and, again, the web remains for a day in the press.

The web is then taken from the press and is carefully measured and examined to see that it is still the required width everywhere and to see that no blemishes are visible. Each blemish – known in the trade as a "damage" – is marked with a bit of coloured thread on the edge of the web and the miserable manufacturer's account is docked of a quarter of a yard.

It is at this stage of the work that certain faults of a serious kind come to light. If for any one of many reasons the cloth has varied in width before being dried or if in general it has been too narrow, the manufacturers' drying machinery hides, but does not necessarily cure, the fault. Or the piece may have been badly distorted so that the checks or threads do not pass squarely across the webs. All such faults are exposed by the shrinking – whether honestly overlooked or dishonestly hidden. Some the clothworker can cure or improve, some he can only make visible.

At the end of all this work, the cloth should be in perfect condition for the tailor or dressmaker. It should not shrink or change its shape even if the wearer fell into the river. Even if kept on the shelf for years, it would unwind in perfect and unchanged order. Of course, as far as Scottish Woollens are concerned, this must always remain a purely academic hypothesis, because no tailor or dressmaker ever kept a web of Scottish Woollens for any length of time on any shelf – it gets sold at once.

We are often enough asked if clothworking is necessary or worth while. It is also often hinted that if we manufacturers did our work honestly and thoroughly, we should be able to deliver our cloth ready for use. It is not possible to answer these questions and charges definitely. There are few pieces of Scottish Woollens that could not be safely used as they leave the mill. It is likewise true that after a skilled clothworker has dealt with a piece of cloth, the difference between a shoddy and a good cloth is difficult to distinguish. But it is always well to make a good thing better. It is not painting the lily, but is adding perfection to goodness. And, after all, where are you to stop? Is the manufacturer to become merchant? – nay more, is he to become tailor? Is he to stand behind a counter and sell his garments? The positions of the manufacturer and of the clothworker might be likened to the positions of the doctor and the specialist. Both clothworkers and specialists are useful in their trades. We do not charge our doctor with dishonesty or incompetence if he suggests a consultation with some big-wig who has made himself master in his own restricted field. So when we manufacturers advise clothworking, it is not to be taken as an admission of failure.

This is the end of the first part of our question: the part we are able to answer. It is an important part, although some might say it is not quite our business to deal somewhat ignorantly with a subject barely on the outer edge of our trade. All the same, we think some idea of how clothworking is done and how and why this shrinking comes about is needed before it is possible to understand what is meant by that other and more puzzling kind of shrinking. That will form the subject of Part II, and we hope to leave our readers with some ideas about the Hows even if we cannot answer the Whys.

AN INTERLUDE ON CONDITION

 N WHAT condition? The condition of wool is the answer. Wool is a curious material. It contains water as part of its ordinary, everyday composition, apart altogether from being damp. The amount of water it contains varies with the state of the atmosphere or climate in which it happens to be for the moment. In scientific language, wool is hygropherous – that is to say, it has the power of attracting and absorbing water. The word "condition" is used by the Woollen Trade to represent the balance of water contained in the wool under any circumstances. The word has by now almost come to mean the actual quantity of water in the wool, though this is more accurately called "regain", which is given as a percentage of the artificially dried wool. This water is not held in the wool as water is held in a sponge or a dish, but in some still mysterious way is absorbed into the very substance of the wool itself. The absorption is not altogether unlike the way water is absorbed suddenly by any chemical when it crystallises and without which the form of the crystal cannot be maintained. Geologists used to hold out the dire threat that when all the minerals in the molten earth had crystallised, all the water in the world would be taken up and we would all be reduced to drinking beer. There is this difference – the water in the crystals is fixed. The water in wool can be continually driven off by heat and it will return to the wool when it cools down. Thus week after week you can air the blankets on your guest-room bed before the fire and they will always steam, yet the bed need not be damp. Thus woollen cloth, although a very perfect insulator, is not suitable for plate mats on your polished dinner table, for they will steam the polish every time a hot plate is laid on them.

Wool is a peculiar material. When wet it, becomes very easily stretched and it loses much of its strength. In this it is the exact opposite of cotton or linen, which become very much stronger when wet – an evident arrangement of Providence for the benefit of the sailor whose sails gain strength with the spray and rain of the storm.

As we said in our description of clothworking, the wool dried under tension retains but temporarily only its stretched form, and we told how it was the duty of the clothworker to remove this temporary stretch. Another job the clothworker has to do is to adjust as perfectly as possible the amount of water in the wool.

Wool should contain about 17 per cent of its dry weight in water to be at its best. This water is not a fixed quantity, but varies with the weather or, to be more accurate, with the saturation of the atmosphere. To get the best out of wool, it should contain about this 17 per cent of moisture. It is then most pliable, softest to the touch, best able to resist wear, best able to retain its shape in a garment. It is most springy, and so will best return to the shape the cutter has designed. Trousers will keep their shape better, skirts will not "knee" – or at any rate they will come back to their correct shape when laid away or hung up after use.

Now all this is not just a fancy theory, but is most practical politics. It has a strange bearing on American as against British cloth habits. For a moment, consider what happens with a mixture of air and water like our atmosphere. As the air grows warmer it is able to absorb and keep more and more water without becoming what we call "damp". Up to this balance point, air will relentlessly absorb water from every possible source. When it can hold no more, the air is said to be saturated. As the amount of water the air can hold is not fixed but depends on temperature, our scientists use the term "relative humidity" for this varying quantity and express the "dampness" of the air by a percentage of the amount of water needed to make the air saturated – "filled to capacity".

The American climate is much drier than the British – we might even say the European – climate. Of course, we are talking very broadly, for the North American continent is much too large to be included in so sweeping a statement, but for the moment let our generalisation pass. A lot of odd things happen in consequence. In Pittsburg, the furnaces give a higher yield in winter because the winter wind contains less moisture. Cosmetics were developed far earlier and to a far greater perfection in America because the dry air robbed the skin of its required moisture. The writer during his first visit to America found that his gold spectacles wore a hole in the bridge of his nose, and thus was he converted to the American fashion of shell frames. Fine old English furniture becomes brittle and easily damaged after the American air has sucked out its blood. Woollen cloths deprived of part of their water become looser because the fibres necessarily become thinner when this water is removed. So to counteract this looseness, the American tailor demands firmer cloths than the British and the American man presses his suits to death to keep their shape instead of wearing them out in kindly and gentle affection. The chief element in this difference is the natural lack of moisture in the air, vastly aggravated by the high indoor temperatures customary in America.

In these papers, we have always avoided figures. Figures are apt to be dull. Unless figures are very carefully guarded, they are apt to be misleading. Unless they are very carefully edited, they leave joints in the armour through which the editor may be brought low. But this is a somewhat novel business about which surprisingly little is known, even in our trade. So a few statistics may be allowed. They were dug out for us by our Research Association, but we do not wish to evade our own responsibility for their use.

Taking a sort of middle from Scotland, the January average temperature of Aberdeen is 41.5° Fahrenheit and 60.8° in July. The relative humidities are 80 per cent, and 73 per cent. This will give us something like 17 per cent, in our Scottish

Woollens, but in a room at 68°, the humidity will fall to about 50 per cent, in winter and will give us only about 12 per cent, instead of 17 per cent. In America, the real trouble is not the summer heat but the winter cold – in particular, the very low lowests, the sub-zeros, which are quite common in most American districts, such as Denver with 30 below, Salt Lake with 20 below, even towns like Boston and Philadelphia with 13 and 6 below. Taking the house temperatures as round 70, you find a very low moisture content in the air, and that is what counts so heavily against woollen cloths. We cannot just dogmatise on these figures, but the probable figures will be something like 14 for Denver, 18 for Salt Lake, and 16/20 for Boston and Philadelphia. Now this is where conditioning of air comes in. Unconditioned these will give wool regains ranging from 5 or 6 per cent at Denver and 6 or 7 per cent at Boston and Philadelphia. The practical outcome of all this is that, reckoning say 7 per cent, as an average, cloths that in Scotland weigh 22 ounces to the yard will scale only 20 ounces, an 18-ounce cloth 16½ ounces, and a 12-ounce cloth will lose an ounce in weight.

It is a queer problem. When our Woollen Trade Delegation went round the United States and Canada in 1931, we were struck by the way our clothes lost "quality". It was just at the end of winter. In New York, our keys crackled as we opened our bedroom doors and we could get sparks out of the carpets! As we got round to Vancouver, there was just a suggestion of spring in the air and a definite reviving of spring in our suits!

Here, then, is the problem. We hand it on to our American friends, whose exuberant hospitality we so greatly enjoyed in that memorable tour. We hand on the problem, but the answer will not be given in the next issue of "Scottish Woollens". Find some process that will retain the water in the wool, or find some chemical which will not dry out and with which the water can be replaced.

AN ENCOURAGEMENT

Some time ago, the Scottish Woollen Export Council sent round to us Scottish manufacturers an inquiry to find out how our deliveries were getting through to the U.S.A. The result was interesting, most encouraging, and a great tribute to our Navy and to our merchant seamen. The question asked was how many consignments had arrived safely and how many had been lost. The answer was 4006 consignments had arrived safely, and 66 had been destroyed by the enemy: under 2 per cent. These figures take us to the beginning of May.

Epilogue

I have been writing this on Sunday during a short holiday in our Highlands, far from the sights and sounds of war. The village is but a small collection of houses scattered amongst the birch trees – hardly enough to call a village. On a high mound near by – relic of ancient glaciers – surrounded by a tuft of pine trees stands the Parish Kirk. Small, bare, whitewashed, it has nothing to mark it as a church but a little belfry above the gable. It is big enough to hold perhaps a hundred people. In these days of empty crofts and overcrowded towns, it is rarely filled. The gravestones crowd round the little building on the narrow space on top of the mound. There is no path to the door. The parishioners, in friendly kinship with the dead, pick their way gently over and amongst these various memorial stones, upright and recumbent.

We lingered amongst the birch trees waiting for the sound of the bell to ring us in. There was no one about. Quite suddenly, we remembered we were at war and that the ringing of bells was forbidden. We were late. The first psalm was being sung as we went in. Above our heads where we sat down was a brass plate recording the names of "the men of this Parish who gave their lives for their Country in the Great War". Most of the names were the same. Of how many wars might not that plate have been a memorial! So many times have the men of the Strath gone off to war, always the same names, always the same epitaph, "for their Country". Always there was the resolve that justice should be done, and in their hearts the hope of peace. Some day it will be achieved, but it is not altogether in our hands. "Vengeance is mine; I will repay, saith the Lord."

WHY DOES WOOL SHRINK?
PART II.

OOL has one peculiar property. This is technically known as the power of milling, or felting, or fulling. This is the property of knitting its fibres together so that they cling tightly to one another and, as it were, support one another in resisting friction and in making a fabric that contains countless little pockets of air. These are the two features that make wool so invaluable as clothing. Wool does not share this property with any vegetable fibre, cotton, rayon or flax, not even with silk. In fact, it does not share this property with any fibres excepting the coats of a few animals, such as camels and some of the goats. This is specially interesting because these animals are not closely allied to sheep.

Perhaps the best way to get at this whole question is to examine wool itself. Wool is not a fixed and definite product like water, which can quite accurately be described as H_2O, even when adorned with the best Scotch. Rather, it is like air, which is a mixture varying quite considerably under varying circumstances, although always fundamentally composed of oxygen and nitrogen. Wool is fundamentally composed of keratin. Keratin is also the basis of skin, hair, horns, feathers, ivory and so forth. It is a very complicated substance allied to gelatine. It is first cousin to the proteins, which dietitians are always telling us we must swallow if we are to be healthy – meat, cheese, eggs, beans and such like. Heated, dry keratin swells up and chars, and this gives us the most useful quick check of whether a fabric is wool or cotton. Put a match to a thread of the cloth. If it curls up and leaves a thick hard ash, it is wool or silk. If it burns right away, leaving nothing but a little powdery ash, it is cotton or linen, or some kind of rayon. Of course, blends make this test a little uncertain in the positive direction, but it is quite infallible in the negative direction. If any fabric burns right away, it is certainly not wool. Again, if treated with heat and alkali, keratin can be dissolved, especially in caustic soda solutions, from which the moral is do not use too much soda or ammonia when washing woollens and not too hot water. So long as your hand can bear the heat everything is all right, for your skin and the wool are both keratin. Even the most inexperienced young woman doing her own washing is not likely to melt off her own hands.

This principle of softening by heat and alkali has given us permanent waving. The hairdresser winds his victim's hair round his myriad curlers. Heat and ammonia are applied. They soften the keratin – that is, the hair. The alkali and the heat are removed. The hair sets. Thus will the barber remould it nearer to the heart's desire. Thus the beautician – most unbeautiful of words – has borrowed a gold mine from the craftsman in wool.

But we must not limit ourselves to considering the behaviour of the raw material of wool, apart from its practical effect on cloths.

We have already said that the peculiar feature of wool is its power of becoming closely entangled into a dense mat. It shares this feature with no other textile fibre, excepting with the coats of most of the fur-bearing animals – camels, goats, and so on. If your pet dog were clad in cotton or linen, you would not be troubled by having to comb and brush mats and tangles out of his coat.

In the traditional treatment of Scottish cloths, this power was of the greatest

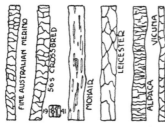

MICRO SKETCHES OF WOOL AMPIED
FROM A.B.WILDMAN'S "ANIMAL FIBRES"

importance. The effect of this milling or fulling on our cloths is so great as always to be one of the most interesting and surprising stages for visitors to our mills. You can hardly convince your guest that the raw, miserable-looking fabric that looks like a kind of canvas and that is treated with scant respect on the floor of the examining room is really a lovely soft, delicious Cashmere or a bright, fashionable suiting for a millionaire magnate. The amount of shrinking that takes place during milling varies greatly according to the type of cloth that is being made. In the usual Scottish Woollens – if the word "usual" can be applied to any such varying product as leaves our mills – the pieces are woven, say, 60 yards long. Such a piece after being milled measures, say, 48 yards. The cloth that the weaver has left about 80 inches wide has been reduced to 58 inches.

That is not an extreme example. It is a pretty fair average for a Scotch Suiting. The old regular Scottish Woollens were a very happy compromise. They were woven loosely enough not to be stiff, to make a good job for the weaver, free of broken threads, and to give the yarns room to swell up during milling. They were felted enough to ensure good wear and to blend their usually rich colouring pleasantly. They were not felted enough to lose their pliability. The openness of the weave ensured that the full softness of the wool could reassert itself after the tight twisting of the thread.

All the same, milling must be watched. A certain disintegration of the wool takes place in the process. It is a queer anomaly that although milling improves the wear of cloth, it weakens it. Just what happens to cause this destruction of the wool is not really known. It happens progressively, and many really heavily milled cloths are quite weak. This is something to do with the other fact that shoddies deteriorate sooner than sound wools, which is an undoubted fact even if it cannot be accounted for altogether. And this is not to say that very useful cloths cannot be made of shoddy. But it does make it very difficult to devise any good mechanical method of testing a cloth for the qualities that matter, such as ability to stand wear.

The extensive use of silk for the "decoration" of both suitings and trouserings, and the long preference of fashion for English cloths have tempted us to work for the brightness and smoothness of surface that is natural to worsteds. Some of the supreme wearing qualities and clothing qualities have been lost in working for this texture. There is much less milling in Scotland than there used to be. This point was dealt with fully in one of our earliest "Scottish Woollens" – No. 2, "Woollens versus Worsteds." It is a loss. It is a gain. You can get nothing for nothing. "Il faut souffrir pour être belle!"

Wool has scales on its surface. These overlap in a way like the slates on a roof, and these scales are built up from the root. They are so irregular in shape as hardly to justify the name of scales. The wool fibre might best be likened to the rough horns of the sheep or to a structure built up out of worn and damaged ice-cream cones threaded on a rope. These scale edges can only be seen with a microscope, for they project very little. Fine Merinos are the scaliest, bright wools like Leicesters are almost without scales. It so happens that the scaliest wools mill the most easily.

Late in the eighteenth century a Frenchman named Monge wrote a paper on "The Mechanism of Felting", and coupled these facts as cause and effect. For a hundred and fifty years, this theory of milling has been taught. He deserved to die on the guillotine for having misled us for all these years. Perhaps that is ungrateful, for he was the first to draw attention to the fact that there was a problem to be solved. The writer never could quite convince himself that the theory was reasonable. It seemed always too small a cause for so great an effect.

The theory was that as you rubbed and pounded at the mass of wool fibres they engaged each other's scales, and owing to the direction of the scales on each fibre, they worked into each other and could not back out. It was the principle of the eel trap or the lobster pot, or the way the Emperor moths make their cocoons – sort of one-way traffic. It was the way you can make an ear of barley creep up your sleeve, or the way a ratchet works on a monkey-jack. It was not a bad theory, and it accounted for most things. It accounted for the fact that the confused mass of fibres in a woollen thread milled easily because they intersected in a thousand directions; that the tidy parallelism of the fibres in a worsted thread milled less easily because the fibres could only touch each other with the scales in two directions. It accounted for the fact that the locks on a healthy sheep did not felt because all the scales were pointing in one direction.

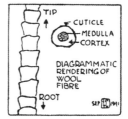

It was laziness on our part to accept this theory, for it was long ago recognised that it did not quite answer all the Whys. For example, it did not tell us why Leicesters and a good many "hairs" could be milled at all. Since we wrote the first sentence of Part I, our Research Association has published the results of a new inquiry into this "Mechanism of Felting". They have not got very far yet – in fact, they have only got as far as the negative result of disproving the scale theory, which was already becoming a little worn out and moth-eaten.

A very interesting and ingenious series of experiments seemed to show that there was a directional structure in all such animal growths, including human fingernails. These experiments included such nice childish amusements as dragging about a wool fibre tied to a string like a child's toy cart. This was to find out if any side drag were set up by the scales. Another was the almost superhumanly delicate job of making a cast in wax of wool fibres to reproduce the scales in some non-wool material, and to discover if it still showed guidance from the scales. All these many experiments built up a proof that the scale edges had little or nothing to do with the directional movements of the wool strands. Further experiments were made, some of them very ingenious, such as the splitting and polishing of porcupine quills to see if the inner surface retained the same trend as the outside. It did. This was another of the small links in the chain of evidence. So this directional trend of wool does not depend on its surface, but on some structural property of the fibre itself. There is a lot to be done before all this business can be sorted out. But it does give us woollen men a bit of very solid comfort. It seems almost impossible to imagine that any real substitute for wool can ever be made.

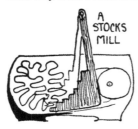

The modern method of milling is a fairly accurate process. The cloth is usually washed clean and is then impregnated with warm soap suds, and in this warm wet state it goes to the milling machines. Broadly, there are two types. The old-fashioned type consists of two heavy hammers that alternately fall on the crumpled mass of cloth that lies in a basin so that the mass of cloth turns slowly under the hammer blows. This is a mechanical rendering of the method of dealing with Harris cloths where the neighbours congregate round a long table and thump the wet cloth by hand to the rhythm of ancient labour songs. It is still used for many types of work.

In the other and more rapid method, the box mill, the cloth is crushed between two very heavily weighted and sprung oak rollers – perhaps a couple of feet in diameter and six or eight inches wide. The cloth is then forced into and through a long narrow box or trough without ends, and of which the lid is held down by heavy weights. By various adjustments of these parts, 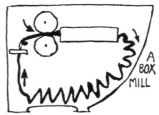 the mill-man controls the width and length felting of his cloth. The two ends of the web of cloth are sewn together and go endlessly round in the machine, like a squirrel in a cage, until the mill-man is satisfied with the result. Our ordinary suitings and such like cloths will run thus for half an hour or an hour; cloths like army coatings for three or four hours, and cloths like Irish friezes may take more than a day.

Before the modern development of soaps, this process was carried through with fuller's earth, a natural clay. For those who like long names this is an hydrous silicate of alumina, and in composition is first cousin to the felspars, sapphires, rubies, topaz and such like Aladdin luggage; also corundum and emery, beloved

146

of engineers, and bauxite, the raw material of aluminium, called after the queer picturesque rocks of Les Baux in that fair France that has temporarily fallen from grace.

After that the earth or the soap is all most carefully washed out and the cloth is ready for drying. We have seen in print, in a trade journal, a statement by someone who should have known better that the shrinker has – amongst other things – to remove sizes, oils and other foreign substances. There are no such substances left, in Scottish woollens at any rate, and cleaning is no part of the work of the clothworker in dealing with our cloths.

We finish up our chronicle of ignorance with a perfectly barefaced bit of advertising. Owing to the balanced compromises of our processes, SCOTTISH WOOLLENS ARE THE BEST. With one eye – as usual – on our promise to be as truthful as we know how, we say The Best is shared by other makers, but there are none better. In some classes, such as sports suitings, many types of coatings, and a great collection of luxury fancy cloths, we are supreme. We have a very good opinion of ourselves, and in spite of our innate modesty we are, and always have been, ready to back ourselves both in Peace and War!

AN ESSAY ON IRRELEVANCE

SCOTLAND was a poor country and still is small – poor till the Industrial Revolution revolved us into the sunlight and made us wealthy by the use of these energies liberated by our Union with England. Before then, most of our energies were spent fighting our neighbours. In the intervals, the rest of our energies were spent in fighting each other. For us, the Union and the Industrial Revolution fell very fortunately, just at the moment when we could make best use of them. This old history and this modern success have left deep marks on our Nation. Amongst other things, they have left our language sprinkled with pithy proverbs for poor people. It is not reasonable to expect our readers to keep beside them a Scots dictionary, so we quote but one very suitable to the present moment. "He that tholeth overcometh." To thole is to endure. And sorrowfully we must admit, that many a true-born Scot can make but heavy weather of Burns. "The day draws near when this illustrious and malleable tongue shall be quite forgotten."

In the old days, we leant heavily on the blood-thirsty comfort of the Old Testament. It was an odd habit amongst our people to decorate their severe stone houses with pithy texts and sayings from the Prophets. The proverb we have just quoted is carved above the door of an old Edinburgh house. Like the Jews, we had endured a hard upbringing, and on all sides this feeling of savage effort was everywhere pressed upon the passer-by. Our Edinburgh Arms display a three-towered strong castle with the motto, Nisi Dominus Frustra, the beginning of the Psalm which in our version reads, "Except the Lord the City keep, the watchmen watch in vain." Our National Beast is a ramping lion, our National Flower, the very prickly thistle, with the motto, "No one shall touch me with impunity." And, indeed, we have been left with a very prickly nationalism, arising in modern psychological jargon from an inferiority complex. It shows itself in a thousand prickly ways and is very deceptive to the stranger within our gates. We keep on offending each other. England keeps on offending us by forgetting our existence. Yet this, after all, is truly a compliment. It is a testimony to our ability to forget ancient wrongs, which in truth we have avenged pretty well, and shows that we can merge our whole forces with an ancient enemy whose ideals and traditions we share. It shows most perfectly that we are no longer "The United Kingdom", a collection of pieces tied together somewhat insecurely by the bonds of common interests, but are at last and most truly just one realm – Great Britain.

There is another effect arising out of our old history. We know the value of things and what we get we keep. As a disgusted Englishman said, we keep the Sabbath and anything else we can lay hands on. We feel sure that Mr Churchill must be a Scot, although the proofs have seemingly been lost. We know that Mr President Roosevelt is a Scot by direct descent from one of our old and war-like Border families. Doubtless it was from the unpeaceful Murrays that he got his leadership and his indefatigable drive. So he also is one of us. So also is the B.B.C. We are not so much part owners as just owners.

This year in the Overseas Programme, there is a series of very Scottish items of very general interest, although most definitely of interest to our Scottish people throughout North America. Once a month, a programme about our Scottish Clans is being broadcast. Each programme contains a sketch of one Clan. The B.B.C. is using its great persuasive powers to entangle the Chief of the Clan in each broadcast, so that he may give a special greeting to his kinsmen, spread over all the States and Canada, and for that matter over the rest of the world as well. The chiefs of many of our Clans still live amongst their people. Shorn of their ancient powers and even of much of their ancient territory, they still take their place in the life of the community. They are amongst the best of our landlords, and the sons still follow the old tradition of military service.

Our Scottish Nationalism surprises and misguides our neighbours many a time – friend and foe alike. It is a somewhat nostalgic sentiment, and to quote one of our own poets, distance lends enchantment to the view. It is from the distance of an alien shore that our somewhat barren and hard-featured homeland is seen through the rosy sunset light and recognised as that lesser heaven that we left behind, half willingly in imaginative ambition, half regretfully because our ungrateful land could hardly even feed us. So the squalls endured on the streets of our gusty capital seemed to R. L. S. "a downright meteorological purgatory", but from the distant mountain top of Samoa, they became "winds austere and pure". Nevertheless, we have a strange capacity for setting our roots deep in our adopted soil and making it our own. We are British first, Canadian first, citizens of the United States first, but in our hearts and always we are Scots. To us there is no difficulty about this double loyalty. George Herbert, who was a divine, a poet, and no Scot, also saw what we see, "Love your neighbour, but pull not down your hedges".

The B.B.C. is always doing the impossible, and is equally expectant of impossibility from others. We were to produce a "Scottish Woollens" from the B.B.C. angle. From what kind of queer angle did our colleagues think we could see them? Perhaps they thought of us as inflicted with the distorted vision of the modern press photographer who must lie at your feet or climb a tree to take your photograph. Still they were broadcasting about our Clans. They liked our northern country life and often projected our Scottish accents on the ether. But what is the connection between Woollens and Wireless? Both begin with "W"? "The time is come, the Walrus said, to talk of many things, Of shoes and ships and sealing wax, Of cabbages and kings" More nonsense swims up in our mind, "She went into the garden to cut a cabbage leaf to make an apple pie". "'Besides I don't see how a man can cut off his own head.' 'A man might try.'"

The men of the B.B.C. have done a great job since Hitler set out to make his "New Order". No easy struggle this against lies and bombs, but they have fought both most valiantly. If we are to value their service at its worth, we must remember that the B.B.C. was an instrument of peace, chiefly designed for amusement and in a mild way for instruction. To our cost in these pre-war days, we took for granted that others knew as much about us as they wanted. Probably they did. We were ourselves no believers in propaganda. We did not advertise. We do not pretend this was a virtue. Our candid friends say it arose out of a monstrous conceit, and it is likely enough true.

The Scots prayer, "Lord gie us a guid conceit o' oorsels", had long ago been answered, and the petition granted not to Scotland alone, but to all our race. Yet ours is not a Herrenvolk conception of the Universe. Behind it lies Lincoln's proposition that all men are created equal. We think of our position, not as rulers by some divine right, but rather as the man at the wheel who must stand his watch until his relief comes on.

However we look at it, the change and expansion of the B.B.C. into a powerful instrument for the dissemination of news and for support of the cause of Freedom was a remarkable deed. They have inherited – or adopted – the old theatrical motto, "The Show goes on." No one can tell the countless incidents from which the B.B.C. emerged, bloody but unbowed. Only now and then we at the other end of the broadcasts heard hints of turmoil. One night as we listened to the news, there was an outbreak of atmospherics, a momentary pause in the calm voice. Another voice said, "Are you all right?" The news resumed the even tenor of its way. Later we learned that the "atmospherics" was the down falling of a large portion of the station under the friendly impulse of the reforming Germans. Another time, when banished to Bristol, there was such a bad raid going on that the usual religious service could not be broadcast from the studio. And thus says the report: "The orchestra could not cram itself into the small emergency studio, but Dr Welch was determined that listeners should not go without their postscript of music. The microphone was placed under a table, and with bombs crashing all round the building, Dr Welch delivered his talk, Stuart Hibberd read quietly from the Bible, and Paul Beard played the violin on his knees."

So they are valiant knights, these B.B.C. folk. People don't do their work that way for pay, although they may be paid for it. Selfishness and money never were motives for great national deeds, no matter what may have set the ball a-rolling. We can hardly overestimate the value of our Broadcasting, and in this we do not only think of microphones with the initials B.B.C., which are the only microphones in our island, but also of the components of that vast overseas net that works with us in the struggle against lies and oppression, some in the open, some in secret with death as the penalty of discovery. May be there is nothing between us and

America but the Atlantic. There's a lot of water there, but not enough to wash out misunderstandings and prejudices and the shadows of old wrongs. Now we can hear the actual words of our King, our President, our Prime Minister, and no politician can come between us to twist mischievous misunderstandings out of plain words. More than that, we have the Commentaries which are anxiously listened to by thousands and which go such a long way to show each of us what the other is thinking and doing. The other evening, listening to one of these excellent American Commentaries, it came as a shock to us to hear the speaker talk of us as "foreigners". Somehow we have never looked upon America as a "foreign" country – we share so much of our blood, of our history, so many of our ideals. Some day we hope we shall not look upon each other even as friendly aliens.

In our own way, we like to think our "Scottish Woollens" also has done something to unite our people. "Scottish Woollens" is, of course, advertisement, but it is advertisement of a special kind. Advertising has developed into a trade – or is it a profession? The skilful journalists who extol the virtues of That or This with lavish superlatives have probably never seen either This or That. They write with brilliance and psychology and they do a good day's work for their pay. "Scottish Woollens" is quite different. We Scottish Manufacturers write the articles ourselves. We write about our life's work. We write about what we ourselves wear for we believe in our own products. We write about things we know so that we write with both knowledge and conviction.

We can hail the B.B.C. as comrades in this great War for Union and Truth and Freedom and Understanding, which will go on long after this present War is over and which will as surely end in Victory.

We shall end this with our comrades' own words by quoting the Postscript of their Diary of the War, "So long as the War lasts, British broadcasting will continue to bring to the homes of this island people". And, we shall add, we hope to our overseas friends and allies "through the hard days, things of strength and beauty and fun... It will continue to sap the spirit of the enemy and to quicken the sense of liberty in the oppressed peoples, carrying the voice of truth and sanity and courage across the frontiers. And when Victory is ours, the high task of radio will be to help in building civilisation upon more enduring foundations, and to a better and a livelier pattern. Once again through broadcasting, 'Nation shall speak peace unto nation!'"

THE SCOTTISH CLANS
PROGRAMME OF THE BROADCASTS

Feb. 21–22. Clan Cameron	June 13–14. Clan Gordon	Oct. 3–4. Clan Mackay
Feb. 21–22. Clan Campbell	July 11–12. Clan Graham	Oct. 31–Nov. 1. Clan McKenzie
Apr. 18–19. Clan Colquhoun	Aug. 8–9. Clan Donald	Nov. 28–29. Clan Macintosh
May 16–17. Clan Fraser	Sep. 5–6. Clan Macgregor	Dec. 26–27. Clan McLean

Wavelengths: 31 metres (alternatives 25 or 49 m.).

Times: Each Broadcast is done twice, first after midnight at 12.45 and then at 4a.m. so as to give convenient times for everyone. The times quoted are Greenwich Mean Time, and here are the equivalents in the Continental War Times: Eastern, 8.45p.m. and midnight; Central, 7.45p.m. and 11p.m.; Pacific, 5.45p.m. and 9p.m. In America the dates of reception will always be the first of the two quoted.

The B.B.C. intends to continue these Clan Broadcasts into 1943, but their further programmes have not yet been arranged.

— 1942 —

A Letter to an
American Friend

MY DEAR SAM,

It is natural enough that you should be so much interested in our personal ongoings over here. You are a long way from the war and need in no way apologise for wishing to know how we fare and what the war looks like closer at hand, and just how it has affected all the friends amongst whom you were such a welcome guest in these far-off days that are only three years ago. We get lots of news of each other nationally, but figures of tanks and ships and prisoners are very chilly and impersonal by the time they have been desiccated for wireless transmission across the Atlantic. I shall try to give you an impression of our little community as the fourth year begins. You have met and worked with many of the very people I shall tell you about and you may be sure it will be a kind of hand sample of many another community in Scotland.

It is a lovely autumn day. You know our countryside; you have travelled over it many times. In these parts, the October sun never rises far above the low line of hills to the south, Everything is quiet. A luminous haze covers the land and bathes the levels in pale sunshine. The tawny fields stretch bare and undulating to the distant hills faint and blue in the level light. The fields are bare. The bountiful harvest has all been safely gathered in, the richest for many years. In the middle distance, a cart and horse moves slowly across the green area of a turnip field, and the thump of the ingathered turnips comes peaceably across the intervening atmosphere. From cottages and farm houses here and there amongst the fields smoke rises straight and bright against the luminous and serene distance. Lines of trees, brown and gold and yellow, separate the fields or crowd together into little patches of wood, giving an added richness to the pattern of the countryside, a lovely web of gold and grey. So it must have looked in all these autumns since the fields were translated from the uncultivated moor. So must that distance have looked to the Picts and the Danes and the Saxons and the Vikings and the nobles and the kings and the priests who gazed across that landscape, and bit by bit built up that idea which has become the Scotland of today. War seems very far from this northern Scottish landscape. Yet there is a sinister background to all this calm beauty. The drone of planes is always there, faint or loud, and at all the road corners the brambles are entangled with barbed wire.

In the midst of this quiet and lovely country lies the little town you know so well. It is just like many another of these little towns that contain the small mills that make up our Scottish Woollen Trade. A small place with old, careless, somewhat bare streets laid out on no special plan, houses each built to suit some long-dead townsman's idea of what was good, showing the fashions of two or three hundred years of slow development. They had seen wars come and go, English conquerors, Highland armies, red-coats and kilts and battledress. To a stranger, the little town looks peaceful enough today; the townsman sees the changes. Army wagons loading and unloading at shops marked "closed for the duration of the war"; a small procession of guns on their thick tyres trailing behind their tractors moves up the street, a Red Cross ambulance or a Church of Scotland Mobile Canteen, perhaps a long aircraft truck loaded with newly-painted wings or the fantastic skeleton of a burnt-out plane. These exotic elements are mingled with the diminished collection of bakers' carts, milk vans, trucks and motor cars; now and then come red and white dappled cows or a little tired flock of sheep. On the pavements, townswomen now all carry large shopping bags – shops no longer deliver; amongst this crowd of women, the usual users of the side walks, quick or leisurely the uniforms of many services move beside our own battle-dress, the inverted chevrons of the United States, tall turban-crowned men of the Indian Army. Amongst our own regimental marks appear the names Canada or Poland or Czecho-Slovakia. There is the dark blue of the Navy, the Police, A.R.P. men, the National Fire Service, the khaki girls of the A.T.S. and the Land Army, the blue of the American and Empire Airmen and our own R.A.F., the women of the Air Service looking very neat and trig, swarm everywhere, boys of the Air Training Corps, older men with lines of rainbow colours on their tunics. Every now and then a lorry load of men in blue or khaki singing or calling greetings to the passers-by. Just occasionally, a kilted figure moves through the crowd, a sort of dim relic of a lost past – the battle-dress of the Clans reduced to a "walking-out dress" to charm the bright eyes of the khaki and blue young women. How many could stand at the street corner of our little town and catalogue correctly all these varied uniforms and markings?

Our population on this island is just over 46,000,000. Of these, over 9,000,000 are children under fourteen, too young to serve in any regular way though many thousands have done good work helping on the farms or as messengers in the auxiliary defence services. The latest official figure for full-time war service is climbing up towards 24,000,000. Then there are about 3,000,000 disabled or over the age of sixty-five from whom only part-time service can be expected. This leaves but 10,000,000. When you think of the number of women required to look after the 9,000,000 children and all the workers' homes, there must be very few able-bodied men and women left in jobs that by any stretch of imagination can be called luxury jobs. That small remnant is steadily falling as new works come into commission. In our fishing villages, every man is at some essential job. A few still fish in very troubled waters. The rest are in that service of the sea that is for the most part unseen from shore and necessarily unknown to our Allies and even to ourselves. Yet it is to these men even more than to our Air Force that so much of our country, like all the Americas, only knows of war by hearsay.

In spite of this defence, by July, the enemy had killed 45,827 civilians and wounded 53,045. It is a horrid proof of the barbarism to which we have sunk that most of these air-raid victims were women and children. We should also remember that it was Germany that began this.

But after all I wish to give you some impression of the effect of the war on ordinary people in our part of the world.

It seems a long time ago looking back to these dreadful opening days of September 1939, when we waited under the first oppression of the black-out for the arrival of the trains of tired and depressed mothers and children evacuated from the threatened cities. Our little town had volunteered nearly double the required accommodation, and then only about half the promised numbers came – so many at the last moment could not face the uprooting of their lives and a day-long journey into unknown parts. So we got them all safely stowed away, a lull in the storm that was to come! The Saturday was perfect. Sunday, the 3rd of September, again a lovely day, overshadowed by Mr Chamberlain's announcement that war was upon us. It is customary to deride the policy of appeasement, but it was an honest effort, and it was right that it should be tried wholeheartedly. It is easy to see now that we trusted men who knew no good faith. Possibly we should have known better, but it was difficult in those days to believe in national treachery. During these months of uncertainty that came before the storm, thousands of our people had volunteered for something. The calling-up of all these volunteers during our last few days of peace caused the most complete disorganisation in our homes. Half our own household went away. Jean went off to hospital service, Tom was called up when the Territorial Army was mobilised, two of our three maids were called up for the A.T.S. In the evacuation scheme, we were a reception area. Fortunately, it was summer. In our thinly-populated land, there was just hardly room, and there certainly was neither blankets nor bedding for the crowds we had to house from the large towns. Mercifully, the weather remained fine, and in a last desperate bid for furnishings, we mobilised the Girl Guides, and they sat all round our mill courtyard sewing up hundreds of canvas bags to be distributed to the farms and filled with straw for bedding. However, somehow things did get done, but on the Saturday our halved household had two large families to look after. Still, again it is wonderful what can be done and they did get put up and fed. Our cook was just brilliant. You will remember her as our very charming table maid.

The local Red Cross was called upon to staff one of the military hospitals, more or less deserted since the last war. There was no professional help, and the V.A.D. members were given a mountain of beds and bedding to turn into a hospital. Again they managed. Our Miss Robertson, whom you remember well, was in charge, and Jean was second in command. They never lost a case, so they did not do badly. The doctors from nearby did what they could to take the place of full-time medical officers who did not exist! John Wilson, who was on the reserve of officers, was whisked off to guard bridges on the railway. Tom, who had newly joined the Territorials, was put in charge of the guard of a wireless station on the coast. A large staff of voluntary wardens patrolled the town all night, watching the blacking-out and straightening out the difficulties of our wretched evacuees.

Then in a few days the second wave broke over us, and we were engulfed in various battalions of the regular Army with trucks and guns and what not. They filled to bursting every school and hall in the place and packed every room in the whole town. We reckoned our population had swelled by a half within a week or two. And still the lovely weather held.

All the late summer work had gone forward night and day on aerodromes and landing grounds; crops were hurriedly gathered, often cut green. Huge levellers roared back and forward in clouds of dust clearing hedges and filling ditches and smoothing down mounds. Planes and ground staff kept arriving, whole villages of huts sprang up, and still troops of all uniforms kept pouring in and settling down. All this time, remember, we were certain of invasion. We were only uncertain where it would start. All this time, we expected heavy air attacks and were sure they would be everywhere. We remembered Guernica. We did not expect any high standard of humanity from Germany, although in those days the horrible massacres of Rotterdam and Belgrade were still mercifully hidden from us. Warsaw was war, but these others were just murder on a large scale.

The troops were housed in the extremity of discomfort as winter came on. The Red Cross started a small hospital, staffed by the members who were unable for their home duties to take full-time work. For an extemporised job, it was really quite good. It had thirty beds ingeniously contrived out of double-tiered bunks from a near-by camp. These contraptions of rough timber were sawn in two and nailed to the floor of one of our small halls. Of course, once the main camps were ready our little hospital dissolved into thin air, or more prosaically the beds resolved themselves into fire kindling! It is wonderful how unnecessary the high standards of medical science and equipment seem to be, and how far common sense can take the place of professional training!

So the months rolled by till Dunkirk burst upon us and started that vast and splendid improvisation, the Local Defence Volunteers, now re-christened the Home Guard. Recruits lined up at every enlisting office. Only the halt and the maim were kept out and many even of them pled for admission, were taken in and did good work. We enlisted about ten times the authorised numbers. It was a strange, mixed crowd that our Colonel addressed that Sunday in the courtyard of the County Jail – boys and young men and a large sprinkling of older men who had served in the Great War. A queer, democratic organisation reminiscent of early colonial days. Our job was to form a screen of watchers to guard against surprise landings from the air or sea. There were no officers, or, at any rate, all were equal in standing. The farmers watched all day, and we others all night from 10 till 6. To many of us these light northern nights revealed new beauties. It is not only in our cities that there is a night life. It was a surprise to most of us to see and hear so many unfamiliar birds and beasts moving quietly about our countryside.

We had neither arms nor uniform. We were deeply impressed by the vast system of spies and fifth column activities organised by the Germans throughout Europe, and elaborate precautions were taken to circumvent them. Our Art School designed and made up special armlets by which we would be known. We were given special code words to be used in all telephone messages. Looking back on those precarious days, such precautions appear needless. In our climate, fifth columns do not seem to flourish.

In these early days, one of Malcolm Inkson's chief jobs was to take the more distant patrols out to their beats in his car. You must remember that although parts of Scotland are quite thickly populated, there are very large areas quite empty or so thinly inhabited that they have not enough residents to make up the necessary guards.

As the Home Guard developed, proper training was gradually introduced, and now the force is no longer purely voluntary. Amongst those in our own mills that you will remember, Ian Cameron and Dodd Mackenzie have blossomed out into instructors and lecture learnedly on bombs and gas and the very varied collection of modern weapons now in their hands. The Home Guard remains voluntary in the sense that it is unpaid, and apart from the bare minimum of drills, the work is purely voluntary – we even graciously expect our men to pay for any petrol they use in the service, and they are allowed the privilege of paying their own expenses! This is no new thing in our history. Did not Queen Elizabeth expect her Admirals to pay for the powder and shot they used to defeat the Armada?

Meantime, our women folk were organising a central canteen for the Services. This was the special work of the churches. The canteen requires a staff of between thirty and forty every day. Each of the principal churches takes a day. They supply light meals and the usual additions of reading and writing rooms and a games hall. A little later, they started the motor canteens that serve the outlying camps, batteries, gun posts, and detachments far out in the uninhabited parts of the hills. In the intervals of acting as our cook, our Margaret is responsible for the drivers and attendants of this field force.

Then there is the big work party organisation of our County Red Cross. It fell to the lot of my wife, when she was not acting housemaid, to look after the work parties. Here, again, the ladies did a great job and almost completely supplied our many auxiliary hospitals with all they needed in equipment. Then there is the Women's Voluntary Service. They are kind of maids of all work, in charge of all manner of odd jobs. They look after the canteens and rest centres prepared against air attacks. They find billets for our evacuees. They are in charge of the stores of clothing so generously supplied by your countrymen for our blitz victims. They do any job no one else can find time for. We must never forget that the women folk have quite real work to do in running the many houses that enclose the more obvious workers. For very many, it is only a few hours a day they can spare and they do spare them. So, one way and another, there are mighty few in all our countryside that are not helping all they can.

The call-up slowly closed about us. Rationing came down little by little. Our petrol was more and more severely cut. Our journeyings were more and more curtailed. But we hardly missed our diminished leisure as we gradually took over the jobs of those who were called up for the Services.

In the mill itself, too, there is a lot to be done. Few of our mills have been "concentrated". Their scattered positions have made this scheme very little applicable, and their small size has made it of no very great importance. But the call-up both of men and women has reduced our numbers by about a quarter and has reduced our skill, too. However, work for the Services is much easier than the work you used to see passing through our plant. It is wonderful how well we get along with goodwill and the ability of every one of us to turn his – or her – hand to anything; that always has been a feature of our trade. Our trade is now under the Essential Works Order. No one may leave his work and no one may be dismissed without the permission of the Powers-that-be, but that does not prevent them being called up for the Services.

Then another question arose. The very primitive town fire brigade was childishly useless against raids and incendiary bombs, and through many stages of developments, the National Fire Service was evolved, and we blossomed into a full-fledged unit with a fire engine of our own. Our engineer in charge, Jimmy Cuthbertson, got trained into a section fire leader with a team of eight to work our new equipment, which is looked after by the team with all the care a mother could bestow on a new baby. Coupled to our fire service, we have three teams fully trained in first-aid under the joint care of Miss Robertson, who has been returned to the fold from her hospital duties, and Miss Sinclair, also well known to you.

Another curious change has come over us. No doubt you remember how quiet you found our house at night. How at first you found it disturbing to your sleep to be surrounded by such complete silence, just accentuated now and then by the hooting of the owls. Now you would find it quite otherwise. Now our visitors have their sleep ruthlessly disturbed by very violent noises. All night bombers and fighters roar over our devoted heads. Night patrols, planes going out on convoy work, our budding pilots learning night flying are never out of the sky. Red and green planets swim into our ken amongst the old familiar constellations. Searchlight beams and the Northern Lights compete for our attention and decorate our horizon. A queer change indeed.

So you see one way with another we are not and have not been idle during that long time of preparation as so many of your fellow countrymen seem to think. We just live in hope that our work may finally prove needless. I shall give you a quotation to round off my story. Oliver Cromwell was an Englishman, of course, and a sore trial to us Scots, but he was of the same race, our race and your race, and his words may well be our words. Said he, and the words are strangely like our Prime Minister's, "Well, your danger is as you have seen. And truly I am sorry it is so great. But I wish it to cause no despondency, as truly I think it will not; for we are Englishmen," –

Yours sincerely, MAC.

NOTE. The figures quoted in this Letter were supplied by the Ministry of Information.

OUR OFFICE

OUR Office is part of one of the masterpieces of British architecture. It is also part of one of the masterpieces of British War-time Organisation, for all the complicated workings of the Scottish Woollen Trade are controlled from No. 27 Charlotte Square in Edinburgh. This work has been undertaken by our Association – The National Association of Scottish Woollen Manufacturers – for the Government. This control covers a very wide field. All the complicated forms that make the manufacturer's life a burden, but yet have kept the trade going marvellously, flow out from this office. The work covers the rationing of wool and other raw materials, the details of the "concentration" arrangements in the industry, agreements for wage rates, Utility Cloth permits – or perhaps we should say demands – and so forth. No. 27 also allocates the orders for a considerable part of the Government requirements of woollen cloths for our Services and those of our Allies. Almost everything needed in our trade is closely controlled, from labour to dyes, chemicals and even wood for export packing cases. Thanks to No. 27 Charlotte Square, this complicated machinery moves wonderfully smoothly. All this business is run by ourselves with our Secretary in control, and so, within the very severe and strict limitations of our National requirements, the administration is entirely in the hands of men who know the Scottish Woollen Trade thoroughly.

Charlotte Square in Edinburgh belongs to that period of human history when western civilisation was awakening to consciousness of the rights of man. Everywhere the new spirit of enterprise and progress was in the air. Our American Colonies, tired of a despotic, distant, and unreasonable rule, had broken loose and had become a new nation under Washington. France was rapidly moving towards that wild explosion that gave the world the great battle-cry, "Liberty, Equality, Fraternity." Even in our own quiet, reserved, conservative country, the leaven of revolution was working, although in our case its chief manifestations were in a great bound forward in Art, in Industry, in Literature. The New Town of Edinburgh was one of the products of this great human movement.

Long and slowly prepared, this strange and – when looked at from the distance of the present age – dramatic change culminated in the time of the French Revolution. The change did not happen suddenly. The same change has happened in many towns and cities of Europe, but in Edinburgh the shape of the land made the development unique in its effects upon the modern city. In many modern towns – even in the New World where the old is comparatively modern – the houses of the nobility and well-to-do have tended to fall in social scale till they have fallen to the very bottom and now house only the dregs of the population. They have usually disappeared bit by bit, probably with great new streets hewn through the tangle of lanes that formed the defensive clusters of most ancient towns. The old has disappeared or has been left in pools or islands amongst the modern avenues. But in Edinburgh the shape of the land gave a queer twist to these universal changes. The Town stood upon a long, narrow ridge rising gradually from the gates of the Royal Palace – a small and poor palace as befitted a small and poor kingdom – for a mile that ended in the absolute and precipitous rock on which the Castle stands. To the north, the ground dropped abruptly to the loch that was, where now on summer days the band plays to crowds below the terrace of Princes Street. To the south, the ground falls as steeply to the Grassmarket and the Cowgate, but no cow now feeds on the old common grazings of the Burgh, long buried under the streets and traffic of the modem city. Houses had grown upwards on the narrow ridge till they reached ten, twelve even fifteen storeys, and must have neared the limits of building in stone and wood. They must have been the highest houses in the world till modern America with its sky-scrapers put all competitors out of the running.

Thus in the eighteenth century matters had reached such a pass that the Town Council of the day looked across at the somewhat inaccessible green fields and thought of bridges. First the North Bridge of 1134 feet stepped across the Markets and the Physic or, as we would say, Botanic Gardens. That space is now filled by the Waverley Station, at any rate till quite recently the biggest in the world. The foundation stone of the bridge was laid in 1763. It was widened in 1876, and finally the modern traffic made up on the old stone bridge and it was replaced by the present broad steel bridge in 1897. Meantime, the line was continued south with the

160

thousand-foot-long South Bridge in 1788. It spanned the old street of the Cowgate, and lastly in 1827 the more modest George IV Bridge was built nearer the Castle. In this way, the old city remained almost untouched by the great new development that went north and south above its crowded roofs and narrow lanes. So it has happened that we still have on its high ridge the Old Town crowned with the Castle on its precipice and separated by the gardens from the terrace of Princes Street, the chief street of the New Town. This result was more than half accidental, but in its final results it has produced one of the most dramatic cities in the world.

Our business is to the north, and this is not a guide to Edinburgh, of which there are enough and to spare. The whole idea of the scheme was bold and imaginative, no less than to make a complete new town across the valley. A competition was held in 1766, and a year later James Craig gained the prize with the layout of the streets of the New Town. The space was limited definitely. The Town Council bought the land, made the roads and leased it to the builders. It is not surprising that the hard and fast details of the plan did not last well. We Scots do not wear shackles gracefully, and we have perhaps gained more than we have lost, for, as R.L.S. says of Princes Street, "Many find ... the confusion of styles induces an agreeable stimulation of the mind." For a while, the spacious proportions of the first plan were followed, but the vast expansion of the nineteenth and twentieth centuries was not foreseen – after all, how could it be? The City got beyond the imagination of those in charge and Edinburgh now melts into the surrounding rich agricultural country with no more dignity than most towns.

So we come back to our Office. Princes Street, on its terrace overlooking the valley that separates it from the Old Town, is without any question the chief street of Edinburgh. This is but an accident of development, for George Street, which lies along the ridge, was the principal street of Craig's plan. It was a limited plan and did not allow for any 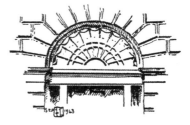 access from the surrounding country, limited also in giving only fleeting peephole glimpses of the glorious views of sea and mountains to the north. It was to be a residential city. Trade was to stay where it had already been established, so each end of the street was closed by a spacious square over 500 feet each way, and our square – Charlotte Square – closed the western end.

Up to this point, the development had been only a plan. Anyone who wished to build took what bit of ground pleased his fancy, although it is true he had to conform to fairly strict rules. The plan thus became clothed with buildings in a rather haphazard fashion. Towards the end of the century, building was nearing our Charlotte Square. Then in 1791 Robert Adam was appointed "architect to the Square".

Robert Adam was one of those family examples that makes us doubt the physical if not the moral soundness of Lincoln's proposition that all men are born equal. His father William, who was born in Fife just across the water from Edinburgh, was one of the most successful exponents of the Baroque tradition and built many great country houses. He lived from 1689 till 1748. He trained all his four sons to his own profession, and his eldest son, John, seems to have continued the family business in Edinburgh. Robert, the second brother, not only studied in Rome, as was the proper course for all artists in those days, but went to Spalato – or if you prefer it, Split – where he made a close study of Diocletian's vast palace, and, so it is said, thereby conceived the idea of treating a whole street or group of houses as one design. This was his most original contribution to town architecture. At home, he followed his father's profession and, like so many good Scots, he, with his two brothers, James and William, migrated to London. Thus anchored in the two capitals, the firm in its second generation rose to the position of dominating the profession throughout the whole length and breadth of Great Britain, as no one has before or since. Their work not only covered stone and lime, but all the sister arts of house decoration, furniture, furnishings, garden design, and the planning of towns and villages.

The Adams' tradition is a development of classic art very strongly under the influence of France, as was so much Scottish work of all kinds. We are always apt to consider the great men of old as isolated phenomena, but as a rule when their work is seen along with that of their contemporaries, we find it only just a little better, perhaps just separated from the work of others by some spark of divine inspiration, just enough to make their work immortal but rarely enough to distinguish it prominently from that of their fellow-workers. The Adams were lucky in being ready to take advantage of a time of lavish expenditure and of great

wealth. It must never be forgotten that of all the arts, architecture is the most plutocratic and alone of them all absolutely requires wealth for its expression. The Adams' art and tradition was quite definitely not British. It owed nothing to the sturdy work of the builders of either England or Scotland. It reflected instead the refined elegancies of the French and Italian Renaissance. France in her borrowing from Italy logically accepted and used the steep roofs and great chimneys called for by the wetter and colder climate of the north and made a feature of them. The men of the Adam revival admitted neither of these modifications of their southern models. They made no virtue of necessity. They hid their low pitched roofs as far as possible and confined their multitudinous chimneys to long rows crowning the dividing walls of their houses. This borrowed finery in the New Town is another element in the contrast between the Old and the New Edinburgh and underlines the change of manners from the old barbaric overcrowding of mediaeval days. In Old Edinburgh, the poor folks lived in the ground floors and next to the stars. The wealthy lived in between and one stair served everyone. In New Edinburgh, it is true the servants still lived in basement and attic, but the social classes as a whole no longer lived together.

The Adam family formed an unusual family group. As one of their literary friends said of them, "they were a wonderfully loving family". Although the brothers all followed their father's profession and worked in close harmony, they do not seem to have been formally constituted into a firm. They were wealthy. They belonged to the great literary and artistic society of the day. Their position was almost aristocratic. John, the eldest (1721–1792), stayed on in Edinburgh, spending much of his time managing his considerable estates. William, the youngest (1738–1822), attended chiefly to finance. The other two attended to the London end of the business. James (1730–1794) was the chief draughtsman, who translated the brilliant sketches of Robert, the most gifted of the brothers, into the most beautiful and delicate working drawings. Two of the sisters kept house for the brothers in London, or at any rate for Robert. The brothers built for their friends. They lived and visited in the houses they built. They moved in the very society for which their vast and lovely houses were designed. They breathed the very atmosphere they helped to create.

Robert's art had in it that element of decadence always present when an idea reaches its supreme and perfect development. It became perhaps too refined, depended too much on a mathematical delicacy of detail. It tended to sacrifice use to appearances. Robert himself was anything but decadent. His energy was wonderful, for not only did he with his own hand draw numberless details of furniture and wall decorations, but he sat as Member of Parliament for Kinross. Charlotte Square was the last and finest of his schemes. Unfortunately, he died in the year following his appointment as "architect to the Square", but his designs were completed and were on the whole conscientiously carried out. His brother James died two years later, in 1794, and the gardens were finally laid out in 1796, probably from plans arranged by John. The Square was not completed till 1814, when St George's Church was finished. Craig's plan included a church to dominate the Square and close the long vista of George Street. The church that was built was not Robert Adam's, although a church to fit the site was designed by him. For some reason, said to be fear of the cost, his design was not followed, which was a pity.

Thus was completed one of the loveliest pieces of town designing in Europe. Time has dealt kindly with Charlotte Square, and though, like so much more of the New Town, it no longer houses "the Nobility and Gentry", its outward form has been very lightly touched.

Do the little clerklets scurrying to snatch a cup of tea or coffee for their mid-day meal sometimes see a coach and four or a Sedan chair stopping at their door? Do they sometimes give a thought to that crowd of dignified and elegant ladies and gentlemen for which their workrooms were designed? Does some bewigged and silk-clad ghost sometimes interrupt the rattle of their typewriters? Perhaps –

for ghosts are everywhere in our old capital city, New Town and Old Town alike.

The Square is now a national monument, preserved since 1929 under a special Act of Parliament. No one can alter it in any way without sanction. At this moment, its sophisticated beauty is somewhat marred by the air raid shelters dug amongst its trees and flower beds, like some fashionable lady arrayed in dungarees attending to a war-time machine. The railings round the gardens have long since gone to make tanks or ships, but the railings round 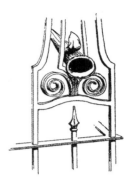 the houses will not be taken away because in the fashion of their day the houses have sunk flats with broad "areas" in which to hide the domestic servants of these unequalitarian times. On the north side, on each side of the steps that bridge the area and lead to each front door, there are still the torch-extinguishers of the days of Sedan chairs and link boys. Before our side of the Square was built some ten years later, public lighting of the streets had banished links and link boys, and another trade had disappeared.

We are not writing for architects, and we hope these notes may give a further interest to our overseas friends who we hope will soon be visiting us again to seek out new things in Scottish Woollens. Some years ago, the editor had the pleasure of lunching with an American architect whose work under Pacific skies had much of the refinement and delicacy of Robert Adam's work. We had been discussing the problem of sky-scrapers. I had said that America seemed to have solved the problem, for the new sky-scrapers were in themselves new and lovely, and were no longer just ordinary houses with the roofs raised. Said I, "If I had a son in the profession, I would send him for six months to the States to study your sky-scrapers." "Well," said he, "we in America think that an architect's education is not complete without visiting the New Town of Edinburgh." I think it was not just an exchange of empty compliments.

"No. 27"

We are indebted to Mr MacRae for the verification in the
City Records of our dates and other facts. Mr MacRae is not
only the City Architect, but is a careful student of all things
connected with the development of Edinburgh.

Our sketches are from photographs specially taken
by Mr J. L. Tweedie, who, like the rest of us, belongs to the
Scottish Woollen Trade. The details are all from the north
side. As that side was carried out before Robert Adam's death,
they seem to have been worked out under his direct personal
care and are more beautiful and complete than those on our
side of the Square.

WHAT IS TWEED?

KING ROBERT II

"WHAT IS TWEED?" Burke used a lovely and penetrating image in one of his orations. No man can tell when day passes into night, but every man knows the difference between night and day. That is true of the very simple question we in the Scottish Woollen Trade are often called upon to answer. In return, none of us can give a definition which cannot be cut to shreds by exceptions. In fact, we might again quote that same Burke's boast that he could drive a coach and four through any Act of Parliament.

In the first of these small papers we told of the derivation of the word. It is true we were rather telling a story – narrating a legend like the old minstrels – than recording the sober facts of history. The story was an old one current in the Borders and certainly has the stamp of likelihood upon it, but truly we cannot quote chapter and verse. As in all old stories of the sort, it has a good many variations in detail, but they all come down to the same basic fact that the name originated in the mistaken reading of the old Scotch word "tweel" for "tweed" under the influence – conscious or unconscious – of the knowledge that the cloth came from the valley of the River Tweed. But after all the origin of a name does not cast any clear light on the nature of the article named, although it may help to do so by inference.

That fact in the discussion is probably the only fact that does stand like a rock in a storm. In those happy far-off days, the Press was not the power in the land it is today, or anyhow its domain was different. It may have been more powerful, but it was much more limited. The Press had not extended its empire to the vast territory of Trade Advertising that it now occupies – somewhat fleetingly perhaps. But there is one particular direction that is quite modern in this influence and that is the artificial introduction of trade names. Looking back on these times round the early days of the nineteenth century, it is not likely that the introduction of the name was intentional. Goods were not written up in trade journals. There was no particular reason why anyone should ever invent or adopt a name for an article excepting that of convenience, and many of the ancient cloth names were derived from the places where they were made – Worsted, Cambric, Muslin, Cashmere, Arras, Gala Tweel. It is an obvious convenience in trade – a sort of short cut across a hill that saves going round by the road. So today the wool man talks of N.Z. Cross, Capes or P.P., and the other wool man knows he means New Zealand Crossbred wool, or fine wool from South Africa, or Merinos from Victoria.

Perhaps we may come to some kind of conclusion by finding out what sort of cloths Scotland made over a hundred years ago when Sir Walter Scott and his Shepherd Check trousers were influential enough to set a national fashion quite unconsciously. At best perhaps we might arrive at a sort of negative definition by discovering what is not a Tweed.

The old cloths were stiffer and heavier than fashion now expects, made to wear and wear and wear. The trade in woollen cloth in the valley of the Tweed was not new. It had been a staple of the country for several hundred years. After the Union of the two Kingdoms, a board had been set up to encourage industry of all sorts in much-harassed Scotland, and amongst other projects, the Board of Manufactures and Fisheries, as it was named, set out to improve this native industry by instruction in better methods and by offering prizes for good work. The seed fell on good ground and flourished. It had no uniform and halcyon weather, but it did survive droughts, frosts and gales. The cloths made were solid, fairly well felted fabrics, and the stage was set to take full advantage of the gradual changing of clothing habits. To begin with, native wools were used, and the cloths were like the strong, dense cloths worn by seamen the world over to this day. They were quite definitely Cheviots, and equally definitely the yarn from which they were made was spun on the woollen system – carded, that is to say, not combed – definitely not worsted.

But in the early years of the nineteenth century finer wools began to be used and by the time of Sir Walter Scott's ascendency the use of German wools became common. It was not till later that Colonial Merinos figured largely in Scottish

demands. We have before us as we write a whole packet of sales catalogues and reports, which by some lucky chance have escaped destruction. They are dated from 1837 to 1844. The chief wools listed are "German Lamb" and "German Fleece". These were the superfine Silesian and Saxony Merinos – the Saxonies that gave to Scottish fine cloths the name "Saxonies," which in quality are equivalent to the English "Botanies." Colonial wools first penetrated the English markets and the early Australian Merinos from Botany Bay gave the name to the English quality. These old sale lists could form the basis of an interesting excursion. One London sales report of 1840 gives the prices of fine Australians and so forth as "ranging from 1s. 4d. to 2s. 3d." and adds the comment "At and below 1s. 8d. clean

German Wools are scarcer and I would recommend English Sorts", and then goes on to quote a long list of English qualities ranging from 11d. up to "Primes" at 16d. and "Picklocks" at 17d. In foreign low wools for blankets from Turkey, he reports 9½d., and for carpets from Russia, 7¾d, to 8d. The expression "clean" most likely does not mean scoured wool, but rather in the ordinary English meaning of "good clean" as might be applied to pretty well anything. The German wools probably lost about 20 per cent against the English wools' 30 per cent, or thereby.

In those early days, "Tweeds" were made chiefly for men. They were mostly dark and dull colours, mostly dyed in the wool, although by no means always. Long ago black and brown Shepherd Checks were made by some pioneer souls by piece dyeing from cloth woven as real black-and-white Shepherd Checks, just as novelty effects are sometimes made now by piece dyeing on top of a pattern produced in the weaving. As the technique of spinning improved, smaller yarns were made and two coloured twist yarns came on the scene. "Pepper and salt" effects appeared and later developed into the more civilized "Bannockburns". The old patterns were chiefly little ground effects in neutral colours.

Like other good Scotch products, such as whisky, our tweeds spread and spread outwards from the land of their birth. On the whole, the English versions ran more to clearer finishes and cloths more suited to dress goods for women, while our tweeds were more masculine, rougher and more woolly in surface. We in Scotland never seem to have claimed proprietorship in the word, for we talk of Scotch tweeds in spite of the evident origin of the word, and at this time of day it might be impossible to produce a definite description that would satisfy everyone.

Now Scotland and the Scottish Woollen Trade never at any time stood still. Always our people poked about for something new, some new material, some new colour, some new process. This takes us back to the old belief that wool dyeing is best. This belief has long ceased to have any basis in fact. In the early days, it was true, because so few colours could stand the long process of the making of cloth.

Some argue that tweeds must be wool-dyed effects or at any rate yarn dyed, and that cloths that are piece dyed just are not tweeds by that very fact. This almost suggests that they claim that it is colour and texture rather than the cloth itself that must be considered.

This fact of wool dyeing against piece dyeing as part of a definition would land us in some queer situations, for a man might buy a patterned cloth for himself and a plain coloured cloth for a skirt for his wife, both the same fabric from the same loom, and one might be incontestably tweed and the other equally incontestably not tweed. Even more awkward would be the case if, for convenience' sake, a colour originally wool dyed were for later orders matched in piece dyed fabric so that the wife might find that she had a tweed skirt but her coat that matched it was not a tweed. That obviously would be absurd if the word "tweed" is to have any real practical meaning.

In early times, only the best fast colours could come through the long and severe manufacturing processes unimpaired. Now dyeing has so progressed that, if properly carried out, shades may be equally fast whether wool dyed, yarn dyed, or piece dyed, and we have only to consider which method is the most convenient for our stocks or is most likely to produce just the effect we aim at. We did say "if properly carried out". It still remains true that wool dyeing has to pass through a more searching test than yarn dyeing, which occupies a middle position, or piece dyeing, which has little to endure once the colour is added.

And what are these considerations or reasons that decide the stage at which the dyeing is done? To begin with, if you are seeking for a mixture effect, it is evident that the wool must be dyed before it is spun, unless the effect is possible by the mixture of raw materials that dye differently, such as wool and rayon. If a large quantity of any particular colour is needed, it may be quite economical to dye the wool even if a mixture effect is not required, but it does tend to lock up material in the yarn store; equally obviously, it does tend to produce a level colour all over the cloth and prevent variation from one web to another.

Then it is obvious that if very small quantities of many different colours are needed, like striping yarns, it is easier to make one lot of white yarn and dye little lots as they are required, and thus save locking up yarn and capital. Also, as there is of course less working on the colour after it is dyed, there is a tendency to achieve more brilliant shades. There is likewise a tendency to advantages and disadvantages. Make more waste in the different processes of winding necessitated by yarn dyeing, and equally, of course, all that working on the yarn tends to weaken the thread and so may delay the weaver. In all these matters it is a balance of advantages and disadvantages that must decide. In some cloths, the use of very soft yarn may be an advantage – even a necessity – and it may be necessary to pay for capital and dye in bigger lots in the wool, for a very soft twist will obviously be unable to stand the processes of reeling, dyeing and winding involved in the dyeing of yarns.

Then, lastly, we come to piece dyeing. The first and most evident advantage is that out of one white yarn, you can produce an infinite number of different shades of finished cloth, and the other equally evident advantage is that by preparing the goods past the weaving stage and storing the half-finished cloth, a much more rapid delivery can be achieved after an order is received. These might be called financial considerations. There are also some real advantages, such as in many types of soft or velvet finishes where raising or brushing comes in or some special milling effect is needed. Piece dyeing enables very soft yarns to be used or yarns of types of raw material that felt badly or otherwise deteriorate in wool dyeing. For example, Angora fur matts terribly in dyeing and also floats about in the dye vessels and so gets lost. Such materials are best converted into yarn as early as possible in their evolution into cloth. And so this choice, wool dyeing, yarn dyeing or piece dyeing, now depends on the manager and the designer entirely. If properly carried out, one method is as good as another in its final effect so far as the wearer is concerned.

Well we have not come much nearer a definition of tweed – at least we have not found a definition that could be embodied in an Act of Parliament, or even very usefully registered for any purpose.

Tweed could perhaps be described rather than defined as a cloth of medium weight, best adapted for suits for men and women. Not very smooth in texture. Tending, but only tending, towards Cheviot qualities. Tending, but by no means limited to broken effects of colour, attained either by pattern or by blends of colour; quite definitely limited to wool spun on the Scotch system – that is, woollen, not worsted yarn. It should show that slightly rough surface and that kind of broken or varied colour that is more suited to informal use than to ceremonial occasions. Such a description brings us back to the quotation from Burke with which we started. The word "tweed" certainly conveys to us all an idea, an image, but like night and day its edges are ill defined.

We in the Scottish Woollen Trade progress and progress. We were and are adventurers in the old true sense. The days when we invented or evolved tweeds are long past. The idea has gone over all the world and our reputation is now somewhat overshadowed by our old pioneering and our old successes with heavy and somewhat primitive cloths. Nowadays we prefer the name Scottish Woollen Trade rather than our old and honourable title of the Tweed Trade, which has served its day and generation. For now we make many things besides tweeds – almost anything that can be fashioned out of wool, and more than that. If new fibres are developed and are accepted by the world, we shall not allow prejudice to stay our hand. We shall turn our old craft to new purposes, for it is the craftsmen that count in such a trade as ours, not the financiers, not the politicians, and certainly not what we made yesterday.

NOTES ON ILLUSTRATIONS.

The somewhat primitive Lion that stands at the beginning of this number is the shield of King Robert II, as depicted in the "Armorial de Gelre", a manuscript of the fourteenth century, which was in the Royal Library at Brussels. Our tracing is from Stevenson's Heraldry in Scotland.

Our two bridges are the first and last over Tweed – Tweedsmuir and Berwick. The first is from a photograph by Reid of Wishaw. For the latter, the Editor is responsible. This great old bridge of fifteen arches dates from about 1634.

CHEVIOT CLOTH

THE Cheviot Hills, for centuries the historic frontier between England and Scotland, have given their name successively to a breed of sheep, the wool from that sheep, and a type of cloth made from that wool. In previous articles, we have told something of the history of the breed and have explained the characteristics of the wool. We now propose to give some description of the cloth that carries the name. This perhaps is not as simple as it looks, for in the course of time, the term, like the word "tweed", has come to bear a much wider significance than was originally attached to it.

It is a happy accident that has associated two of the main features of the Borders landscape with its principal manufacturing industry. The river that winds like a silver ribbon through the whole breadth of the Borderland, to make its exit into the North Sea in a majestic sweep round the grey old walls of the ancient town of Berwick, has given its name to the staple industrial product, and the hills to which many Borderers daily lift their eyes have stood godfather to the most important section of that product.

As a matter of convenience, Scottish Woollens are broadly divided into two categories: Saxony and Cheviot. This classification is helpful both in manufacturing and marketing. Saxony yarns and cloths are those made of Merino wools. The name is enlightening, the first Merino wools to be used in the South of Scotland, at least in relatively modem times, having been imported from the Kingdom of Saxony.

The term "Cheviot" is now used in Scotland to cover all Crossbred products. The more limited meaning of an all-Cheviot wool cloth has, therefore, been superseded.

With reference to wool, the word "quality" has one primary meaning – that is, the fineness or thickness of the fibre. The quality is designated by a number, and this is fixed by the length to which theoretically the particular fibre will spin. The "count" itself is reckoned by the number of yards of thread to the pound and is stated as the number of hanks of 560 yards to which a pound of wool can be spun. Incidentally, the word "grist" is usually substituted in Scotland for count. Thus the answer to the question of what is the quality of a particular wool would be, say, 40s, 64s, or 80s, generally qualified by the breed or country of origin or some further particular, according to circumstances. The quality number is the theoretical limit to which the wool will spin in combed or worsted yarn. Thus 50s Cheviot means that one pound of this particular wool may be spun to 50 hanks or cuts of 560 yards each, say, 28,000 yards.

In carded – or what are technically called woollen – yarn, it is not possible to spin a given weight to the same length, but the wool designation remains. Another point that may be confusing to the lay mind is that say 50s quality of wool and 50s yarn are by no means the same thing. 50s describes the considerable thickness of the fibre, but the actual yarn may be spun to something thicker, say, 36s. The description of such a yarn, if it were two-ply, as is usual in worsted, would be 2/36s 50s quality.

The dividing line between Saxony and Cheviot is 60s quality. This represents a very fine Crossbred, almost returning to Merino. Cheviot wool itself ranges between 48s and 56s, the bulk being generally 50s.

Saxony or Merino cloth is fine in texture and soft and kindly to handle; it may be a loose and pliable fabric or stout and leathery according to the setting in the loom or the amount of milling or felting to which it is afterwards subjected. It is extremely sensitive to the milling process – indeed, as a general proposition, the finer the wool fibre, the more quickly it felts. There are exceptions, but we can only deal with generalities.

Cheviot cloth, on the other hand, is crisp to handle and broader in texture, due, of course, to the "quality". Being of a thicker fibre, it is usually stouter in the yarn and bolder in the twill or more open in the weave. It therefore presents to the eye a bigger pattern or effect. Saxony lends itself more to quiet colourings and restrained designs, while Cheviot offers unlimited scope to the designer for bold patterns and gay colourings. He does not always avail himself of this liberty, for in men's wear at least, a certain restraint is usually necessary, but Cheviots being as a rule more lustrous, take a brighter dye than their finer rivals. Lustre indeed is one notable sign of breeding; it appears in the best bred Merinos, but is more observable in the broader-haired wools such as Cheviot.

The evolution of the woollen textile trade from a purely peasant industry to its present development has been a very gradual process and covers several centuries. At times, its progress has been suddenly accelerated by events of world-wide importance. Three of these followed each other rapidly at the end of the eighteenth and the beginning of the nineteenth centuries. Firstly, there was the advent of power-driven machinery; secondly, the increase of transport facilities; and, thirdly, the great augmentation of the world's wool supply brought about by the colonisation of Australia, New Zealand and the Cape Colony, all of which were actually and potentially great sheep-rearing countries. The population of the more or less civilised and wool-wearing portions of the globe was then rapidly increasing. The wool production and means of transport kept pace with this increase, and machinery gave its all-important contribution in meeting the growing need. In or about the year 1895, world wool production probably reached its peak and has more or less remained slightly below this level. Whether this is in excess or short of the demand has depended on many factors and, more recently, on the challenge of artificial fibres.

All this may appear to have little bearing on our subject, but we mention it because the peasant character of by far the greater part of the Scottish Trade has long been merged in the greater commercial organisations, and even at the moment in the distant Hebrides and the remote Highlands it appears to be undergoing "rationalisation"; the Homespun tradition still lingers in an important section of our products, such as Harris, Shetland and the true Cheviot.

The raw material of the peasant industry was locally produced, and, in earlier times at least, the weaver might also be the owner of the sheep that provided the wool for his yarns and cloths, and even much later, the master weaver, or "clothier" as the manufacturer was originally called, did not look beyond his own countryside for his supplies. The growing ease of obtaining foreign and colonial wools about this time introduced a radical change. The old rough Homespuns, the Galashiels blues and greys, made of the native product, had for the time being seen their day when two famous Scotsmen, Sir Walter Scott and Lord Brougham, stepped into the breach to give Scottish Woollens a much needed fillip, about 1826.

Now the curious thing is that it was not the old Homespuns to which they gave the required advertisement, but to cloths made by Scottish manufacturers from wools imported from Saxony. From a reference to old pattern books, still extant, it would appear as if designers during the earlier days of the Tweed Trade were solely occupied with the finer cloths, and the batch books of the same period seem to confirm this view. The description of wools that crop up most frequently all seem to be of a Merino type. A batch book dated 1847 lies before us as we write, and with the exception of some Down Fleece, there appears to have been no Crossbred used by this particular firm at that time. The name that occurs most frequently is Odessa, while German Lambs, presumably Silesian, New South Wales Botany, and various American wools are often mentioned.

Notwithstanding, it would seem that parallel with this cult for fine wool and small yarn cloths, the old tradition of a coarser-fibred cloth was carried on, and, indeed, was a large and essential part of the trade. The new types varied from the old in milling, finish and very definitely in the great variety of colours now introduced. While Cheviot wool remained the basis of these cloths, Colonial and foreign wools of comparable quality were largely blended with the home product.

It is certain that even in the era of stiff conventional outer garments, the landed proprietors and gentry, at least when on their own domains, would occasionally, for ease and comfort, relax into a more homely garb. Galashiels blues and greys, although possibly more utilitarian, could not be considered any more comfortable than even the conventional upper class attire of that period, but here was a class of cloth that could be worn with comfort and distinction, and, moreover, had the seal of fashion set upon it. During the years following their break from the older tradition – that is, from 1830 onwards – the Scottish manufacturers catered increasingly for the exclusive London West End trade, and side by side with the new fine Merino cloths, developed cloths of a Cheviot variety made largely from Cheviot wools supplemented by Colonial Crossbreds now being imported in ever-growing quantities.

From the colourful and picturesque male attire of the Georgian era, there was a gradual transition to the more sombre and uglier garments of Victorian times. Against this uniform dullness, there must have been at least a tendency on the part of blither spirits to revolt. This found its expression, among the leisured classes at least, when placing their seasonal order with their Savile Row tailor, and decided then to include one or two more brightly coloured Cheviot suits in their annual outfit. London has always held the same sort of pre-eminence in men's fashions as Paris has in women's, and Savile Row in its own sphere rivals the Rue de la Paix. It was natural, therefore, that male visitors to London from all parts of the world should take the opportunity to replenish their wardrobe. Thus the new fashion caught on and Cheviot suits became popular in all the temperate climates of the globe. It has been no fleeting popularity, because the sterling worth of these cloths, and their handsome appearance and wearing qualities, have commended them to the many millions of Central Europe, and in their lighter forms to our American friends.

We have so far been thinking chiefly in terms of what, for want of a better word, we have called the true Cheviot – that is, a cloth made of a distinctive Cheviot quality and therefore necessarily in a fairly round yarn and of a medium to heavy weight. These probably reached the zenith of their popularity in the eighteen nineties. A few of the older generation can still remember with pride and pleasure the beautiful colourings and designs that were then evolved by some of the leading Scottish firms. There was at that time, too, evidence of the gradual breakaway from the stiffness and conventionality of the Victorian era, for which the silk top hat stood as a symbol, and which received its final knock in 1914.

It is not to be supposed that the vogue for Cheviot confined itself merely to the wealthy or leisured classes; the cloths had qualities that commended them to the masses, and, where style alone had not to be paid for, they were capable of production at very moderate prices. But customs and fashions do not stand still, nor do the Scottish designers. During the last fifty years, there has been an ever-increasing tendency towards ever lighter suitings. The same remark does not apply to overcoatings, as these are designed to protect us against the rigours of winter and the biting blasts of spring. The weather is not interested in fashions.

This difference in weight over the period is very marked. In 1894, an inhabitant of these islands might cheerfully and comfortably have worn a cloth of 26 ounces to the yard in winter and of 22 ounces in summer. His descendant may now complain that 16 ounces is on the heavy side. The three main causes of this change have been the development of the knitting machine, central heating and motor transport.

How has this change – and it has been a very gradual one – affected Cheviot cloths? In overcoatings, not at all. However, in suitings, the problem became an ever more acute one for the manufacturer. Lighter weights meant finer yarns. It was met at first by spinning the old-quality yarns to a finer count, but there came a time, and that very soon, when wool of a purely Cheviot character would not go any further, and it was necessary to introduce wool of a finer Crossbred quality in blend, or possibly altogether. As time rolled on, even this was not enough and a proportion of Crossbred worsted had to be used in the lightest weights, thus preserving the crisp, bright Cheviot character, although the fabric might not contain an ounce of Cheviot wool. These lighter-weight cloths, with their finer yarns, lend themselves to neater designs and are more suitable for town wear than their hardy predecessors that depended more on colour and relatively simple effects. They have indeed offered a field for development in which the Scottish designers are supreme.

As in our previous article "What is Tweed", we have endeavoured to steer clear of strict definitions, knowing the pitfalls that one must encounter, but we hope we have been able to convey an idea of Cheviot cloth.

The name of Cheviot is dear to the heart of the Borderer, and the exile from that land often longingly wonders will he ever "see the bounds o' Cheviot mair". The cloth has naturally had its imitators, and on a very large scale. These imitations have not always kept it in good repute. Like "the grand old name of gentleman", it has not altogether escaped being "soiled with all ignoble use", but in its genuine manifestation, it still remains the aristocrat of Scottish woollen cloths.

THE FIFTH YEAR
Another Letter to an American Friend

MY DEAR SAM,

Often since I sent you my impressions of our little town in war-time you have asked me for another letter about our country – something less parochial, more national, but still about Scotland. Each time on reading your welcome letters, I have resolved to try to satisfy your curiosity. Each time I have run away from the difficulty of giving you anything like a true picture of what we are doing and thinking, and especially of what we are thinking. I started a letter months ago. As things occurred to me, I kept adding bits to my letter, trying to make a picture for you. At last I had got together some more or less coherent whole. And still I hesitated. In spite of its date, most of this letter was written in spring. Since then, the vast Tide of Victory has swept over devastated Europe, a victory in which your people have taken so magnificent a part. I wondered if circumstances had changed so much that my letter would have lost interest, but after all it is an account, not of a few days, but of a long period that even yet is substantially unchanged. Our faith has been justified and hope has grown to certainty, but still the shadow of war lies heavily upon us. So I thought I should send my letter to you after all.

In some ways, looking back on these last few years the war seems to have filled all time and space. It is an incredible time since Mr Chamberlain stepped down from his plane waving his promise of peace in our time. We sometimes wonder if we ever had known peace or if our time will stretch out far enough for us ever again to know peace.

When I last wrote to you about our district, it was autumn. Autumn has come again and has gone, and again it is not far off. Still we live in a sort of disturbed oasis in this wide desert of war. We are nearer its sounds and turmoils than you are, "but still a Ruby kindles in the vine, And many a garden by the Water blows".

I am sitting on the edge of the wooded ground just below our house. Let me recall to you that view, which you have so often looked down on from our windows. The ground falls some 70 or 80 feet to our little river that wanders so waywardly through our landscape. The river is spangled with a myriad sparks of light and dappled with golden brown in the sun. In front of me is a crab-apple patched with white blossom and young green leaves and filled with the wandering traffic of flies and bees and butterflies. Birds flirt and flicker in its branches; coal tits and blue tits, the sober slim wheatears, chaffinches, and now and then the almost tropical brilliance of a bullfinch, all against the bright blue of the sky or the pale green of the young oats. The wild cherries are just over, and an occasional drift of petals on the gentle breeze reminds you of their newly past glory. Our mixed halfwild Scottish woods are a joy and a delight in early spring. There is an infinite variety of greens, poplars of several kinds, from the fawn of the Italians to the grey of our own aspens, sombre Scotch firs, brighter larches, the wild cherries now bright green, the golden tone of the oaks, the silver leaves of the whitebeams, the intense and vivid foliage of the young beeches, the quiet grey of birch and rowan and willow. Away to the not very distant horizon lies a country infinitely detailed with farmhouses and varied crops. Now and then a train bustles by, trailing smoke and a line of cars to break – or to accentuate – the sleepy spell that lies on the landscape. The jarring and long-familiar note is the ceaseless sound of aircraft lining up, taking off and landing on the level stretch of the distant aerodrome. The constant sound, loud or faint, never seems to leave the sky empty. As I watch, the vast shadow of a plane rushes up the opposite fields and vanishes amongst the trees.

As you know, one of our characteristics is fondness for living in a rut. We are conservative, very conservative. It takes a great upheaval to jolt us out of our rut – be it personal or national. It took a dire national necessity to induce Oliver Cromwell to desert farming for the command of an army, but once started his motto was "Thorough". It is in this conservatism that much of our power rests. Now it seems to me that the country has settled down into a war rut. All your friends that I catalogued in my last letter are still at their war jobs, with just one exception. Pattern making in our mills has almost ceased. Partly it is needless to trouble about novelties, partly the staff is otherwise needed, partly there is an official recommendation that almost amounts to an order against pattern work, so our Miss Sinclair has become a "hen-wife" – that is to say, she has been "directed" to look after a poultry farm. Otherwise, privates have become sergeants, captains, majors, but there is little other change. We hardly imagine any other state. Everything for war needs is accepted almost without comment. We growl not at the imposition of the really very hampering restraints, but rather because we are not quite sure they are going to give us the effect we want. As a somewhat extreme example of this state of mind, there is an area hereabouts that the Admiralty thought they would like for practising "combined operations" for the much demanded "second front". It was to give the last stages of training to the assault troops.

This involved the complete clearance of every individual and of every beast. The area was surrounded by a deep safety zone from which for a day or two at a time the population might be warned out. The fleet was bombarding with live shells and some might easily go astray. Tanks, large and small, also were careering up and down the country. In the cleared area, they and the Navy paid no attention to houses and farm buildings. In the safety zone, the tanks paid no attention to such minor property as field-fences and dykes, as we call the mortarless stone walls that in Scotland surround most fields. For over half a year "combined operations" did their worst till hardly a field would keep the cows from wandering, and here and there a farm was flattened out. No one seemed to mind a bit. The schools would close at a few hours' notice for a day or two, and the children would be carted off to the nearest centre not affected. No one seemed to mind. The animals were the greatest difficulty, for most farms have no guest rooms for cows and pigs and horses. The poultry had to take its chances against shells and machine guns, and it says something for the men collected from every part of the Allies' territories that the birds did not find their way into the camps. I have told you a good deal about this because in a somewhat extreme way this attitude is typical of what is happening all over Scotland, and doubtless all over England as well. Remember this was not invasion or enemy action or any such things that just must be suffered as best you can, but just an area selected for very violent and destructive army manoeuvres. Our folks' attitude is not just tame acquiescence – sufficient unto the day is the evil thereof – but is a deeply-rooted will to do anything possible to further the destruction of the enemy.

But along with all this, we are not good personal haters. The other day, a German airman baled out and was captured by a farmer. He seemed to expect some dire fate and was surprised to be taken to the farmhouse and given breakfast and a cup of tea before his "host" telephoned for the police. That remains a typical reaction. I must also tell you a good story I got first hand about the Italian prisoners in our district who are working on the land. Every day, the gangs go down in lorries from their "cage" to their selected farms. They are under armed guards. As one of our farmers' wives was motoring home in the evening, a figure stepped out and signalled to her to stop. This was one of the Italian prisoners. No one was within sight: "Please, ma'am. If you see our sentry, would you send him along? We can't go home without him." "Home" was the word he used. I think many may even look back with pleasure to the days of their captivity, and that should be good propaganda for the peace of the world.

Travelling is not comfortable: sometimes the trains are empty, sometimes full twice over, and there are far fewer trains. Dining cars have all been taken off and made into ambulance trains. Both trains and stations are thoroughly blacked out, so that travelling is to be feared after dark. Loud speakers at all the important stations do not compensate for the lack of vision. As your train draws up in Edinburgh – let us say – a vast feminine voice from somewhere overhead fills the air. You grope your way along with the dense crowd, burdened with unseen baggage. This voice says, "Passengers for London hurry up please, train leaves number-one platform in ten minutes." Other instructions follow, and then the message begins again. The crowd feels its way to the exits, mixed up with goods and baggage trucks, guided by faint blue lights here and there – a queer scene.

To many, this black-out is the most dreaded of all the everyday effects of the war on our everyday life. In the country, of course, dark nights always were dark and all country folk are accustomed to darkness outside their doors, but in the towns it is very oppressive. The great reduction of traffic has helped, so far as roads and streets are concerned. Petrol restrictions have almost removed private cars from the roads and traffic is the ghost of what it was. Even now, when the Luftwaffe is so much less able to visit us, the regulations are almost fiercely administered, and on the sidewalks on dark nights those on foot still bump into each other.

All rationed food is well and evenly spread. No one has any difficulty in getting his share punctually and without trouble. Fruit is very scarce, vegetables in the towns not easy to come by.

Of course, there are queues – but not for anything very essential, and only in the larger towns, excepting for 'buses. That is a horrid exception. Like all other forms of transport, the 'buses have been cut and cut till they – or their absence – constitute a real burden to many thousands of war workers. There are queues for such luxuries as cakes, and mighty early in the day they are gone – and they are rather apologetic cakes anyhow. There are queues for fish, which so far has successfully defied control and remains as erratic and ungovernable as its native seas. And all this leads up to another queer development of war – the British Restaurants. They were started by the Ministry of Food during the bombing of London to feed the workers and the people, and the idea spread all over the country. It is an interesting development. The Ministry supplies the outfit – everything – tables, cooking apparatus, knives, forks, everything, including permits for the supplies. The local authority, the Town Council or whatever it may be, does the management, and has to arrange prices so as to repay the capital at the rate of at least one per cent each month. Finally, when the capital is paid off, the local authority can do what it likes with the Restaurants. They are worked on the cafeteria system, and you can get a good square three-course meal for between 9d. and 1/3. Also from these British Restaurants radiate streams of trucks with insulated containers taking hot meals to country schools, where want of ordinary 'buses has made it hard for the children to get home for dinner, or to groups of workers under the various voluntary schemes run by the Ministry of Agriculture to help farmers, or for any of the many gangs working at special war jobs of too short a duration to have proper canteens. The Ministry of Information claims that we are the most mobilised of any of the countries now at war, and I could imagine it may be true.

In the hotels, service is at the minimum, the menus are sprinkled with As and Bs, and the instruction is that you may only have one A dish and one B dish or two B dishes if you prefer. Still, the variety is remarkable and the quality is not bad. Some things, such as fresh eggs, have almost vanished for the townsman for they used to be largely imported. Butter and jam are severely restricted. But there are still some unrationed foods that help to compensate, such as salmon and other fish, tongues, poultry and rabbits, of which only the prices are fixed. To this extent, we are better off than in the Great War, as we do not need to give up coupons for meals in hotels unless we stay over four days.

We are, generally speaking, an orderly folk. All the same, the almost total absence of black-marketing is not caused by orderliness, but by a universal recognition that rationing is for a good cause. Fairly often prosecutions are reported, but they form an almost invisible percentage. They earn such sentences in the Courts that he must be a bold man who at the same time can ignore public opinion and the Courts of the Realm.

The chief black-marketeers are the boys of our Air Forces, and it matters mighty little under which flag they serve. Fresh eggs are the chief articles and they are captured not by coin, which is the currency of most black-markets, but by smiles. No farmer, or at any rate no farmer's wife, can resist the blue uniforms. They can almost wile the birds off the trees. They never fail to wile the eggs out of the basket.

The most awkward part of our rationing is the restraint on buying clothes. Food rationing leaves no good cause for grumbling. There is plenty and we get our shares without difficulty. But we are getting very shabby. It's an ill-wind that blows nobody good. Through the scarcity of coupons, our people are finding that Scottish Woollens are worth paying for and cheap clothes are almost unsaleable. We just cannot afford to buy poor stuff.

So, as a natural sequence I suppose, auction sales have gone quite mad. There always was a considerable crowd of sale addicts – folk who never could resist the auctioneer – now they are having a wonderful innings. All the blandishments of the Government have not managed to borrow all the spare cash that cannot be spent owing to rationing and the coupon system. We are bound hand and foot in the amounts of pretty much all new articles that we may buy, but sales are sales and are still outside Government control.

Another change is the shaving down of our newspapers. Even the great dailies are reduced to six pages so many days a week and eight pages on the other days. The more local papers seldom exceed four small and very thin pages. I don't know that we miss them greatly for the war news comes red-hot over the wireless and no other news counts for so very much nowadays. The newspapers have also most loyally kept secrets out of their columns. In fact, it is altogether wonderful how whole communities have kept essential secrets. For example, the "Queen Elizabeth" slipped unadvertised out of the Clyde. The vessel is as big as a sky-scraper and her movements must have been known to many thousands. We won't know of lots of wonderful happenings until after the war. And yet it is not so surprising. In 1745, after the collapse of the last Jacobite Rebellion, Bonnie Prince Charlie, after his final defeat at Culloden, was long a fugitive over Scotland, with £30,000 on his head. Scotland was a very poor country and £30,000 a splendid fortune, but it remained unearned.

Perhaps of all the new features in our national life, our craze for planning is the most curious. We who never planned anything, who always extemporised something when something turned up, who "muddled through", now seem to talk of nothing else but plans. The air is darkened with "blue prints" for every imaginable improvement. The end of the war should herald in the Millennium if planning can do it. But it is good that we should do all this thinking out methods for the future of mankind. Without exception, they are for the improvement of the common man. Beveridge Reports, Highland power schemes – a small echo from the Tennessee Valley – prevention of unemployment, and if that ghastly and crushing load can be lifted from the shoulders of our Industrial Democracies, half the ills of modern civilisation will vanish. These are but a few of the larger plans that are going forward just now. Even if the schemes fail, the mere fact that the evils have been recognised and that men of goodwill throughout our Democracies are working hopefully for their extinction is something to cheer us all. Here in Scotland, special committees have been set up by the Government to report on every aspect of life you can think of: housing, town planning, where our industries are to be put, how they can be improved, the best systems of technical and other forms of education, how to improve our local government and ways of taxing, our methods of electing Members of Parliament, our supplies of milk, the development of our natural resources, our agriculture, the design of our manufactured articles. All the pigeon holes in St Andrews House and in Whitehall are filling up with reports.

Sometimes amidst all our planning for this rosy future rises the spectre of debt. How can we Allies hope to pay off any important part of these vast mountains of debt we have already incurred or have promised to incur? For we have promised to set the wheels once more going in the desolated countries slowly emerging from the clutches of Hitler's Gangsters. How can we look forward to the time when we shall have money to spend on any of our glorious plans? I think the hope and the solution lies in the huge extra force, the new energy the war has developed, and which would never otherwise have existed. So far, it has been dissipated in smoke and fumes – but that is not the end. There will be left behind a great mass of mental training, even many useful articles, and many new services and organisations, and what is less visible and more important, the spread of knowledge of organisation. If all this enormous force can be turned to the uses of peace in a few years this should go far to undo the measureless harm and destruction that Hitler has brought upon the world.

And so when next you visit us, you should find a new country, very like the old, but more thriving, more prosperous, less class conscious, altogether better, only you will miss many of the lovely old buildings in which our national story was enshrined. You will not see them for they are dust and ashes.

Yours sincerely,   MAC.

P.S. – Up till the end of July, the Nazis have killed 56,154 civilians in this country and have seriously injured 75,881. How many deaths and how much misery they have inflicted on Europe it is unlikely we shall ever know.

ALPACAS AND OTHER QUEER BEASTS

NCE upon a time in Scotland there was a Farmers' Club that held a show of livestock every year. It was a great place for sheep and cattle. Farmers came from far and near to compete for the cups and prizes, to gossip with their friends and neighbours, and to celebrate all the news of the farms round about. In the same district there also lived a Public Spirited Merchant of Woollen Cloth, who said to himself: "These farmers do not know the best kind of wool for cloth making. I shall give a prize for the best fleece of wool for this purpose on any sheep in the show. By that I shall add to the prosperity of our Farmers and to the fame of our Show." The Farmers' Club accepted this good offer and the Committee invited a real Wool Man to be the judge. This real Wool Man had never looked at wool growing on a sheep and he was rather doubtful about his ability to judge a growing fleece. So he asked a friend of his who was a Manufacturer of Cloth to go with him to the show yard. Neither of them had ever been to a cattle show before and they felt rather lost amongst the crowd of rosetted judges. There was a vast crowd of sheep, all baaing and being pushed about and debated by the judges. The Wool Man and the Manufacturer were completely terrified and did not see how they could hope to disentangle this muddle of noisy, woolly beasts. They were given one of the pen-men who looked after the sheep to guide them and to protect them from danger. However, they put a bold face on the matter and set about their job. It did not appear so impossible when looked straight in the face, like so many other problems that beset us in this life.

Almost at once they saw they would have to divide the prize into one for fine wool and one for coarse wool. The sheep space was divided into three parts – lambs, ewes and rams – so they decided to pick the best of each lot first and then to compare their three selections. They started with the lambs of the fine group.

After a while they got them down to two lambs, both busy keeping the quality up like our Association, but there they stuck. They could not make one better than the other, try as they would. Despairing, they said to their guide that the two were as like as two peas. "Nayther wonder," said the pen-man, "they're twinnies." So the two lambs were marked as first equal.

Next they started on the ewes, selected one and said to the pen-man the beast was as near as nothing to the lambs. "Weel," said he, "that's nat'ral; she's their mither." And just in case you may think it very unlikely that the pen-man would know all this, you must understand that at a country show every countryman knows the family history of every beast on the field. He knows the beasts as individuals just the same as he knows his own friends and neighbours.

Much heartened and steadily growing in respect for their own knowledge, our Two proceeded to the rams' stockade, selected one and once more made the same remark to the pen-man. "Aye, aye," says he, "yon's the lambies' faither."

That's the first part of the story. The second part we shall shorten. Of the coarse-woolled sheep, our Two – feeling much less inferior to the other judges now – picked five separate beasts and there stuck. Not one was better than another. The pen-man's comment was "They're a' frae the same flock." "But," objected the Two, "we were told there was only one competitor allowed from one flock." "Aye," said he, "that's richt. There's but ae competitor, but for the Butchers' Prize, there mun be five beasts on the ground and ye've picked the five.'

This tale has a moral. Moreover, it is strictly true. If out of such a collection of one part of one race of animals such a selection was inevitable, how much more must the characteristics of totally different races count? Remember, being in Scotland, there were not even any Merino sheep concerned. Just think of the value and variety of texture to be got by the knowledgeable use of camels or goats, or Vicunas, or rabbits, or Alpacas, or any of the rarer wools.

And so we come to Alpacas. They are cousins of the camels, and this number of "Scottish Woollens" should be considered as a continuation of No. 16, which dealt with Vicuna. In that article, the Editor was wrong in writing of the introduction of Vicuna to this country, and to Europe, as very probably 1847. Messrs Ronald & Rodger of Liverpool have traced transactions there to 1844, and Walton, in his book on Peruvian Sheep published in 1811, quotes Vicuna as better known in France and Germany than in England. He also quotes "fine cassimere shawls" of Vicuna being worn at the trial of Lord Melville in 1809 (he was tried by the House of Lords for embezzling Admiralty funds but was acquitted). Walton records that the colour "was not satisfactory", which prevented the material from becoming popular. He does not say where these shawls were made nor why they were "unsatisfactory". There were four entries of Vicuna in the catalogue of the Great Exhibition of 1851. There were three from Yorkshire besides our own.

There are four South American camels – Llama, Alpaca, Guanaco and Vicuna. More strictly speaking, these are the four representatives of the Camelide. They are almost like four assorted sizes of the same animal. They are all the same shape – light, neatly made like deer but with long necks and heads that proclaim them for small relatives of the camels of Asia, as does their nasty habit of spitting at you if they don't like your looks. The hair of them all is distinguished by softness of touch.

Of the four, the Llama is the biggest and its wool the coarsest. It stands about four feet high at the shoulder and its upright neck raises its head another two feet. The Alpaca is only a little smaller and for general purposes its wool can hardly be distinguished from that of the Llama – in fact, the finest of the Llama is finer than the coarsest of the Alpaca. The beautifully soft touch of these wools is, unfortunately, off-set by its coarse and wiry appearance. It is like a straight and strong Cheviot in its rougher samples and comes down to the fibre of a fine Cheviot at its best. Like Cashmere and some types of sheep's wool, as, for example, Scotch Blackface, Alpaca and Llama have a finer, shorter and more curled under-down that may be removed in the process of combing for worsted spinning. This becomes "noil", and is much more easily dealt with in the Woollen or Scotch process, for the fleece is often as much as twelve inches long. Both by itself and as part of a blend, it gives a lovely soft yet goodwearing finish in coatings.

Both Alpacas and Llamas are used as beasts of burden. Before the coming of the Spaniards, there were neither horses nor donkeys on the Pacific Coast, and the Llama and the Alpaca did all the carrying. The Llama was the more prized. Both these animals are of mixed colour, most of them are piebald, and they vary from black – which is really a very dark brown like "black" sheep – to white through a great variety of colours – grey, russet and fawn, both solid colours and mixtures. Walton in his "Historical and Descriptive Account of the Peruvian Sheep", which we have already quoted, gives the proportion of black as nine-tenths. The Indians preferred black. One of the principal importers gives the figures of the present day as more or less constant at 10 per cent white, 12 per cent black, 10 per cent light brown, 22 per cent dark brown, 22 per cent grey, 12 per cent piebald, and 12 per cent fawn. These are the seven standard colours into which the wool is classed for marketing. It seems improbable that before Walton's time all that was not "white" could be reckoned as "black", because about half the total quantity of these colours is nearer white than black.

It is particularly interesting to see how so important a feature as the colouring of these great herds could be modified in so short a time as 130 years, even in a market so ill-organised as that of Chile and Peru. The modern manufacturers, like gentlemen, prefer blondes. The lighter the colour of the wool, the more general its application for dyeing. Of course, Walton's figures must be taken with caution. At that time, it is not possible that his figures could be based on any really accurate statistics, but the difference between then and now cannot be altogether wrong.

Now natural colours are not fast enough for most modern requirements, even though these South American Camels are faster than coloured sheep's wool. Beyond question, undyed natural colours have a peculiar and beautiful quality not to be achieved by any dyer. Moreover, even under modern processes, any dyeing tends to take the fine edge off the touch of wool. Traders also fight shy of these undyed colours because natural colours cannot be matched accurately to any standards. It is not possible to run counter to general trade prejudice that demands a standard of matching with little relationship to utility, so natural colours remain for the connoisseur and for the buyer of craft products.

One of the smaller sacrifices we have made to the Allied cause has been the complete abandonment of all this careful, specialised trade. Why, we cannot really say, for as is the habit of diplomacy the "reasons" shift and change from day to day like the fragments of coloured glass in a kaleidoscope. We always hope there is a good foundation for these ministerial decisions, but the reasons given to the miserable victims would rarely pass muster in a first-year class for apprentices. Perhaps it was really one of our contributions to Lease-Lend, but the fact remains that in the war years all these rarer wools of South America have gone to the United States. If this is the reason, we need not grudge this small return for such a vast and friendly service as Lease-Lend.

Authorities differ a good deal about the total quantity of Llama and Alpaca produced each year. Estimates vary from 4,500,000 pounds to 8,000,000 pounds. This variation may, in fact, be real because the beasts are usually only clipped on alternate years and various matters such as prices and weather might easily cause the total numbers clipped each year to vary quite a lot. After all, the total quantities of these rarer wools is really too small to guarantee a constant average. In the primitive markets of China in a season of bad prices, the innumerable little farmers just did not sell their Cashmere wool, but kept it for a better day, or possibly used it up themselves, and so probably it may be with Alpaca.

Whatever the total quantity may be, we in these islands were by far the principal users. Our imports varied round 5,000,000 pounds a year, rising at times to 7,000,000 pounds and falling as low as 2,000,000 pounds. Although in the figures of the world's wool consumption, these quantities do not sound very important, as the whole of a highly specialised trade, they do represent a very real sacrifice to the Allied cause, for Vicuna, Alpaca and Llama have all gone – lock, stock and barrel – to the United States during the later stages of the war.

The real pioneer of the trade in Europe was the young man who afterwards became Sir Titus Salt, one of the creators of Bradford and one of the earliest builders of a model village – Saltaire. The story is one of the romances of industry, celebrated or mocked at by Dickens in "Household Words". It was in 1836. A quantity of over 300 bales had accumulated in the stores of Messrs Hegan & Co. of Liverpool. Some say it had been used to prevent cargo from shifting – anyhow, it was unsaleable. Before this, experiments on a small scale had already been made in England so that, of course, our young man was not literally the first to use Alpaca. Titus, greatly daring, and against the unanimous advice of his friends and family, who were all in the wool trade at one stage or another, bought the lot for 8d. per pound. He overcame the considerable technical difficulties of dealing with a material so unlike the sheep's wool that Bradford knew. By 1844, his cloths were established and the price of Alpaca had advanced to over two shillings. It was for ladies these cloths were made. Fortune lay before him and fame. So out of this individualist's energy and love of adventure rose the great firm that bore his name, Sir Titus Salt, Bart., Sons & Co., now Salts (Saltaire) Ltd., and England became established as the almost sole user of Alpaca, a position it has held ever since.

No lasting success has ever been made of introducing any of these South American camels to other parts of the world. They live in such high country that this is not very surprising. Where the borders of Peru, Bolivia and Chile meet, the land ranges from 10,000 to 16,000 feet, and it is fairly obvious that an animal evolved in such an atmosphere is unlikely to enjoy itself in the low and luxuriant pastures beloved by cows. This high land is not so very dry. The rainfall is round about 25 inches, which is much the same as the driest parts of the east coast of Scotland. In 1926, a small collection of Llamas, Alpacas and Vicunas was sent to the Edinburgh Zoo where as visitors they lived quite comfortably, but there seems no greater prospect than there

ever was of establishing any of these beasts on a commercial scale outside their native land. An earlier experiment found its precarious way across the Napoleonic wars. A choice little caravan of twenty-five arrived in La Plata in 1805. Next year they were "interned" at Buenos Aires where some of the animals were killed by the guns of the British Fleet. What was left of them went on not to England but to Seville in Spain, and when in time Seville was captured by the French, they somehow arrived in the park of Malmaison, the home of the Empress Josephine. In 1800, she already had two Llamas, so we suppose they all lived happily ever after.

Sir Titus Salt tried them in Yorkshire, but his flock just faded out by 1877. This flock had been bought from Lord Derby; parts of it were sent to Australia and the Cape, but with no better luck.

It is surprising how little is known about so important a pair as the Llama and the Alpaca, or perhaps it is more correct to say how little information is ordinarily accessible. Quite a lot has been written, but it is nearly all buried in the transactions of various learned Societies or in private or semi-private publications.

The country of the Alpaca is round Lake Titicaca and the great tableland of the Puna. From the collecting centres of Cuzco, Sicuani, Checacupe, Santa Rosa, Juliaca and Ayravire, the fleeces go to Arequipa where they are sorted and packed for shipment through Mollendo Tacna,and other Peruvian Ports. From there, most is sent to Liverpool Wool Sales.

Now, the new Science of Salesmanship seems to he a quaint mixture of psychology and humbug, and one of its most important achievements is the evolution of "selling points". One of these most important points is the word "pure". So we are forced to make "pure" Alpaca or "pure" Mohair, or anything else even when a much better and more serviceable article may be made from a blend. For many purposes, the lustrous and silky nature of these fibres makes slipping at the seams of a garment a marked danger. This can be overcome quite satisfactorily by blending with sheep's wool. This would abolish the definitely bad reputation of both of these beautiful wools. But sad to say the reign of humbug is by no means over!

Colonel Stordy, who is one of the greatest authorities on Peruvian wools of all kinds, says the natives of Peru looked upon the Llama and Alpaca as a present from Heaven, and so may we. Some day, we may look forward to the development of these luxurious and beautiful wools till not only captains of industry but even "other ranks" may hope to shelter under their genial warmth.

Our illustrations are from photographs by Col. R. J. Stordy, C.B.E., D.S.O. The little landscape is typical Alpaca country at La Raya, 14,153 feet above sea level. The head in the initial letter is from Mr Stroock's "Llamas and Llamaland."

VICTORY

A Third Letter to an American Friend

MY DEAR SAM,

It is nice to know you are as interested as ever in our comings and goings. I had not intended to give you any more full-dress reports, but perhaps you are right that I should round off that particular phase of our letter writing by setting forth our experiences of Victory Year. Victory Day has just slid into history – a day of mild gaiety, something like the weather, not very fine, not very bad.

Just a year ago, the first part of the war finished. In November, we collected to commemorate the final victory. It was a subdued and quiet crowd that waited in the market place round the memorial of the last war. A line of ex-service men with felt hats and rows of medals stitched to their Sunday jackets; another line of young men in khaki, not yet decorated with medals; a third line of the blue-grey of the Air Force; in the middle the town council with their red robes and cocked hats linking us with the Middle Ages. Wreaths are laid. The kilted pipers play "The Flowers o' the Forest", that outpouring of grief for so much youth and heroism and hope gone forever. The air dies off into the silence. Then the lovely cadences of the Last Post tremble up and vanish in the thin November sunshine. The crowd melts slowly into the kirk. The service is short. On the reading desks before the magistrates lie the great Bibles presented by the Guilds of Craftsmen nearly 200 years ago. We are reminded that we are commemorating all who died in these great contentions, friend and foe alike: "So long as men do their duty even if it be greatly in a misapprehension... we may be sure they will find a safe haven somewhere in the providence of God." We are reminded of the blood and hunger, treachery, heroism, disaster and glory that has made up our long history. We are reminded of these lines of Laurence Binyon inscribed on so many war memorials.

> "They shall grow not old as we that are left grow old,
> Age shall not weary them, nor the years condemn.
> At the going down of the sun and in the morning
> We shall remember them."

And so we move out again into the pale November sunlight. There are no decorations on the grey stone houses. But Victory has come home.

Most of us were, at least in our secret hearts, optimists. We hoped, we expected, to find Utopia just round the corner. I suppose we did not really expect to find it if we strictly cross-examined ourselves, but there was a good time coming when we would get all the things we had fought for – Freedom and Safety and Brotherhood and Friendliness. We have not got any of them yet. We seem even to have lost some of these things we gained during the war. We are less brotherly. We have forgotten some of our friendliness. Perhaps the rather childish word "cross" applies to our state of mind. "Nature is often hidden, sometimes overcome, seldom extinguished."

Quoting is tempting. I remember the leopard and his spots. It is rather comforting, as is one of Bacon's tight-packed phrases: "but custom only doth alter and subdue nature". So I suppose we were wrong ever to expect six years of war could make any great difference to our natures. I suppose it was only the terrible intensity of those six years that for the moment allowed our fundamental and better qualities to overcome our old habitual selfishness and caution. Now we must wait a little till custom can alter and subdue our natures.

But I daresay you can do all that moralising for yourself, Sam. My present job is to report.

Controls are still with us in full force. We groan and grumble and fill up endless forms – definitely less willingly than during the war – but in our inmost hearts we agree with Mr Attlee that only the "lunatic fringe" really demands their immediate extinction. It just can't be done yet. We dare not risk a repetition of what happened after the Great War, when the whole intricate structure of commerce came crashing about our ears. Millionaires came over from your side and had to work their passages home. You cannot have forgotten how men who had never known a day's idleness stood on the street corners of your towns trying to sell apples. In our trade, it took us all the years between the wars to recover our lost stability, and when Hitler attacked us, we had by slow patience hardly built up what the Great War and the Great Slump had destroyed. If our governments have not learned enough to save us from a new disaster, then we may despair of democracy as a method of management, however much we may continue to believe in it as a political system.

Yet in spite, of all our groans, we must admit that in many details we are improving. Controls are little by little disappearing and we are no longer being plastered with new decrees to take their place. Our folk are little by little and rather reluctantly filtering back through the mesh of demobilisation. Production is rising a little but not very fast – not nearly fast enough to counteract the constant rise of wages. Hitherto, we have with some success held out against that most dread curse, inflation, but we are already mounting the spiral. Wages are chasing costs, although slowly so far, partly held in check by taxation, partly camouflaged by subsidies.

There is still no serious black-marketing. What there is is but a mild and sporting gamble on the part of those who buy, just as during your dry years your Bright Young Things took to hard drink, not because they liked it, but just because it was against the law. Of course, there are always some ingenious gangsters who make money by directing their skill to the service of these innocent law breakers.

It has always been possible to get our rations in full and without much trouble in queues. In the towns, certainly there is a great deal of queueing for the ornamental and unrationed articles of diet. Since the nominal return of peace, our folk are quite noticeably more impatient of restrictions, but unlike Italy and some other parts of Europe, the country is better than the towns. The black market has not been nearly strong enough to attract supplies from the country.

In travelling, everything is slowly coming back to normal. Railway trains are creeping back on to the lines. They are much more punctual, much less crowded. We are still desperately short of engines and carriages, but the dining-cars are being demobbed from their war duty of carrying wounded and most of them have had their Red Crosses painted out and, on the long distance trains at any rate, they are now running once more. Uniforms are definitely less conspicuous and most of the troops are out of our countryside. Some aerodromes are once more growing grain. Some are utterly cluttered up with countless planes. Overseas uniforms no longer dominate the streets of our little town, and on the roads military trucks no longer replace private automobiles. We are no longer limited to permits for special purposes. We once more have a "basic" ration of gas, although not very much. The roads are filling up little by little. A queer mixture of very ancient and battered war veterans and brand-new shiny beauties. The air has been full of the unwonted machine-gun chatter of pneumatic drills removing bomb shelters, pill boxes and road blocks.

In the stores there is more of many things. Early in the war our aluminium pots and pans were collected and turned into aeroplanes. Now the planes are being turned back into pots and pans to the relief of our womenfolk. Clothes are still scarce and apart from Utility horribly dear, but still people are more concerned in the value of valueless coupons than in the value of money. Production still trails far behind requirements. Scotland has stood up for quality. We have acted up to our motto "Keep the Quality up". Our special cloths and garments have been given all the skill and care bestowed upon our usual productions. In all utility goods, standards, qualities, and prices are fixed. They are not subject to our Purchase Tax. As this tax varies from one-third to the total value of the wholesale price of the article, there is a vast gulf between utility and ordinary prices.

The Scottish Woollen Trade stood out strongly, even violently, against the Government policy of cheapness, for the Government listened to the cheap ready-made clothiers. After a severe struggle, we got permission to make our pure wool Scottish cloths, 227 for men and boys, and for women we share No. 209 with the English Worsted Makers. Our numbers are 209 and 209B with the distinguishing description "Scottish Tweed" added to separate ours from the fabrics made in England. To begin with, a National Bunch was produced. Only a limited list of patterns was permitted and the minimum length that could be accepted was, and is, 200 yards to a pattern. In this way, production was simplified while variety was assured. Of course, these utility cloths were limited to the home trade. The cloth prices are fixed and the prices of the garments made from these cloths are also fixed. We are expected to devote 80 per cent of our machinery to the utility programme. Before the war, our mills exported somewhere about 75 per cent of our output. We are just now still working with about 35 per cent shortage of workers. Our want of coal still prohibits overtime. We are told the life of the Nation depends on our increasing our exports by 75 per cent over our old level. As Alice said, "Curiouser and curiouser". If you work all that out, you will begin to understand how little we can do for you.

There is another thing that does not encourage cheerfulness and that you folk don't quite know. For generations, we have sent our men and our money all over the world. You are one of the results. Another result was that we in the old country drew about 1,000,000,000 dollars a year from the savings we had spent on helping to develop other countries. Almost all these savings have been spent in war materials, and nearly all the cash now lies in your pockets. All our overseas investments were taken by our Government and were used to pay for war supplies, before your great Lease Lend scheme was on foot and before you joined us in the Great Fight. We had not enough savings to pay for our defences and ran badly into debt besides.

But there is another aspect of the war that is not nearly so bad as we had feared it must be. The figures of our losses have just been issued. Our losses in killed and wounded are only one-third of what they were in the Great War. In killed we lost 357,116. Of these 60,595 were peaceful citizens, and out of that heavy total 25,399 were women, 7,736 children. One figure tells of the hell through which so many passed during these six years. It was impossible to classify 537. This massacre of civilians is almost a new feature of war and it suggests the horrid carnage that must have been inflicted on the ruined cities of the continent. You at least were spared that. The Navy lost 50,758. The Merchant Navy 30,248. There are many other illuminating figures in the White Paper and another lot of figures may help you to recognise the intensity of our effort. There were finally 640,000 of our women in the Services and 4,683,000 men. Besides these on full time there were 3,002,000 on part time Civil Defence and 319,000 women. A heavy burden for 45,000,000 of a population.

You will be asking what about all our folk? We have been extraordinarily lucky. Our Margaret no longer careers around amongst our lost and forsaken Coastal Batteries and aerodromes with her mobile canteens. She is at home, cooking and looking after our house – domestic service still being an unknown trade. Jean is back from hospital service up and down Europe, decorated with various bits of ribbon. The Germans gave Tom a bash on the head in Normandy and the War Office mentioned him in dispatches. He also is back at work. Miss Robertson still counts our money. Miss Sinclair has been captured by Country Life and the Friendship of Hens and, like a lot of others who have tasted the open air of the Services, does not want to return to patterns and indoor life. John Wilson, after spending the war years guarding bridges, controlling Naval comings and goings in the islands, stamping passports, looking for spies and many other varied jobs, is now mostly engaged counting coupons and filling up forms in our own mills. All our Home Guard men are back trailing clouds of glory.

I must not fail to thank you and many of your friends for your unvarying kindness in sending parcels to us. They are opened at home surrounded by a smiling and interested crowd. It is a kind of recurring Christmas. You know amidst all that enjoyment we feel just a wee bit ashamed. We feel we are getting all those candies and other delicacies under false pretences for we are not anywhere even on the outskirts of want and hunger. But it is very good of you and we are really grateful for so much kind thought and warm friendship.

I hope you don't think we are down-hearted. In spite of our groans and complaints, we are not. Not a bit. There is one cure for all these rises in wages that we cannot spend, this clipping of our liberties that we cannot evade, these controls that we must still endure. When we have cured these things, Friendship and Brotherliness and Freedom will all come back to us. Most of this letter seems made up of quotations and I shall end up with another. It gives us the magic spell that will cure all our ills. It is from an out-of-fashion sage old man, Thomas Carlyle:

"Be no longer a Chaos but a World or even a Worldkin. Produce! Produce! Were it but the pitifulest infinitesimal fraction of a Product, produce it in God's name! 'Tis the utmost thou hast in thee; out with it then. Up, up! Whatsoever thy hand findeth to do, do it with thy whole might. Work while it is called To-day, for the Night cometh wherein no man shall work."

Yours very sincerely, MAC.

THE LADIES' TRADE

"For we that live to please, must please to live."

ONE of the facts that all historians sooner or later come up against is that few movements have definite beginnings. It is only when looked at from a long way off that they seem simple. The grand design of the New York skyline is quite undreamed of in the streets behind the water front. Nevertheless, it is from that grid of gloomy chasms that springs the vision of fairy palaces that charms and delights the voyager from the Atlantic. So this historian of that little niche in industry, the Scottish Ladies' Trade, has found it pretty well impossible to put a date on its start. Of course, in the ultimate view, it never "started" at all for the women of Scotland have necessarily always worn Scottish Woollens, but we are really dealing with a definite and special phase of the clothing of our women folk when we use the term "Ladies' Trade".

We mean, of course, that phase when our Scottish Woollens were designed and used for those people who consciously dressed decoratively and ornamentally, and not just to protect themselves from the weather and to keep themselves warm. Or perhaps it would be truer to say used our cloths for decorative occasions, for the making of clothes for decorative occasions has from very early times been a feature of human behaviour.

The first thing to remember is that our Scottish Woollen Trade is still very young as an industry. That is one of our advantages. The dew is hardly dry on our fields. We still preserve much of the freshness and keenness of our youth. We still enjoy ourselves, are still interested in experiment and adventure, are still seeking after something new. Our mills still remain small enough to be very personal in outlook.

In Scotland in the days of the youth of the Nation, while we were struggling for our existence against our strong and aggressive neighbour, England, our fine ladies made their ceremonial clothes – as in fact did our fine gentlemen – from cloths imported from Northern Italy, from France, from the Low Countries. A little later, when we had subdued our unruly neighbours, our gentlefolk wore English silks and satins as well, and even men wore "guid braid claith" from England. That took us up into the early years of last century. Then Queen Victoria led the great invasion of the Highlands and perhaps that was the beginning of our movement. Of course, that again goes back to the "Author of Waverley", the Great Unknown who turned out to be a lame Edinburgh lawyer, Walter Scott – undoubtedly the greatest national advertiser we ever had. But, again, how far back are we to go? When the

Pilgrim Fathers sailed on the "Mayflower", how many years of oppression, what local persecutions had been needed to goad them to forsake for ever their country, their friendships, and their old-established habits?

Anyhow, by the middle of the nineteenth century, quite a few of our wealthy invaders boldly made costumes for use on their Highland mountains. Of course, in those days even the young ladies did nothing so unladylike as shooting, but they followed the guns and they went out with the picnic baskets and the ponies, and helped to escort home the day's bag and the whiskered gentlemen with the guns and dogs.

Then about the eighties these same ladies began to appear in London wearing "tweeds", and the term "tailor-made" was added to the fashion journalist's vocabulary, but these cloths were for the most part really men's cloths. This was the stage in the movement which we have described in our papers dealing with the development of our Scottish District Checks ("Scottish Woollens", Nos. 6 and 7). In one direction, this movement led to the adoption of protective colouring for our army and then of the armies of all the world. In another direction, it led by slow degrees to the present active stage of our entry into the Ladies' Trade proper.

About 1880 the Hillfoots district led off in the production of cloths quite definitely intended for ladies' wear. This group of small towns had always been on the border line of the Ladies' Trade for it was in Alloa, Menstrie, Alva and Tillicoultry that the shawl trade had been developed. It was, of course, to Paisley in the west that fell the honour of naming the finest and most elaborate of these garments, which had become an essential part of the trousseau of every bride.

The weaving of tartan shawls in the Hillfoots started about 1800. It was so successful that by the thirties the population had doubled. The weaving was carried on by small manufacturers owning two or three looms. They went to market twice or thrice each year to sell the shawls they had made. Up till the sixties, this was the staple trade of the district. As it was a seasonal trade, many of the weavers tramped back to the Borders or to Yorkshire for the other half of the year.

By 1870, there were some forty of these little manufacturers in Alva alone. Then, gradually, the hand looms were displaced by power looms and the trade changed from a handicraft to an industry in the modern sense.

In this way, these little towns formed a channel for the flow of highly skilled craftsmen from Yorkshire, who were one of the strongest influences in adding refinement and intricacy to our somewhat stolid weaving craft. A fine export trade to America was the natural reward of so much skill and energy. And then in a night the blow fell. It was silent and invisible, but it was no less devastating to these little towns than the great fire was to San Francisco or the eruption of Mount Pelée to Saint Pierre. The blow was the McKinley Tariff of 1890. Perhaps if the politicians were imaginative enough to see the results of their work beforehand, they would more often hesitate to impose destruction and misery on a helpless population. It is a long time since the question was asked: "Am I my brother's keeper?"

All this time technique was improving – in the woollen trades as in all other

THE REAL AND ITS IDEAL

trades. The historian looking at ancient Persian work or the tapestries and brocades woven in France and Lombardy in the Middle Ages may demur at this, and it would really be more proper to say mechanics and power and knowledge of their application had spread vastly. In our own life-time, appreciation of beauty and the possession of beautiful things has gradually ceased to be the privilege of the few. We were among the first to pioneer this new knowledge, but as knowledge spread, we Scottish manufacturers found that our neighbours in the South were improving their cloths and their colours and were little by little trespassing on the field of quality and beauty which we had considered our own. Then after the Great War, the clothier trade took a great bound forward and at the same time – spurred on by the example of America – gradually improved the qualities they worked. Thus they came up into the price category that brought Scottish Woollens within their reach.

While all these tendencies were moving our Scottish Woollens nearer and nearer to the Ladies' Trade, a few of the great designers, seeking after new effects and ideas, discovered that in the foundations – the "set-up" – of the Scottish Trade lay the possibilities of a most useful development. They saw that the small size of the firms went far to guarantee exclusiveness. This was further influenced by the scattered positions of the mills. And there is still another element. In provincial France, the innkeeper has long recognised that his goodwill lies in his kitchen, so with great common-sense, he is his own cook and no one can spoil his trade and hold him to ransom. So in the Scottish Woollen Trade, the owners of the businesses recognise that designs and specialties are their goodwill and they are usually their own head designers and devisers of cloths. Moreover, we are an extremely conservative people and our "labour turn-over" is very very small. Still further, there is a very tough core in Scottish folk: we hate to be beaten and will go almost any length before we admit some idea submitted to us is impracticable. The combination of all these features has made the Scottish Woollen Trade of great value to those sections of the Ladies' Trade that appreciate quality and originality. It is a type of trade that calls for co-operation between the dress designer and the cloth designer – but for the dress designer who cares to take the trouble, the reward is certain.

The light weights needed in the finer part of the Ladies' Trade have always been a real difficulty, for yarn spun on the Scottish woollen system cannot be made so small as is possible on the English or worsted system. We have dealt with these limitations inherent in the two types of yarn in several of the earlier numbers of "Scottish Woollens" and so need not elaborate on them here. This has largely been overcome by the extended use of English worsteds along with our own woollen yarns.

Partly the clothiers have ceased to demand firm cloths and have learned how to use open, soft, fine, draping fabrics. A generation ago, any clothier would have thought any manufacturer offering such cloths just silly.

Now there is opening before the trade still another possible development in the use of soluble materials in conjunction with wool. This is not so much new as showing lively signs of new development. In the past, cotton has been used in some fabrics to act as a scaffolding for the weaver, the cotton being afterwards burned out by "carbonising" with acids of one sort or another. This ingenious use of a well-known process has been little more than a technical curiosity, but there are great possibilities in the soluble threads or fibre blend of the new alginate rayons made from seaweed. This development is not likely ever to become used on a great scale for it is obviously expensive to use a fairly dear material just to wash it out, but in the fine trade it promises a new scope for the novelty man.

We have not found it easy to discover what proportion of our trade is now devoted to the Ladies, but probably the estimate of one of our most experienced members is pretty near the mark when he suggests half, and that is a remarkable development for, say, twenty-five years. It is a proof of the liveliness and adaptability that we have always claimed for Scottish Woollens.

Today the range of materials for women made by our Scottish manufacturers is very wide and is growing. Six ounces to the broad yard is no longer a curiosity. We have seen samples almost as fine as cotton gauzes, making quite a serviceable appearance at less than two ounces. In a few years, it is not unlikely that such cloths may be in fairly wide use.

Another change that has influenced this development in Scottish Woollens is the great spread of all kinds of sport amongst women. With all our modern science we have still no control over the weather and so for outdoor use the old requirements of clothing still govern us. Knitting has come in for outerwear and our Scottish Woollens blend better with knitted garments than the more dressy types in which Roubaix and Bradford excel.

But fashion is a fickle jade. No one can tell what she may be up to next. There is no saying what further changes may be in store for Scottish Woollens, but that blend of conservatism and adaptability that has always been a national characteristic is not likely to fail us in the future. Fashion changes in the Ladies' Trade are rapid and somewhat bewildering to the cloth maker trying to plan his programme of production. His stocks are expensive and the variety of his raw material astonishingly great. The fashion trade and the manufacturer have not yet settled down into that

ADAM AND EVE (*circa* 1830)

practical understanding of each other's needs that is essential, but that understanding will come. Meantime, transport and fashion journalism have made changes quicker and quicker. Not so long ago it took fashions six months to travel from New York to the Pacific Coast. Now there is hardly any lag.

We finish up with a story. One of our members was lecturing to a fashion group in London not so long ago. To illustrate this terrific speed-up, he said: "Nowadays, fashions created in the Rue de la Paix on Monday reach London on Tuesday, New York on Wednesday, the Pacific Coast on Thursday..." At this point, a voice in the audience mockingly interrupted, "When do they reach Scotland?" To which our lecturer replied, "Scotland has been busy all the week preparing the fashions for next week."

OUR ILLUSTRATIONS

By the kindness of Messrs Geo. Bell & Sons, Ltd., the London Publishers, we have been privileged to borrow from their illustrated edition of Carlyle's "Sartor Resartus", published in 1898. These illustrations were not so much illustrations in the usual sense of the word as an artist's comment on Carlyle's text. Edmund J. Sullivan, R.S.W., R.E. (1870-1933) was without doubt one of the finest pen draughtsmen of our times. He was trained in press work and started with the "Daily Graphic". He gained a world-wide reputation in his own medium. He also worked in watercolour, lithography, and was an etcher of some repute.

"BY REQUEST"

A Fourth Letter to an
American Friend

MY DEAR SAM,

You are not easy to satisfy. What more can I say about us? Peace is now a couple of years old, and nothing much is happening. This letter can be little more than a chronicle of negatives, but it seems to me that is by no means to say it is a chronicle of despair – or even of down-heartedness. In the Great War – I mean the one we used to call "The Great War" before the Greater War happened – there was a popular gag. Someone would call out, "ARE WE DOWN-HEARTED?" and all the people responded with a vast "NO!" Regiments on the march, crowds at railway stations, sports crowds, at concerts or at public meetings all knew the required response, and gave it with enthusiasm. We are still not down-hearted, even if we are a bit quieter about it, even if some don't remember the response.

Of course, Sam, you are a sort of narrow-minded chap – or perhaps it is your courtesy that makes you pretend to be interested chiefly in our small concerns, in Scotland, in Scottish Woollens, in our small community. Also, of course, the antics of the Big Four are so well reported to the whole world that everyone knows all about them. Also, we are surprisingly little interested in the Big Four, and I expect you are only mildly interested, too. Do you remember R. L. Stevenson's lines about the sermon in the country kirk? – "The braw words rumm'le ower his heid, Nor steer the sleeper; And in their restin' graves, the deid Sleep aye the deeper." It would be a pity if so much heroism, so much courage, so much sacrifice should go for naught, but I still cannot believe that such a disaster could befall us. We are still optimists, and we still are not down-hearted.

Controls are slowly going off in our particular trade. All unprepared wool can be bought by anyone who can find it and has money enough and nerve enough to pay for it. We still receive, every four months, permissions to use what we can according to our machinery standards, but – joy of joys – the need for export permits has just been abolished, and we may send you anything we are able to make. Prepared wool, such as tops, the raw material of the worsted spinners, is still rationed strictly, as are the resultant yarns. The output of the great English Combing Trade is increasing slowly, although it is still not much over half of its normal level. In Scotland we are well over the 70 per cent now. Everywhere the week has been shortened to forty-five hours or thereby. It was a universal argument that the shorter week would enable people to work harder, and so would not reduce output. It is really a testimonial to our workers in most trades that they have not been able to make up for the shorter hours. After all, it is only in trades that are physically exhausting that the shorter hours could have that effect. We are still very short of coal, and our electric supplies are still suffering from the Government's policy of prohibiting expansion during the last years of the war. In almost every part of the country, factory hours have to be "staggered" in order to prevent the complete breakdown of supplies during the peak periods of the day, and by all accounts we shall have to stagger along as best we can all next winter.

In the solution of this power question, we in Scotland are deeply involved. Scotland is the most mountainous part of our island. Our west coast being right upon the Atlantic intercepts most of the rain you send over to us. England and Wales only get what Ireland leaves. Our usual winds are west, so our Highlands are the obvious source of water power. Not power on your vast scale, for Scotland is a small patch of land compared to your country. No Boulder Dams or T.V. for us, but a great collection of little schemes with which we mean to bring a new youth to our dying and deserted Highlands, just as you have brought new hope and new vigour to the exhausted lands of Tennessee. These schemes are going forward with almost war-time energy. We hope gradually to attract industries and people to the Highlands once the plants are working, but for a good many years most of the current will flow south to maintain the mills and factories of the industrial belt, and so release some of our diminished supply of coal for export. We cannot risk any return of that desperate fuel crisis of 1947, compounded of short supplies of coal and the most Arctic weather Great Britain has experienced for several generations. Many mills of all sorts in England were totally shut down for weeks, and have never been able to make up for this lost time. We in Scotland were more fortunate, although we had an unpleasantly close shave. It will be at least a couple of years before we will get anything more than local help from our water-power, but this at least is a great piece of planning that has not stuck at the blue-print stage like most of our other schemes.

And what of our financial state? It is not easy to impress on folk that we are in the midst, or anyway on the verge, of a crisis. Yet, in principle, our situation is simple enough. Your magnificent Marshall Plan is really needed if we are to get on our feet again. It is as though you had a wealthy friend who had all his life worked hard and honestly. He was always ready to help on any likely enterprise, and had courage enough and energy enough to enjoy adventures. Then, like Antonio, in the "Merchant of Venice", whose ships did not come home a month before the day, he found himself penniless – suddenly. Trying to help him out, you bought his books, you bought his pictures, you bought his stock-in-trade, all at good prices, for you were an honest friend. It was not enough. He could not keep his various enterprises going, enterprises that were beneficial to you both. You had to get him to accept a loan. We are in the position of your friend. We need not be ashamed to accept a loan, or for that matter we need not be ashamed to accept a gift. We should, and I am sure we will, work as hard as ever, or even harder, to repair our fortunes and show that we were truly worth your help.

Many of your newspapers spread the idea that we were slacking – that we were sitting around twirling our thumbs and living or hoping to live off your charity. You know us well enough, Sam, to treat that propaganda for what it is worth, but everyone does not. Let me quote you some facts and figures. I'll not take you through all the details of how the taxes work, but all over we are said to pay about 40 per cent of the National Income, about double your levy. It is true that the machinery for exacting all this levy is horribly expensive, but that is cold comfort for the rest of us. Our purchase-tax figures will also interest you. A cloth or other article for which we manufacturers get, say, 10s. pays from 9s. 8d. to 8s. 3d. according to the length the jobber sells – a scarf or such-like contributes 4s. 2d. An Auto Robe 8s., and our supply of coupons is even more important than the price! And just to show we have not lost our old energy in spite of taxes and coupons, we held a International Music Festival in Edinburgh last summer where many of the finest orchestras, opera companies, and soloists were assembled for a "couple of weeks". The weather was glorious and our fantastic old Capital was a dream city. Then, trade, not to be outdone, staged a really beautiful Exhibition of Industrial Design with the enticing title, "Enterprise Scotland". So, you see, we are not giving up – in fact we are holding another Festival this coming summer.

In the Great Slump that followed the First World War, many a man, in both our countries, lost every cent he had made. Many a man borrowed money and started again, and again made good. The hope of our recovery lies in the fact that the power of a business is in its built-up skill and knowledge, its organisation, its staff. Even if you take away all its bank balances – which, after all, are only figures made with pen and ink on the pages of books – even if you bomb its machinery and its buildings into dust, the real business remains. It does not start again as it started originally in a little shack. Provided the people have not lost their faith and their enterprise, it starts again with all the backing of a great reputation and a fine organisation. It will not be long before it regains its place. Provided the people have not lost their faith... Well, we have not lost our faith, and with the help you have so generously, so understandingly, given us, it will not be so very long before the Union Jack once more flies over full cargoes and busy ports.

We are suffering very definitely from inflation – again, simple in theory but not so simple in practice. Or, to put it otherwise, to diagnose a disease is not the same as to cure it. The basic economic fact is that all the money in the country must inevitably equal all the goods. Thus, as John Ruskin states in "Munera Pulveris": "If the wealth increases but not the money the worth of the money increases; if the money increases but not the wealth the worth of the money diminishes." Your heap of dollars must always be totally exchanged for your heap of loaves. If you have a hundred dollars and a hundred loaves, your loaves are worth one dollar each. If you coin a hundred dollars more but bake no more loaves your loaves are worth two dollars each. That is inflation, and the only cure is fewer dollars or more loaves. In actual fact, the coining of dollars is such a vastly complicated business that it is doubtful if even the greatest financiers can quite follow the intricate interaction of wages and credits and savings and capital equipment and taxation. But the rule is absolute and can by no means be evaded – all your money is equal to all your goods. This governing of the cash situation is a Government job, and we poor fish just can't do anything about it.

I feel sure we are as full of energy as ever. Up in Scotland, we have always been ready to fight for our rights. Most minorities are, I dare say, and we are a minority in Great Britain. The other day, I attended our Convention of Royal Burghs. The Convention is one of the oldest popularly-elected bodies in the world. It started to advise and restrain our Kings away back in the twelfth century, and without a break, through all the changes of eight hundred years, has gone on admonishing and advising the Sovereign, and sticking up – often with violence – for the rights of the common citizen. Every burgh is represented by a Commissioner and an Assessor, as we are called. At the annual meeting we muster well over four hundred. We meet as guests of our Capital, the City of Edinburgh. We meet high up in the Old Town, and the windows of the Council Chamber look over the streets and gardens of the New Town far below to the sea and the distant hills beyond – a sort of birds-eye view of Scotland.

The Convention is opened with prayer and the solemn administration of the oath of loyalty. In our two days of deliberations, every possible aspect of local government comes before us. In the last few years, it has become the habit of the Secretary of State for Scotland to open our proceedings by giving an outline of what the Government has in store for us, and reporting generally on the past year's events. We are a curious, a very British body. We have no legal powers, but we run a great network of committees and can focus a vast fund of knowledge on any subject. The Government regularly consults us on all Scottish legislation, and we are a power in the land.

I have dragged in the Convention because it is an absolute proof of our liveliness and vigour. Each year, attendances have increased and the indifference that clogged our progress and that seemed growing steadily in the inter-war years has vanished. Our people are once more keen and alive. Yes, Sam, you have backed the right horse.

But your demands for news have brought home to me once more the impossibility of giving a true general picture of our country – or I suppose of any country for that matter. The other day, I was travelling along our northern coast in the somewhat lugubrious train that skirts our little fishing villages and this impossibility was borne in upon me once again. We had carried out a terrific experiment in socialism. We had nationalised the railways, the carriages were as old and as shabby as ever. The little stations and the crowds – or their absence – were as they always have been. About all that had happened was that on the engines the old varied initials were being replaced with the simple letters B.R., and thus the British Railways heralded in the revolution.

But the people were just the same. Our fisher folk are curiously separate from the rest of the population, their lives are conditioned by the sea and its tides. The men come and go on the tides and all the communal life of the village moves slowly round the clock, for the moon and the sea observe an eleven-hour day. Even the schools, which for the children at any rate measure out the day, have not succeeded in counteracting the domination of the sea. So even in our little country in our small slice of it you have three totally different ways of life that hardly change in the lifetime of a generation. The seafaring folk, the general farming and business community, and just across the narrow belt of fertile country the totally different mountain life of the Highlands.

Few people know this land except people like you who so often have been among us. The visitors from abroad spend their time amongst major history, literary and political, in Edinburgh and in the south generally, or pursuing the theatrical beauties of Highland lochs and mountains. But along our northern coast, from Aberdeen to Inverness, the visitor is apt to take full advantage of easy roads and to rush along deaf to the gentle appeal of the country.

The outstanding character of this northern land is delicacy. It is not savage and rugged, but has a wide and spacious aspect full of small detail and long horizontal lines. Its colours are quiet, pale shades infinitely varied. You see a red-roofed farm-steading, then with surprise you note that it is hardly different from the brown ploughed land in which it is set. The gentle gold of a haystack makes quite a bright note in the pattern. In appearance, it is wonderfully like the desert when spring is coming, but it is an amiable desert. The trees are small and infrequent – in fact, they just give scale to the prospect. Quite a small rise in the road may open out mile after mile of country. Small streams, bordered with reeds and alders, give little inlays of brilliant blue. Over all this landscape is pitched the vast arch of the sky of that pale and tender blue only to be seen in these northern lands, and through it all move the clouds whose shadows accentuate with long dark lines the diversified delicacy of the view.

The fishing villages of our coasts are not beautiful in any conscious way, but they achieve a pictorial value very much like the countryside. The small, crowded houses have all the same dominant warm greys of the land, but some roofs are of a delicate rose tint, some purple slates, some the pale shade of the native flag stones. Here and there are surprising and beautiful notes of black where a leaking roof has been tarred. These houses are sprinkled over the ground without any formal plan, each facing the way its owner fancied; all more or less alike in design. A door, a window on each side, two dormers in the roof, a gable and a chimney-stack at each end. The design of a toy-house, diversified at the back with various little sheds for fishing gear, and decorated with drying nets and groups of brilliantly-painted net buoys. The fisher folk, thriftily brought up to paint their boats every year, practise the same art on their houses. These, although most solidly built of stone, are often painted with most brilliant colours, so that they have something of the gaiety of the wooden houses of Scandinavia. Their owners are a freedom-loving, hard-working, most individualistic race.

And just a word about your friends. Our Margaret still cooks, helped largely by Jean. Both still look after troops, but they are troops of Guides and Brownies now. Tom has sensibly got married and is rearing a family. Miss Robertson still counts our money – more of it than in the old days for we also are inflating gently. Miss Sinclair still dotes on hens, and has not returned to indoor life. John Wilson still counts endless coupons. Our Home Guarders, Ian Cameron, Dodd Mackenzie and Malcolm Inkson, now spend their days trying to hit a different kind of target for Sir Stafford Cripps, and so we go on somewhat unadventurously from day to day.

I used to boast to you about the absence of black-marketing. Peace and Government restrictions are steadily making inroads on our honesty, and we are sinking slowly from our – I was going to say "amazingly" – high war-time standard. It was not amazing truly, for this country was never so unanimously in earnest about anything as about the war and the need of winning it. Nothing was too hard to ask the people. Generally speaking, the Government, even under the fire-eating and beloved Churchill, rather fearfully lagged behind in its demands on us all. Clothes are very scarce – largely, many say, an artificial and coupon-made shortage. Food in some ways is more difficult; in some ways, such as fruits, easier, but in the towns there is still a good deal of queueing.

And that brings me to a quite personal note – parcels. I have thanked you before, but I must end with a poem I have been allowed to take out of the pages of our immortal *Punch*. I do not really know whether Sir Allan Herbert is best known as a most active Member of Parliament, as a playwright, or just as A.P.H. the versifier of *Punch*, but I do know that no one could more perfectly express our feelings than he does in these lines:

"Dear friend across the seas,
   I wonder if you know
How perfectly you please,
   How gratefully we glow.
"A parcel! A parcel!"
   The day has a smile.
"A knife! A knife I"
   No, wait for a while.
Let it lie on the table,
   A joy in the mind.
We look at the label;
   We cry "How kind!"
We feel – and we guess:
   We wonder and mutter,
"Cheese? Possibly – yes.
   It couldn't be butter."

Then the great Opening.
   Children again,
Slowly, slowly
   We make all plain:
Magical packets,
   One by one,
Lovingly wrapped,
   Gently undone:
Cake-powder - jellies –
   Unless I'm mistaken –
It can't be - it is
   A morsel of bacon!
We give some away –
   You're glad, I know –
And always we say
   "It's from So-and-So."

The neighbours leave
   Like men with inherited
   wealth:
And we, at eve,
   We nibble your noble
   health.
Think not our bellies
   Are the only affected parts:
You help us to live,
   But we eat, as you give,
With our hearts.
   Yours is a gift of the spirit:
Ours is a feast of goodwill—
   The friends of freedom
One family still."

Ever yours affectionately, MAC.

CARBONISING

NE of the incidents of a misspent youth was my attendance at the Geology Class at Edinburgh University. Part of the equipment for our fieldwork was a small phial of acid with a glass stopper and a little dropping rod. This was to test rocks for lime. If the stone fizzed when moistened with a little of the acid there was lime in it. If it did not fizz, there was at once a whole list of common rocks that we need not bother about. So properly clothed in vest and jacket – not in the slovenly pullover habit of the present generation – I carried the little phial snugly in my waistcoat pocket. On one of our expeditions, as I walked along white dust kept appearing down the front of my trousers and, though brushed off, the supply was continually renewed. Later, the phial fell at my feet, and on taking off my waistcoat I found all the lining and the pocket burnt out through the leakage of the acid. I thought it almost miraculously good luck that the outer parts of my suit were quite undamaged. It was not till years later that I recognised that this was no miracle, but that I had just been introduced to the ordinary process of carbonising. The cotton linings and pockets had been reduced to powder, but the wool had remained unharmed.

Carbonising is the process of removing by chemical treatment vegetable matter of all kinds from wool of all kinds. It is based on the fact that vegetable matter, that is to say, cellulose, can be destroyed or reduced to something very like ashes by the action of acids, whereas wool, that is to say, keratin, is more or less impervious to their action.

"Revolutionised" is a badly overworked word, but it is often used with less justification than in describing the effect of carbonising on the Woollen Trade. Burrs and seeds used to be a very serious deterrent to the wool buyer, an equally serious loss to the wool grower, and a heart-breaking problem to the manufacturer of woollen clothes of all kinds at all stages. Well do we remember as children the discomfort – almost agony – of new underclothing until we had located and removed the little burr hooks that even the most careful knitter could never remove entirely from the thread. In those days, carbonising was not applied to high-grade wools, and the manufacturer relied on a wide variety of machines devised for the removal of the burrs. None of them was perfect and, in spite of care, individual burrs broke up and there was nothing for it but to hand-pick the finished product, at best a slow job, at worst an almost impossible problem.

Although the burr is by no means the only bad seed to be found in wool, it is by far the most difficult to remove. It is the seed of *Medicago maculata* or arabica, a small low-growing plant allied to clover and alfalfa. It is moreover a valuable fodder plant in hot and poor country where fodder is scarce, as over a large part of Australia.

As it appears in the wool, the ripe seed is about the size of a large pea, but is a little flatter. On close examination, you will find this is really a tightly coiled pod about two inches long, and when you uncoil the neatly packaged pod, it drops the ripe and shiny seeds and leaves in your hands a couple of strands with sharp little hooks all down one side. These strands look rather like some kind of wiry centipede with little horny hooks for legs. It is these hooks that become utterly entangled

ERIGERON BONARIENSE

in the wool and make it almost impossible to pull even fragments of the pod clear of the wool. This very curious construction is one of Nature's ways of getting her products hitch-hiked round the world – most ingenious and completely successful. There is probably no other seed in which this spreading mechanism has been so perfectly developed. The parachutes of thistles and dandelions and the explosions of the broom pods are amateur efforts compared with this spreading mechanism of the burr. There are now few wool countries in the world, excepting Asia, where the burr has not gained a footing. It has even forced its way into the British flora, although it is still looked upon as an enemy alien. It is an attractive little plant, and we have illustrated, in the initial letter of this article, the appearance of the seed under the microscope.

Perhaps the next worst seed is the Australian Bidi-Bidi, but nothing is really a good second to the burr. The burr has named the machines that it defeated. It has named the process of picking out bits of vegetable matter – "burling" or "birling"; the vegetable bits themselves – Burls; and the trade of taking them out in which the women are called Birlers more often than Pickers.

Burrs and Bidi-Bidi are by no means the only seeds that infest wool. There are many grasses that are a considerable nuisance, and of these the worst from the grower's side is *Hordeum murinum*, the aulns or ears of which even pierce the skin of the sheep, sometimes so badly as to cause death to the sheep and in any case serious damage to the hides.

The Central Wool Committee at Sydney has published a monograph on seeds annoying to the sheep farmer. Its title is "Vegetable Matter in the New South Wales Wool Clip", and in it over seventy types and species are listed or illustrated. Unfortunately, it is one thing to recognise and name your enemies, but to deal with them is a very different matter. In the vast areas across which the flocks of the world graze, no control of these plants seems possible.

The variety is astonishingly large, and includes many of the clover group – which bear away the prize for efficiency – many grasses, some even dangerous to the sheep themselves like the *Hordeum* I have mentioned; ferns, which are chiefly mischievous as staining the wool a golden brown; thistles; and even forest trees such as some of the Australian oaks and blue gums.

All the time while the burrs were triumphing over the mechanics, another form of warfare was developing. It had long been known to the chemists that cellulose, which is the principle material of the frame-work of all plants, could be destroyed by most of the common acids. So away back in the years about the middle of last century, very extensive efforts and experiments were made to find a controlled process by which the vegetable matter could be removed without

destroying the wool in which it was mixed. In Great Britain alone, between 1855 and 1876, sixty-nine patents were taken out. Mr Jarmain of Kirkheaton, near Huddersfield, very kindly had this list extracted for me from the records of the Patents Office. French and German names appear on the list besides our own English names, and show how wide-spread was the effort to solve the problem. The early difficulties of making the trade efficient and profitable can be deduced from the number of patents that subsequently lapsed. It was in 1865, in the middle of this strenuous period, that H. Sikes and G. Jarmain took out their patent. The date was 12th April and the patent No. 1042. This was the first real commercial success, and may

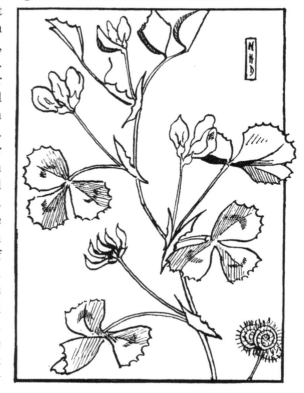

be claimed as the foundation of the large carbonising trade of this country. It is still fundamentally the process used by Jarmains of Kirkheaton, where the grandson of one of the original patentees is now the head of the business. Europe was also working on the problem, but our prominence was natural enough for we were, and are, by far the biggest manufacturers of woollen materials in the world.

Sikes and Jarmain in the preamble to their patent indicate the wide-spread efforts that were being made to improve the process of carbonising. They use the word "improvement" and only apply the word "invention" to various details of the manipulation of the wool. These articles are not the place for actual instructions of how to do the various processes we describe, but some of our readers who like figures might like to know the patent gives instructions for both hydrochloric and sulphuric acids. With hydrochloric of the density of 1–14 a bath of one part of acid to six or eight parts of water was to be heated to 200°F., and the wool soaked for fifteen minutes. Alternatively, sulphuric acid of 1–85 density was to be used 4 to 6 per cent, and in the cold bath the wool was to soak for about twelve hours.

Then in any mill a certain amount of cotton inevitably strays into the material, and especially into the wastes made in each process, because at so many points and in so many machines and processes are used string and ropes, and packing cloths and thread, canvas and dusters. In former days, in New Zealand and Australian wools, wax matches were a dreadful plague. The shearers and the scourers used "vestas" and, of course, many got swept up with the wool or were thrown into the scouring machines as a safe way to extinguish them. The scouring there, or later on in the mills, washed off the wax and left a whole lot of little bits of soft spun cotton, which broke up in the preparatory processes and contaminated a whole lot of wool. In the same sort of way, in Chinese wools, such as Cashmeres, there was and is constant bother over little rags and fragments of the blue cotton that is the usual workman's clothing in China. The trade has now overcome most of these troubles by closer supervision in the packing and sorting.

Now you may ask why all this fuss over a few specks of cotton or such-like. The answer is simple. Very few wool dyes dye cottons. The result is that cotton, invisible in the undyed wool, stays undyed, and so in the dyed and finished goods, every scrap or tick or tiny fragment of cotton stays white and becomes glaringly evident. To darken those snowflakes, often "burr dyes" are used, usually by adding them to the soap in washing off the cloth, but this is only a palliation, not a cure. These burr dyes are really simply cotton dyes that have no effect whatever on the wool.

Mechanically, then, the problem was to get the acid into contact with the sticks and seeds in the wool without spoiling the wool itself – for wool is not entirely acid proof. As in all the processes of woollen manufacture, the principle is very simple, but it takes a high degree of skill, care and experience to do the job well. On the continent, the gas method has been most fully developed. In this, the acid in the form of gas is passed through the wool and as the vegetable matter has greater affinity for the acid than the wool, it attacks and destroys the vegetable matter first. The wool is then put through crushing rollers to reduce the burned seeds to powder, dusted, and then the acid is neutralised in an alkaline bath.

We shall describe the wet process a little more in detail, although fundamentally it is the same as the gas process. Usually the wool is first washed to remove the natural oils, which tend to waterproof the vegetable matter and prevent the acid from getting at it. The wool is then passed through a bath of weak acid, generally ordinary sulphuric acid, but within limits any acid will do.

The wool may then be very lightly washed off in clean water just to remove any surplus acid – but this is not essential. The surplus water is then removed by squeezing or otherwise as the carboniser may fancy, and then the wool passes into the drying chamber. Here heat is applied slowly, and at the end, when the wool is nearly dry, the heat is raised to about 200°F. It seems that during the slow drying, the acid, which does not evaporate, gradually concentrates in the vegetable matter and helped by the heat reduces it to black cinder. This cinder is then crushed or beaten and the dust is removed by suction fans. The clean wool then passes to the neutralising tanks where all trace of any acid remaining in the wool is removed. This is one of the simple details that must be very thoroughly performed, for if the acid is left in patches, the wool will dye unequally. Acids have great fondness for one of the principal groups of dyestuffs, the acid dyes. Any excess of acid in one part of the wool will pretty surely precipitate the colour unevenly into the yarn and then into the cloth or knitted garment with dire results. Moreover, it is one of these faults that cannot be seen at all by examining the wool or the yarn or the cloth, and the fault only shows when it is too late to do anything about it.

It is quite beyond our idea to give the long list of "noxious weeds" as they are officially called, with which the carboniser has to deal. We have mentioned how many plants contribute their quota of trouble. To the carboniser, they are all just vegetable matter dealt with in the same way by being burnt up with acid. The acid process has almost completely superseded all the mechanical processes, so that they can really be ignored by every modern manufacturer. It is as well that this is so, for in the last fifty or sixty years the "noxious weeds" have spread and multiplied all over the world, and were it not for the perfecting of carbonising, our troubles would be endless and, what is worse, increasing. This is, of course, part of the price we have to pay for modern transport and world-wide trade. It is another way in which we are now "One World".

For some purposes, it is easier to deal with the wool after it is woven into cloth. Here the process is virtually the same. It is entirely a matter of convenience, like dying in the wool or the cloth. The woven cloth as it comes from the loom goes through the usual processes of inspecting, darning and so forth. It is then washed as usual to remove the working oils. It is then put into a bath of acid and water and thoroughly impregnated with the solution. The web of cloth is then passed through an ordinary drying machine, but rather hotter than for the usual drying. When absolutely dry, the piece is crushed or shaken, most usually in an ordinary cloth milling machine. As has been described in the treatment of the wool, the cloth is then thoroughly neutralised. It then steps back into the ordinary routine of the finishing processes. The whole work would be perfectly simple if it were not that acid destroys a lot of materials besides burrs! But for many purposes it is much easier and better than having to pick the cloth in the finished state with all the risks of damaging a fine surface or of making actual holes in the fabric.

But there is another side to this business of carbonising. Wool as a raw material is very valuable. It is the most perfect clothing material that man has discovered. It is vastly more adaptable than furs. It can be made into an infinite variety of materials and used for an infinite number of purposes over and above our clothing. In the form of bunting, we cheer ourselves with flags and banners. It covers the ink rollers of our printing machines. In the form of felts, its uses are almost as various as in our particular form of woven cloth. We sleep on it and under it. It covers our windows, our furniture, our floors, but to mention all the uses of wool would fill the whole of this "Scottish Woollens".

Just because of this universality of wool, we cannot afford to waste any. So a vast world-wide trade has slowly grown up for the collection of all these wool materials when they are worn out. All these old worn-out articles are carefully sought out by little men who wander through our streets collecting rags, bones bottles and such-like. Gradually these little trickles converge on the waste merchants, who classify the rags. They also collect the even more valuable waste products of the cloth and knitting mills, the tailors, the clothiers and the garment makers in general. All this huge mass of material is dealt with as carefully and as skilfully as the original wools are dealt with, and for the most part it is sold at such great centres as Dewsbury in Yorkshire. Before the war, material from every corner of Europe and much of Asia used to find its way to the skilful classifiers of Dewsbury. A great amount of complicated machinery and a vast amount of ingenuity, experience and skill go to the proper preparation of these "wastes" before they are ready to be re-absorbed into the Woollen Trade. Nor are these re-incarnations to be despised, although each re-incarnation shortens the fibre, for so varied are the original raw materials and so varied the rags that many "shoddies" are better than many "virgin" wools. Here is the great stumbling-block for the wool labeller, for many a cloth containing what must be described as "re-used" wool, that is, "shoddy". may be far better and more expensive than a cloth that can honestly be described as "pure new wool".

A queer, romantic trade this in-gathering of old clothes if we look beyond the unsavoury presence of this ceaseless salvage. The collectors in the hidden parts of eastern cities bartering little trinkets for an old coat; new blankets for old all over the civilised and uncivilised world; they visit alike the slum and the palace; all the capitals, all the villages of the world. Slowly, as by some mysterious attraction, the old garments and scraps of material make their way to such centres as Dewsbury. There, knowing eyes appraise their value and allocate their use. On the preparing

These burrs are enlarged varying amounts to illustrate their shapes and variety. They are selected from the New South Wales book mentioned in the text.

1. Bathurst Burr (*Xanthium spinosum*): Native of Chili: came to Australia from Valparaiso in the tails of horses about 1840. (X2.) 2. Corkscrew (*Erodium cygnorum*): a geranium seed; often even penetrates the skin. (X3.) 3. One of the blue gum or eucalyptus seeds: about half natural size. 4. Mexican Poppy (*Agemone mexicana*): introduced from Mexico; the seeds are about $\frac{1}{12}$ in. 5. Khaki Weed (*Alternanthera achryantha*): introduced from tropical S. America via S. Africa; natural size about $\frac{1}{3}$ in. 6. Sheep's Burr (*Acaena ovina*): native; seeds quite small, about ¼ in. 7. Wallaby Grass (*Danthonia*): of several species; a group of native grasses widely spread; seeds barely ½ in. 8. Noogoora Burr (*Xanthium chinense*): a native of N. America; introduced in the '90s; a high shrub bearing as many as 10,000; the burr is the seed case and is very troublesome as it is hard and woody; about 1 in. long. 9. Shive (*Aristida*): of many species; produced in such vast numbers as to be a real plague. 10. THE BURR!

The initial letter is from a micro-photograph of a burr case in wool: about three times natural size. On p.177 is the Burr (*Medicago denticulata* or *hispada*). On p.176 and at the end are plants with seeds of the dandelion type now trespassing in our country.

Miss Margaret H. Doig did our illustrations. She took her facts from the New South Wales Book and "The Adventive Flora of Tweedside" by Hayward and Druce. Miss Hayward belongs to one of our best-known Scottish Woollen families.

SENE CIO
LAU -TUS

tables, skilful hands rip out the seams, cut away pockets and linings, every scrap of the structure of the garment that might contain cotton or linen. These bits are handed over to the carboniser, who burns out the sewing cotton, and the linings, and then the whole goes through the complex and careful processes that will start the wool on a new life of usefulness. There is a subtle distinction between the product of these old garments and the more aristocratic cuttings from the makers-up that have never been in use. These are "shoddy", the old clothes are made into "Mungo," a word of mythical origin. The story goes that the carding foreman in the mills of one of the early experimenters sought out the master with the complaint that his blend wouldn't go. "It mun go, lad," was all the comfort he got. Well, the Yorkshire spinner does claim now that he can spin "anything with two ends!"

Up till the time of the First World War we in the Scottish Woollen Trade knew nothing of these mysteries. But wools were becoming scarce. The whole woollen manufacturing districts of Europe were devastated and we were left to clothe the armies of our European Allies and a good deal of yours too. Men and women worked night and day and made a vast and marvellous quantity of every variety of cloth needed. But supplies were low, so the Government organised the intricate salvage system of the United Armies. We were given up to 35 per cent, for our battle-dress khaki, a "shoddy" with a picturesque and strangely romantic name that told tales of battle-fields and camps and hospitals. "Old trousers seamed; seams carbonised and returned to bulk." But in the Scottish Woollen Trade, we are not to be beaten. In a short time, we overcame our fear of a material we had all been brought up to despise, and we did as well as the best.

A young man regretted to the great Dr Johnson that his attempts to become a philosopher had all ended in failure because cheerfulness would break through. The late Mr Mombert also found that even in the Wool Trade cheerfulness would break through, so we end on a somewhat frivolous note by quoting lesson VII of his "The Wool Trade: A Guide for Beginners". Those who wish to continue the course will find the complete set in "Rhymes of the Wool Market".

"A Burr is quite a common seed
That looks just like a centipede,
When, in the combing, it uncoils
And spreads itself among your noils.
When you observe them first, no doubt
You do your best to pick them out;
But in the end you'll find it wiser
To send them to the carboniser.
For, if they're woven in a shirt,
Men scratch themselves until they hurt;
And if girls get them in their undies
They musn't go to Church on Sundays,
For, when they're kneeling down in prayer
They shouldn't scratch themselves and swear."

THE PAISLEY SHAWL

HE PAISLEY SHAWLS have been long regarded as masterpieces of design and weaving, worthy to rank with the best tapestries and greater than the finest brocades. It is to be regretted, therefore, that there is so much misapprehension and even ignorance among their admirers, and that the art and craft of their manufacture is almost forgotten. The generation that made them is dead and gone, those who knew them a little are almost gone, and only a modicum of knowledge of the technique of both design and weaving has survived. Even in 1903, Matthew Blair in "The Paisley Shawl" deplored the loss of all information regarding the bead-lam lappet, the deil or douge, and other strangely named objects. We cannot hope to compensate for this loss. We can only offer a brief sketch of the evolution and history of the Paisley shawl for the benefit of those whose knowledge is even more imperfect than ours.

The production of "Paisley" shawls in Paisley lasted only seventy years, but the industry had its origin very much further back than the weaving of the first shawl about 1800. The shawls of Kashmir, which were copied by the Paisley weavers, were known to the Roman Caesars. Their designs are prehistoric.

Kashmir made shawls which were famous all over Asia from very early times, but although many went to the Russian nobles, few reached Western Europe till the latter part of the eighteenth century. Napoleon's officers are said to have been the means of introducing them from Egypt to France. A famous beauty, Mme Emile Gaudin, made them fashionable, and a regular trade in them sprang up with the Levant. The British Fleet was active in the Mediterranean about that time, which may explain the arrival of Kashmir shawls in this country.

A Kashmir shawl might take three people more than a year to make, so fine and so laborious were the methods of embroidery and hand weaving used. They were consequently very valuable, and such shawls became the property of princes and nobles, and were commonly given as royal gifts. The specimens that reached Europe fell into similar hands. A French trade journal, "Le Cachemirien", of designs copied from Indian examples cites the owners of the shawls – the King of the Belgians, the Duc de Berri, and others. It was the nobility of Britain who acquired them, too. In spite of their high price, the demand for Kashmir shawls became so great that it could hardly be satisfied. Then, inevitably, a cheaper variety was desired. Efforts to copy the Indian examples were made. These soon succeeded, and eventually the Indian trade was almost entirely superseded. This happened first in France, where Paris and Lyons became the centres of manufacture, next in Norwich and Edinburgh, and only lastly in Paisley, where about 1800 a Mr Paterson made the first attempt to copy an Indian shawl.

Paisley was important as a weaving town from Stewart times, and had profited from the teaching of Flemish weavers to become one of the leading producers of cloth in Scotland. In the eighteenth century, its silks and gauzes eclipsed Spitalfields for a time; it also had a name for fine lawn and for damask. Its weavers had therefore a command of the technique necessary before the copying of Indian designs could be attempted. But even the technique of damask weaving, which used a harness "draw-loom" to produce patterns, was inadequate for the task. The complexity of the Indian designs, the number of colours and the nature of the materials employed raised problems that were only gradually overcome. Paisley's eventual supremacy over the other imitators of the Kashmir shawls can be ascribed to the practical and speedy way these problems were solved. Although the greatest advances in the art of weaving – the invention of the Jacquard loom, and the spinning of "French" thread (wool yarn spun round a silk core) – were due to the French, Paisley's refinements led to a cheaper shawl that retained good qualities of colour and wear. It should be remembered that Paisley did not claim the superfine qualities of Edinburgh or Paris shawls, although Paisley shawls became popular in France, and were even exported to India.

The first Paisley shawls were different in many respects from the large cashmere plaid, covered or bordered with rich pattern, which is regarded as typical. The draw-loom of that period could not execute such elaborate designs, no suitable woollen yarn was found, and fashion demanded smaller shawls of pale colours. The earliest shawls were of two distinct types – square shawls with borders applied to centres either plain or sprigged with a small object known as a "spade", and long shawls with a deep border of Indian design at each end of a plain centre, with a narrower border applied all round. Both styles were copied from Indian models and were made of silk. Commonly, the centres were white, but occasionally buff or red. It was not till nearly 1820 that black became fashionable. The shawls often had ornamental corners or central medallions known as "pot-lids". The plaids more rarely had patterned centres. Shawls such as these may be seen in some of Raeburn's portraits painted about 1815, and these styles were fashionable until about 1830, with minor variations. In the latter part of the period, wool was introduced as a weft, and darker colours were worn. The white long shawl retained its popularity throughout the whole seventy years of the shawl trade, the beautiful white-centred plaids of the eighteen-fifties and sixties being their logical development.

The ten-box lay, invented in 1812, increased the range of colours used, but no more than six were employed as a rule; eight or nine are rarely found, except on later and more expensive examples. The first all-woollen shawl was made under French supervision about 1825, and was produced commercially by Mr Robert

Kerr as a "Thibet" shawl in 1828. Before that time, no woollen yarn capable of standing the strains imposed in the lifting of the warp threads by the harness had been found. The French had their speciality, the "French yarn" aforementioned, but permitted little of it to be exported. Paisley later copied this yarn, but silk warps were generally used throughout the whole period, except for the best grades of shawls. Cashmere, and mixtures of silk, wool and cotton, came to be used for wefts. Various other inventions enabled more elaborate designs to be woven, including the striped "zebra" patterns that were so long favoured. It was no longer necessary to weave borders separately, but the draw-loom had limitations imposed by the nature of the harness and its drawboy operator. It was not until the Jacquard loom was adopted about 1840 that any great advance was possible. It was not till then that Paisley became a rival to Paris, which had used the Jacquard machines much earlier. With the Jacquard machine and the ten-box lay, practically any design could be woven. The more complex patterns of the Kashmir shawls could now be copied, and they were. To be more exact, the French copies of the Kashmir shawls were in their turn copied, as is proved by the existence of many French design sketches in Paisley Museum.

From 1840, the shawls became more and more elaborate in design. The long shawl grew in size to cover the fashionable crinoline, and became known as a plaid. Queen Victoria purchased several shawls in 1842. She preferred long shawls to square ones, and so set a fashion that endured until plaids in their turn went out of favour. It is the productions of this later period (1840–1870) that are typically Paisley shawls. Their appearance is too well known to need description. It will suffice to say that designs became more and more elaborate, tending at last to a stiffness never found in the Indian originals. At the same time, the white-centred long shawl with its delicately coloured borders of simple pines, which came to be known as the "pale-end" plaid, maintained its popularity and in its cashmere version formed part of the trousseau of every well-to-do bride. It was worn to church after the honeymoon and at christenings, and so was sometimes called a "kirking shawl".

It was in the late eighteen-forties that a very different imitation of the Indian shawls was first made in Paisley. These were the printed shawls, which have been held to have contributed largely to the destruction of the shawl industry. They were, of course, much cheaper than the woven shawls. They were not, moreover, primarily imitations of them, as they were so different in weight. Many of them were made of the fine silk or wool gauze for which Paisley was famous, others were of Cashmere. They were more suitable for summer or evening wear, and could not take the place of a winter coat as the harness plaids did. Some of these gauze shawls were exquisite productions, but they were perishable. They cost a tenth of the price of a harness plaid, but they only wore a tenth as long. They are seldom found nowadays in good condition.

Yet another type which was manufactured in Paisley was the "doublcloth" shawl. This was a reversible shawl made by a process invented about 1860. The inventor thought to make a fortune by his patent, and refused all offers for it. But before he could get the terms he wanted, someone else discovered the principle and made it freely accessible to the manufacturers. This kind of shawl, however, was not very successful. The double cloth enclosed all the threads not appearing in the pattern (which would have been cut away from the back of an ordinary web) and so made it weighty. A plaid of double cloth would have been insupportably heavy, and shawls were out of fashion, so double-cloth shawls never caught on. The process limited the design to a comparatively small repeating one, and the colours employed had to be few, to keep down the weight. The finished article, therefore, was not as beautiful or as artistic as the ordinary harness shawl. That probably contributed to its unpopularity.

A question that is often asked is "How long did it take to weave a shawl?" The answer is a week, or a fortnight for a plaid. The questioner is usually surprised, however, to be told that before weaving could be begun, five months' of work had been done in the processes of design and the setting-up of the web in the loom. The design processes, as any weaver would realise, were necessarily elaborate. The designer first drew a sketch of his idea in miniature, then parts in detail and colour. These drawings were traced on to oiled paper and coloured, and the sketches passed to draughtsmen who transferred the design to squared paper, and coloured it. The enlargement that this involved meant that the sheets of design paper for a plaid would cover the floor of a large room. The process might be compared with the similar one of carpet designing, but the work was very much finer, and demanded more time and skill. The design paper used for shawls to be woven on Jacquard looms had a peculiar ruling to represent the diagonal effect of the twill weave. This was another French idea, which is now obsolete.

There must have been almost as many artists as poets in Paisley at one time – and history relates that once, when the toast of Paisley poets was proposed, every single guest rose to reply. There were several firms of public designers, and the more important manufacturers kept staffs of artists – in one case, as many as twenty-six. Some idea of the amount of work turned out can be gauged from the design books of John Morgan and Son (now in Paisley Museum), which show 500 different designs for 1844–1845 and mention five different artists. While the importance of the industry generally is attested by the setting-up in Paisley of a Government school of design. The work of English and French artists was also used, as is shown by the number of sketches in Paisley Museum bearing the stamps of designers in London and Paris.

The setting-up of the loom was also a complicated business. The tying up of the harness of a draw-loom originally occupied three people: one to "read the flower" – that is the design from the squared paper; one to take it down; and a third to "lash the flower", tying the harness cords into the appropriate arrangement. When the Jacquard loom was used, the cards were cut by an operator who read the design line by line from the squared paper. The harness of the shawl looms, in order to execute such fine and elaborate designs, was fine and elaborate, too. Unfortunately, no example of such a harness has survived. Looms that once made shawls were later adapted to other uses, or destroyed.

The processes of making printed shawls did not differ from those employed in making other printed fabrics. At first, wooden blocks were used, then blocks with the pattern lines inlaid with metal, and latterly metal rollers. The Paisley printing was notably excellent in registration, although it employed many colours and therefore numerous blocks, which were often of large size. It is notable, too, that all the work of designing, weaving, dyeing, block-cutting, printing and finishing was performed in Paisley itself.

The two varieties of shawls we have discussed, although known as "Paisley", were not the only kinds made in Paisley. Queen Victoria's choice in 1842 included velvet, satin and tartan shawls, as well as harness ones. Tartan had been woven before the Indian imitations were thought of, and tartan shawls and plaids were continuously made in Paisley up to 1941. From the year 1823, Paisley imitated the Chinese crepe embroidered shawls very successfully for at least twenty-five years. Chenille shawls were invented about the same time by one Andrew Buchanan. These shawls were reversible; an arrangement to bring all the velvet to one side suggested the carpet patent that was the beginning of the great Templeton manufactures. Another variety was the Angora shawl, which was a kind of blanket with a coloured pattern. It was not a great success, as gentlemen escorts objected to the number of fibres it shed, but it remained popular for export, and its development, the "fur" shawl was the last variety to be woven in Paisley. It was made by the last two shawl manufacturers in the town, both of whom scrapped their looms in 1941. One of their looms was presented to the Museum, and the last Paisley shawl, albeit only a "fur" one, was woven there. The last "harness" shawl had been set up in 1886.

The industry is not likely to be revived. Costs nowadays would be prohibitive and knowledge of the craft is already lost. It goes to join other arts and crafts, such as Ayrshire needlework, in oblivion. But the shawls are still there, and will be for many a day, a delight to their owners and an inspiration to designers and craftsmen all.

Mrs JAMES CAMPBELL

219

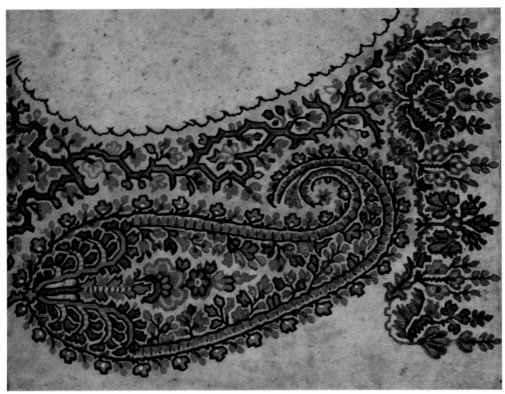

PLATE II

NOTES

THIS NUMBER has been written for us by Miss Dorothy Whyte, B.A., who was acting curator of Paisley Museum during the war. The shawls used as illustrations are from her collection. We would like specially to thank Messrs Hislop & Day, who have taken infinite trouble over the blocks for the illustrations, and our printers for their patience with a troublesome job.

PLATE I shows in use the type known as "the common red silk shawl". This is Sir Henry Raeburn's "Mrs James Campbell" (30 x 25) painted early in the nineteenth century. In "Sir Henry Raeburn", Sir Walter Armstrong, Keeper of the National Gallery of Ireland, considers this perhaps the greatest of Raeburn's portraits. Sir Walter calls it "the astounding Mrs James Campbell". Mrs Campbell died in 1815, aged seventy-six. The portrait belongs to Lieut.-Colonel Thomas, D.S.O., of Glasgow, and is on loan to the National Gallery of Scotland in Edinburgh. It is to his courtesy and to the help of the Director, Mr Stanley Cursiter, R.S.A., that we are able to include this portrait.

PLATE II. Part of a designer's sketch on oiled paper. This and all the other colour plates of shawls are reproduced full size without any reduction.

PLATE III. Part of a design, dated 1824, hand painted on squared "point paper". Each square represents one thread on the surface of the shawl.

PLATE IV. Left Upper: White Cashmere shawl with silk warp, pine border and corner sprig – about 1830. Left Middle: White Cashmere shawl patterned with twining design, and with a knotted fringe

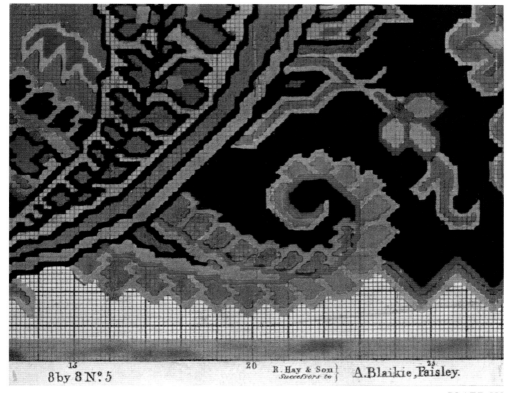

8 by 8 Nº 5   20   R. Hay & Son} Successors to { A. Blaikie, Paisley.

PLATE III

added; about 1842. Such a design could be woven in the piece and cut to any size. Left Loner: White Cashmere shawl with silk warp spade" middle (not shown in the illustration) and medallion corners. The border and fringe are added; about 1825. A late example of one of the earliest types. Right: White Cashmere plaid with wool warp; about 1850. A typical "pale-end" design.

PLATE V. Detail from the left upper shawl on Plate IV showing a typical "pine".

PLATE VI. Upper: Shawl with medallion centre and corners. This is an example of printed warps. Each quarter is a different colour: red, yellow, green and black. Made before 1840. Middle: Shawl with deep border and black centre – about 1845. Bolder in design and coarser in weave than the others shown, this shawl uses silk and cotton threads in the weft as well as wool to achieve brilliance of tone. Lower: All-Cashmere shawl that is really fine wool, not Cashmere in the real sense. It has stained or printed warp round a white centre; about 1850. Its fine weave and elaborate design are typical of later specimens, although the design of this particular shawl is unusual. Note the border next to the fringe, known as "tail-pieces". These are not found in shawls of pre-Jacquard manufacture, although almost all Indian shawls show them.

PLATE VII. Detail from the upper shawl on Plate VI showing the employment of a stained warp. The centres of many shawls of one or more colours often involved the printing of warps, as did the small coloured patches of the "tail-pieces" at each end.

PLATE VIII. Detail from the lower shawl on Plate VI.

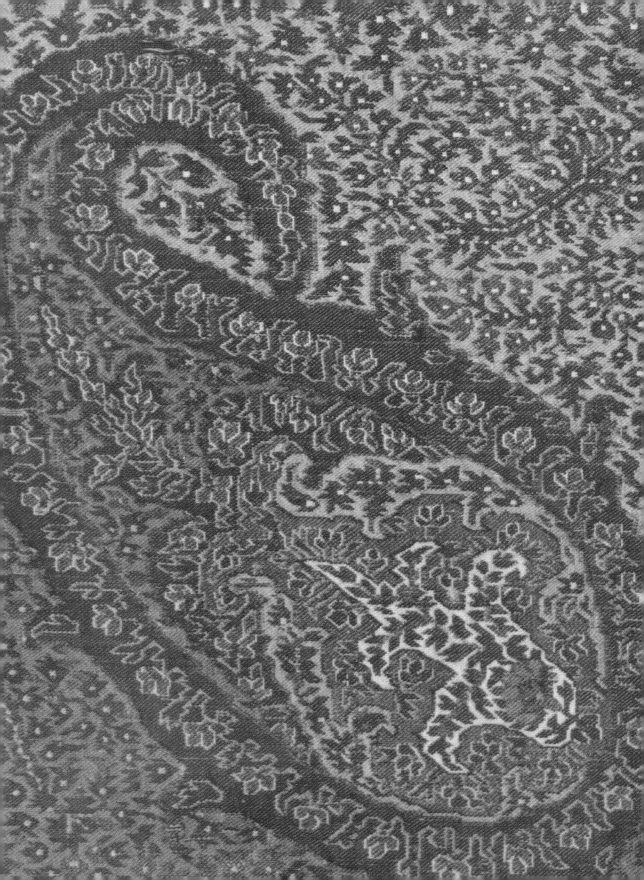

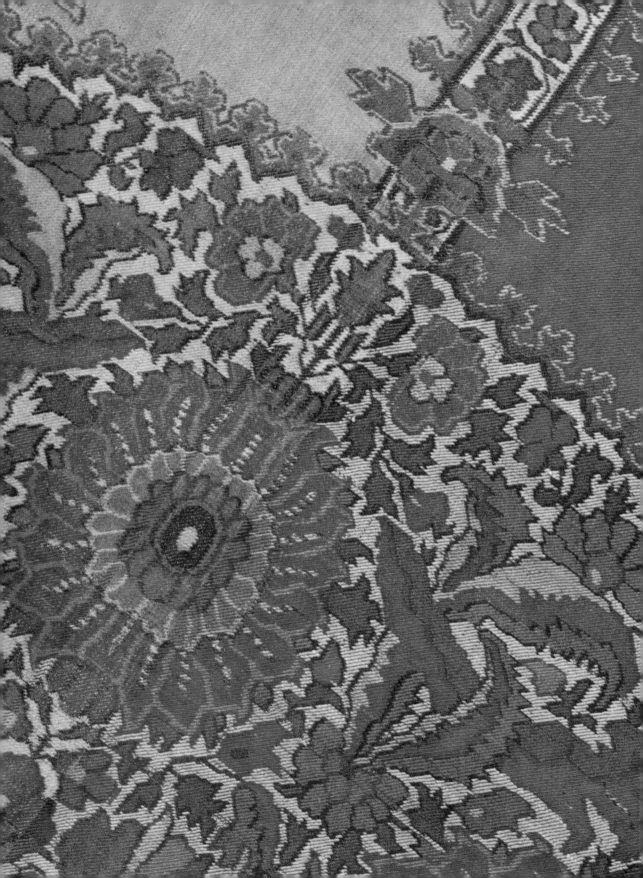

NETHERDALE – AN EXPERIMENT

HERE was a surprising campaign for a while to prove that our Scottish Woollens had deteriorated since the war, English Woollens likewise – in fact, that we British weavers no longer cared for the quality of our cloth and the reputation of our craft. Perhaps it was in part true because during a war standards necessarily deteriorate in such trades as ours, for a man can be quite adequately clothed without the refinements of colour and quality on which we have built up our reputation. The war had gone on so long that it would have been quite natural if we had forgotten our standards. All the same, we were not working under the violent pressure of the Great War when we were left alone to clothe the Allied Armies for so long. Then the only limit was human endurance. All limitations went overboard – legal and otherwise – only quantity counted. There was no doubt then that it took our trade several years to recover old standards. But in the Second World War, the urgency was not nearly so great and there was very little lowering of standards, in Scotland at any rate, even during the war.

All the same, it was good for us to be pulled up and made to look at our laurels to see if they had faded a bit, and one of the directions in which we looked was our education. For years past, the apprentice system of learning a trade has been decaying. The Great Slump that followed the Great War had left parents with a doubt in their minds about the security of their children in our trade. This increased the doubt planted in their minds by the long earlier depressions. Also the spread of the demands of the developing semi-professions and local government and clerical work generally had enticed away a steady and increasing stream of our young people, and intellectually at least the best of them at that. It seemed our only hope was to develop our teaching outside the mills. In 1909, we started our Scottish Woollen Technical College at Galashiels, well equipped with experimental machines. We had fifty little looms, a set of machines for yarn making, good laboratories, and all the trimmings demanded by modern teachers, but – and it is a very big "but" indeed – all that did not come up to the practical work that was required in an actual mill. All who have been concerned with technical education have been up against that problem. In a school, it is not possible to handle the quantity of material to make boys or girls even moderately expert in practical work. In a cookery school, you cannot cook enough food to make your students into real cooks whose work must stand up to the test of supplying a daily dinner to a hungry family. So we concluded our only hope was to start a mill of our own.

One of the victims of the Great War and the Great Slump that followed was Netherdale Mill in Galashiels. The plant had been dispersed and the buildings were standing empty. Galashiels had clung to the hope that some day something could be done with this large and substantial ghost, and had refused to pull down the walls or even to take off the roof, the only way to avoid taxation under the law of Scotland. So there was our chance. A group of citizens bought the property and set up a whole collection of businesses in the old mills – a large, modern bakery, some light engineering works, a hand-loom factory and others, and then the College governors took one of the two big blocks in our illustration and therein set up our Mill. It is called a Production Unit, which sounds much more learned.

Netherdale Mill consisted of extensive sheds and the two big blocks shown in our sketch. We bought the nearer of the two high blocks and the hostel and canteen on the opposite side of the open space beside the trees. Here we are in the act of setting up a complete plant. We work on commission for members. We take in wool, dye, spin and weave. Soon, when we have finally overcome the infinite delays in getting machinery, we will be able to finish the cloths we make.

In the top flat, with excellent roof lighting, we have set up the laboratories for our Scottish Branch of the Wool Industries Research Association, whose laboratories are in Leeds. So now we are well on the way to having the most complete and modern technical college in the Woollen Trade – in fact, one of the most complete and practical trade schools in the world. We have that ideal organisation where the student can learn the most intricate theory of his trade and can himself see the actual practical application to the machines of what he has learned in the classroom and the laboratory. We are not yet in full blast, but last year we wove 432 webs of cloth, and our learners practised their skill in darning over 50,000 yards of broadcloth of all kinds.

It is very much worth while for anyone interested either in our trade or in education to visit our experiment. Such a visit is entirely stimulating. We seem to have managed to combine the busy, purposeful bustle and energy of a flourishing industrial undertaking with something of the thoughtful and deliberate air of a university. This is really something of a feat, and so far at least this atmosphere – to use a somewhat threadbare word – seems to be appreciated quite widely. We have students from many countries and our corridors and workrooms are almost as polyglot as Berlin or New York. Our College and our Mill, in fact, form a small but real contribution to that international understanding so ardently sought for and so difficult to attain.

Besides teaching learners, we hope to have the chance to teach ourselves, and one of the ideas we have is to install experimentally all manner of new inventions and try them out on a working scale so that we may see the newest and best that textile machine makers invent. For a beginning, for example, we have eight power looms, of four different types, including automatics, so that any of us can experiment in the suitability of any new machine for our various requirements. We have space arranged for two more looms, when we can get them.

NETHERDALE MILL, GALASHIELS

Another scheme that looks like being very useful is the development of what our war-time army called "refresher courses". The College arranges such courses for any tradesman who wishes to be brought up to date or to gain experience of some new machine. We have two hostels, one for men and one for women, where those coming from a distance can be put up at moderate cost and in complete comfort. This has overcome what has long been one of our most definite troubles in dealing with a trade so scattered as our Scottish Woollen Trade, for Scotland being truly a wool country and our trade truly native, our mills are scattered over every part of the land. Not a very big country and not a very big trade, but a country not so very easy to get about in, and a trade so dependent on novelty and change that our College is an absolute necessity for our very existence.

But our Mill is not at all highbrow or snobbish. We have not equipped it with all the latest automatic plant, although we try out all the newest devices. We aim at putting our learners through a routine they will find all over the country and to teach them these fundamentals, which are much better learned under simple circumstances. We are teaching principles, not production-line technique. Our whole scheme is to serve every workman in our varied trade from the Highland hand-loom weaver to the modern mill manager. You can take a two- or three-year course covering every stage and process of manufacture. You can take part-time classes in any special branch you fancy. You can arrange to refresh your youthful energies if you think you have lost them, and you can have as big or as small a dose as you may feel you need, and if you are one of the bosses, and so of course have no more to learn, you may attend Specialist Lectures by other bosses, and argue with them during the discussions that follow.

These little monographs that we christened "Scottish Woollens" have now been going for twenty years, and thus have had not only an unexpectedly long life but they have had a totally unexpected success.

This may be the swan song of our venture in literature. The venture was definitely limited in aim. Our aim was to give simple accounts of the various processes involved in the creation of the great range of different cloths our mills turn out so that those who distributed our products all over the world might know something of the intricate and absorbing history of our materials. These monographs – perhaps too pretentious a word – have all been written by members of our trade whose life-work has been devoted to the subjects about which they write. What they have written is therefore reliable and practicable and authoritative. We hoped our readers might find a new and undreamed-of interest in the world-wide commerce on which we depend for the collection of our wools, our dyes, our chemicals, and all the stuff we weave together to make a suit or a dress or a scarf of Scottish Woollens. There may be one or two more numbers for we have not kept all our promises, but there is no important section of our trade we have not dealt with. During the war, we used a few numbers to show our friends how we were living and working under that infliction, and this essay is again a departure from our intention for it is really a piece of special pleading for our conviction that Scottish Woollens are still in the very forefront of British industry and for our resolve that we intend to keep them there.

HIGHLAND ORNAMENTS AND WEAPONS

The lyf so short, the craft so long to lerne

HE truth about the ornaments and weapons that accompanied the Highland dress in its heyday has been obscured for more than a century by a mist of romantic enthusiasm. We do not want to disperse the enthusiasm, but the truth – how often it is so! – is so much more interesting and exciting than the fiction that hides it. The few authorities on the subject have to go like men picking their way over a peatbog for fear of the expostulations of this clan-chief or that when they imply his proudest family heirloom is quite two hundred years later in date than Bannockburn or could never have been carried at Culloden. Indeed, there are times when the correspondence columns of our newspapers suggest that the furor Scotorum is now largely spent on fighting about what our ancestors wore and how and when they wore it. It is a pity that greatest of authorities on Highland ornaments and weapons, Charles Whitelaw, died before he could write the book that would at once have become the standard one. It would have set out the whole story, documented beyond argument, and for ever shamed the spurious by the beauty of the real thing.

Let us begin with the sword. It epitomises all the misconceptions. I was passing through Speyside a few weeks ago when some charming little girls got into the train on their way to dance at a Highland games. They had with them a case of swords, which – to my dismay – turned out to be cavalry officers' dress-swords. Now there is nothing more pleasant on a fine afternoon than a green, grassy meadow on which brawny, kilted men toss the caber against a background of dark pines and purple hills; but if those occasions are not to be the means of keeping up

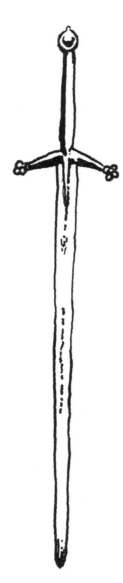

CLAIDHEAMH-MOR
(CLAYMORE) OR
"GREAT SWORD"
OF THE HIGHLANDS

the true customs and traditions of that lovely countryside, then I see no purpose in them at all. The proper weapon for the sword-dance is, of course, the basket-hilted blade, which Walter Scott speaks of as an Andrew Ferara, the sword which – again, quite wrongly – is now generally called a claymore.

The story of the Highland sword opens with the claymore, the real claymore. The real claymore is a great, double-handed weapon that takes its name from the Gaelic "claidheamh" – mor, meaning "great sword". Its quillons are depressed – that is, the guard or cross-pieces drop slightly towards the point of the blade. There is no ornament except a small quatrefoil at the end of each quillon. This type of sword must have come into use about the beginning of the sixteenth century, and those who know the collection of tomb slabs at the Priory on the island of Oransay may remember one slab carved with a fully-developed claymore, dated 1539. The carved slabs on Oransay and Iona supply us, too, with some hints about the origin of the claymore. They depict numbers of smaller, probably earlier swords with drooping

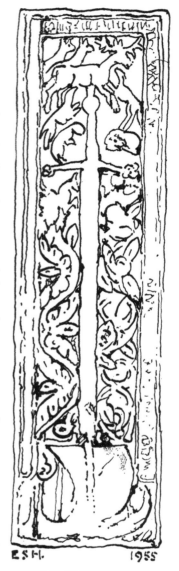

TOMB-SLAB SHOWS THE
TYPICAL SIXTEENTH-
CENTURY CLAYMORE

quillons that have a Norse look about them, and a single one of the earlier swords survives in the National Museum of Antiquities in Edinburgh. Those beautiful sword portraits – Whitelaw was convinced they were portraits of actual weapons – suggest that the claymore came into being in the domain of the Lords of the Isles. It is just possible it was common to the whole of the Celtic west, for several fine claymores have been found in Ireland, but whether they really are Irish or were brought in by marauding Scots is an open question. The typical claymore seems to have gone out of use about the middle of the seventeenth century. Survivors are exceedingly rare now, and the appearance of a genuine one in a saleroom causes a stir among connoisseurs of arms and armour.

The well-known basket-hilted swords, on the other hand, survive in considerable numbers. Even quite good swords are within the reach of modest collectors. Many hundreds must have been picked up as loot on the field of Culloden, and for a long time the blades of some of them formed a railing at Twickenham House near London. They appeared in Scotland probably about the time Jamie the Saxt moved south to occupy the throne of Elizabeth. However, the Scots cannot claim to have invented them, because basket-hilted swords were in use on the continent perhaps half a century earlier. The English also used them a good deal. Both English and Scots must have got the idea from the Germans, because a big proportion of English and Scottish blades carry the famous Wolf of Passau and other marks of German bladesmiths. On the other hand, one who is perhaps the most popular of all eighteenth-century Gaelic poets, Alexander Macdonald, hints at another source —

"Gu'm beannaich Dia ar claidhean,
'S ar lannan Spainteach geur ghlas."

This, in Sheriff Nicolson's translation, reads:

"God's blessing be upon our swords,
Our keen gray brands of Spain."

Whether or not the Scots made any great proportion of their own blades – and by 1600 the armourer's essay-piece had become "ane mounted braid sword sufficiently wrought" – the distinctively Scottish contribution to the development of this fine weapon was the basket hilt itself, and it is mainly by the hilts that specimens can now be dated. The earliest hilts are built up from ribbon metal. Then comes a type in which the iron is forged into thin bars welded together with a small junction-plate at the meeting-place of the crossed counter-guards. From about the middle of the seventeenth to the middle of the eighteenth centuries occurs a more ornamental, pierced basket with notched and incised designs. Some rare baskets of this sort are of brass, or are

BASKET-HILTED HIGHLAND
BROADSWORD

inlaid with brass or silver. Rarest of all are the silver baskets. His Majesty the King possesses two broadswords with such silver baskets, pieces made for presentation to winners of race meetings. William Scott the Elder, the Elgin silversmith, is the maker of one of them, which is inscribed:

"Win at King Charles fair at Huntly Castell the secund Tusday of September 1713 all horsess not Exciding ane hundred Marks of price ar admited to rune the rideres staking Crounes a peace, Which ar givin to the poor who may Pray that Monarchie and Royall Family my be lasting And glorious in thes Kingdomes."

Stirling and Glasgow, however, seem to have been the chief centres of hilt-making.

The blades, of course, at once conjure up the legend of Andrea Ferara, whose name became synonymous with the best of the swords themselves. It will be found, in various spellings, on many a blade that has lost none of its whip or temper or keen edge, and most of those associated with the great Jacobite champions bear it. There is no doubt it is a hallmark of excellence. There is also no doubt it is not in the nature of a signature. According to the legend, Andrea was a celebrated bladesmith of Ferara who slew an apprentice because the young man spied upon him and discovered his secret for tempering steel, and his wanderings are supposed to have brought him to Scotland. He would, however, have had to be a phenomenally long-lived and energetic craftsman to have made all the blades that carry his name, and there is no evidence that he ever came to the country.

A cut-down blade of a back-sword – that is, a sword with one cutting edge instead of two – was often adapted to form a dirk. But the Highland dirk is a weapon with a history of its own. Its progenitors are the knives and daggers in use throughout Europe, more precisely the dagger-knife with hilt of heather or ivy root used in Scotland in medieval times. This may be called a dirk as soon as the craftsman began to carve the hilt with Celtic knotwork, which happened some time in the seventeenth century. Such decoration appears first as two bands of simple interlaced work,

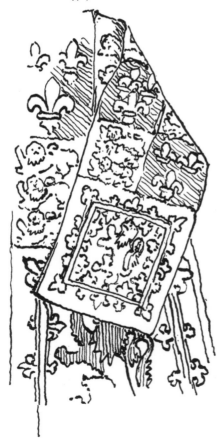

HERALD'S COAT, OR TABARD

one above and one below the grip. Dirks of this kind are very rare indeed and difficult to date; but the Colville Collection in the National Museum of Antiquities in Edinburgh possesses one carved with the date 1696. It must have been just about this time that the fully-formed dirk came into use. At first the carved decoration covers the grip only, and has the functional purpose of insuring a firm grasp. The carving finishes on the haunches with a neat triquetra.

The pommel is surmounted by a flat plate, and the tang – the extension of the blade that passes up through the hilt and pommel – is secured above by an iron nut. In time, the entire hilt was given to decoration, and the strands of the knotwork tend to become narrower as the eighteenth century progresses. The patterns show considerable variety, but, as a rule-of-thumb method of assessing age, the simpler and more workmanlike the form of the hilt, the older the weapon is likely to be. The notion of mounting Scotch pebbles on it arrived about 1800, and this developed into the crystal and cairngorm-stone elaborations that have since prevailed; while the simple grip eventually took on an extraordinary baluster form that not even the most powerful fist could grasp with confidence, and the final absurdity has been to make the pommel a mere setting for a vulgar display of semi-precious stones.

HIGHLAND DIRKS

The "biodag", the dirk, was a general-purpose implement, used for domestic as well as military occasions. There is a tale told that the Bruce first had his resentment roused against the English by a taunt that he used the same knife to carve his beef and his countrymen, against whom he had just been fighting. Later dirks have sheaths fitted with knife and fork. The celebrated little knife known as a "sgian dubh", now worn in the stocking, was formerly concealed under the armpit. It was a weapon made for strictly practical use rather than for show, but the hilt was carved with some semblance of Celtic knotwork. Blade and hilt were generally about equal in length, and the pommel might be mounted in some such metal as pewter. Genuine "sgian dubh" are now very rare. It is commonly the case that plainer relics from the past were less treasured and less carefully preserved than more ornamental ones, and so they have now become collectors' prizes. It is not altogether easy to translate Gaelic sounds into English letters but "sgian dubh" is very nearly pronounced "skee-an-doo".

The clansman probably used his broadsword and his dirk in right and left hands, as the Italian of the seventeenth century used his long rapier and his main gauche dagger; but on his left arm he carried the targe, a light but tough shield that served him well in parrying cut and thrust. The targe and dirk were used together, the dirk held point down to prevent an enemy from closing. Targes are invariably circular, about twenty inches across, and they weigh on an average about 6 ½ pounds. They are built up of two plies of oak or fir boards. One ply crosses the other at right angles, and the boards are pegged together with considerable numbers of wooden pegs. The front is covered with cow-hide, bent in over the edge, while deerskin is stretched over the inside, which is fitted with a hand-grip and a loop for the forearm. The beauty of the targe lies in its outer face. This may be ornamented with metal studs arranged to form a pattern, and the central boss is sometimes fitted to take a long spike. The surface of the leather is often beautifully tooled with a Celtic design. Heraldic emblems of the owner may be incorporated, as in the case of the superb targe of Macdonald of Keppoch, who fell at Culloden. This is now in the Royal Scottish Museum in Edinburgh. Few targes are dated, but the Hunterian Museum in Glasgow possesses one of 1623 – nearly a century earlier than most surviving pieces of its kind.

It is a solemn thought that the instinct or impulse behind the beautiful Celtic decorations on weapons little more than two centuries old is the same that inspired the ornament of the West Highland crosses, of the magnificent jewellery and relics in the National Museum in Dublin, and of the great treasures of pre-Roman Britain such as the Battersea Shield and the Torrs Champfrein.

How the continuity persisted is largely a mystery. This mystery is less baffling in the West Highlands, where the tomb slabs that have been described bring the traditions of the early Christian monuments right down to the sixteenth century; and it may be that in other parts of the Highlands, such as Perthshire, Pictish Monuments served as inspiration for the clan armourers and other craftsmen. Powder-horns provide some of the best pieces of this late Celtic decoration. They are a useful index to the development of the strange renaissance, because many are dated. They are made of cow-horn flattened under the influence of heat, and the decoration is sometimes carved, but more usually engraved. In a very few instances, the engraving is ambitious and some attempt at representation is made, the most notable case of this being the charming hunting scene, reminiscent of Pictish animal carvings, on the horn identified with Sir George Mackenzie of Tarbat, now in the National Museum

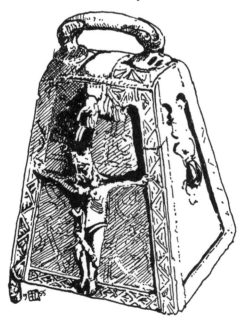

BELL-SHRINE

236

TWO HIGHLAND POWDER-HORNS

of Antiquities. This, like so much of the best Highland equipment, is pictured by Drummond in his "Ancient Scottish Weapons", a volume that is itself now a collector's piece. The engraving of powder-horns was, of course, an art found in many European countries, but the only foreign horns that resemble the Highland ones at all closely are some from Scandinavia.

The one branch of Highland weapons about which there is much authoritative published material is firearms. Whitelaw happily published some of his researches as a chapter in the beautiful book by Herbert J. Jackson, called "European Hand Firearms". Before that, in 1907, appeared an essay by a French scholar with the unlikely name of Georges Stalin. It was called "Notes sur un Pistolet Ecossais", and was printed in Beauvais. It is pleasant to know that the other partner in the Auld Alliance was the first to make a systematic study of the Highland pistol. M. Stalin was keenly appreciative. He says of the Highland pistol: "C'est une arme de luxe, un petit chef-d'oeuvre de precision et de bon gout…"

Pistols of Highland type were made in Scotland over a period of about two centuries. The earliest known pieces are a pair of "dags" dated 1598, which – until 1939 at least – were in the Dresden Museum, but the records of the Incorporation of Hammermen show that a firearms industry was in being in 1587, which means firearms were being made in Scotland perhaps as early as the middle of the sixteenth century. The cumbersome, expensive wheel-lock was never fitted to Scottish pistols, and the type of lock employed until late in the seventeenth century was the snaphaunce, a variety of flintlock believed to take its name from the similarity of its action to the head of a pecking hen. In the earlier weapons,

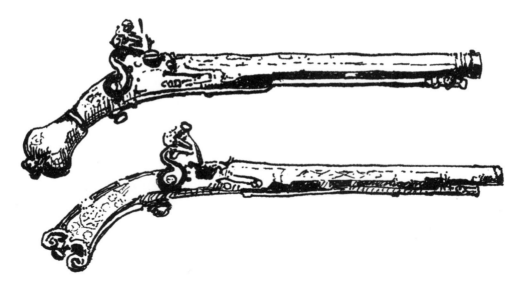

THE HIGHLAND PISTOL, OR DAG, IN THE SEVENTEENTH AND EIGHTEENTH CENTURIES

stock and butt are generally of brass, sometimes of wood. There is a beautiful wooden-stocked example with silver mounts in the Royal Scottish Museum. In later pieces, butt and stock are of iron. The typically Highland form has a butt that ends in a double scroll, or "ram's horns", and this begins to appear about the middle of the seventeenth century and is perfected in the second quarter of the eighteenth. In this period, nearly all the surface of the pistol is beautifully engraved and stock and butt are inlaid with designs in silver wire, while the trigger and pricker knobs are of silver. As the iron parts of the pistol were originally blued, the contrasting effect was rich and full of appeal for the Celt, with his love of colour and brilliance. Indeed, the appeal went far beyond Scotland. Several of these pistols are preserved in the armouries of the Continent, and although some of them may have been left behind by Scottish adventurers, the Curator of the Royal Armoury in Stockholm recently assured the present writer that he believed them to be presentation pieces. A very few of the pistols are inlaid and mounted not in silver, but in gold, among them a superb pair in the Royal collection at Windsor.

It is all the more astonishing that the chief centre of manufacture of those little masterpieces was the village of Doune, in Perthshire. Here, right on the Highland Line, worked several families of pistol-smiths, who passed on their skills from father to son. Their names can be read on the lock-plates of the weapons: Robert and Thomas Caddell, John and Alexander Campbell, John Christie. The last of them all is that John Murdoch who is mentioned in the "Statistical Account of Scotland", with a note that with his passing the old craft will be at an end. The factor that killed it was competition from London and Birmingham, where some clumsy but gorgeous imitations of Highland pistols were made in the early nineteenth century, the most interesting of them being the pistols worn by Macdonell of Glengarry in

Raeburn's famous portrait, the originals of which still exist in perfect condition. But the Sassenach who must have profited above all others by his imitations of Highland pistols was a man called Bissell, whose crude, mass-produced weapons seem at one time to have been issued as a regulation arm to Highland regiments. Many hang on the walls of the Banqueting Hall in Edinburgh Castle.

The musket, too, was carried by the clansman. It is strange that hardly more than a score survive of the true Highland musket, a lovely weapon with lines rather like those of an Afghan gun. J. G. Mackay attributed some of them to Spanish manufacture, and called to mind the ill-fated Spanish expedition that met its end in Glenshiel during the rising of 1719. Some of the finest are much earlier than that – a superb one in the Seafield collection is dated 1667 – but the locks in themselves point to foreign influence and strongly suggest a type used on the shores of the Mediterranean. The carving of the butts and the engraving of the metal parts give the guns their chief beauty.

To wearers of the Highland dress today, the most important accoutrements are not weapons at all – for the dirk and sgian, after all, no longer have a function. The articles that have still some sort of practical use are the sporran and the brooch.

The sporran is, of course, simply the Highlander's pouch or purse, and in the early days it was worn on the waist-belt, together with the dirk. Whitelaw dated the wearing of it on a separate strap at no earlier than the end of the eighteenth century, when the quite fantastic long-haired, tasselled sporrans first came into use. Originally, the sporran was nothing more than a bag of leather gathered together at the neck with thongs, and the only decorative features were the small tassels which terminated the loose ends of the thongs. A leather flap covered the mouth of the bag. The material from which the leather was made is generally deerskin, but otter, badger, seal, wild cat, goat or any other wild animal would serve.

Sporrans with metal clasps were certainly in use as early as 1700, and there is one with a silver clasp dated 1706. Normally, however, the clasp is of cast brass. It may be semi-circular, semi-octagonal or rectangular. Decoration is extremely simple, even crude. Sometimes a running leaf-scroll is introduced, but the commonest motif is a small concentric circle repeated. Whitelaw suggested this might be traced back to prehistoric times, but it is such an easy and tempting device for the craftsman's punch that there seems to be no need to look for special significance in it. Simplicity was the keynote of the genuine old sporran; and to those today who argue that gaudiness is in keeping with the Highland temperament one might well quote the verse of Donnachadh Ban, cited by Mackay:

"We got a hat and a cloak,
The sort did not belong to us;
A buckle to close our brogues—
The thong was neater by far."

Even the brooch in its finest periods was never gaudy. The extraordinary articles contrived from Cairngorms and Scotch pebbles date only from the Romantic Revival of the nineteenth century, and are in keeping with the great fiction it produced. The only real basis for the use of semi-precious stones in this manner is the small group of reliquary brooches now generally accepted as belonging to the sixteenth century. Their centrepiece is a big rock-crystal, and it is mounted in silver in various designs.

The Lochbuy Brooch, which found its way from the Bernal Collection into the British Museum, is typical, and the tradition is that it was made by a tinker from silver found on the Lochbuy estate in Mull and handed down by generations of Macleans. The crystals used had a special significance and were probably regarded with superstitious awe. The Clach Dearg of the Stewarts of Ardvorlich won a reputation for curing cattle disease. It is quite possible that some of those crystals were venerated before they were made into brooches, and this may account for legends claiming that certain of the brooches were in existence centuries earlier than any authority would admit.

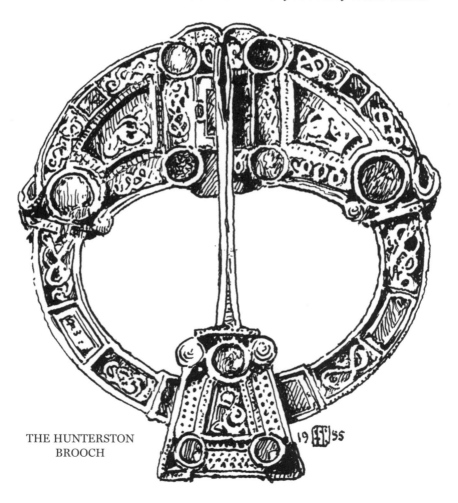

THE HUNTERSTON
BROOCH

The typical Highland brooch of the seventeenth and eighteenth centuries is annular – that is, ring-shaped. The travelling tinkers, or ceards, who seem to have made it, hammered an ingot of metal into the flattened ring shape, or cast it and finished it with the hammer. Brass is the usual metal, although silver is not uncommon. The diameter may be anything from an inch or two up to 8 inches. The pins were of the metal of the brooch and iron ones should be regarded as replacements. The decoration of the surface is simple and consists of engraved panels filled with Celtic interlacing and sometimes with strange animals, which might have come out of a medieval bestiary, but are probably conventionalised deer or wild cats. A few seventeenth-century brooches are dated. Silver examples are often enhanced by the use of niello. Niello is an amalgam made from silver, copper, lead and sulphur, which, finely powdered, is spread over a surface on which a design has been worked with a graving tool, the surface having been carefully brushed over with a flux such as borax in solution. When the metal is heated over a charcoal fire, the powder fuses and fills up the design. When the surplus is removed and the surface polished, the design shows up in greyish-black against the bright silver. It is not known whether the makers of

BROOCHES: FROM MEDIEVAL TIMES TO THE SEVENTEENTH CENTURY

Highland brooches used precisely this method. Those silver-and-niello brooches were sometimes called Glasgow brooches, in the belief that they were made in that city, but there is no reason to think the tinkers did not have the skill, and one sort is known to have been made by a tinker called Ross, near Killin. It is not until the end of the eighteenth century that the making of such Highland brooches came into the hands of city silversmiths, and from then on the elusive charm of the unsophisticated pieces was lost. The finest of the Highland brooches are early ones, and Whitelaw records that they come from Aberdeenshire and the neighbouring counties. Such brooches were, of course, used to fasten the plaid, but by the women, not by the men, who used a pin for this purpose. Evidently they were often given as tokens of betrothal, for a number of them are inscribed with two sets of initials and a date.

It is difficult to describe the accoutrements and arms of the Highlanders without leaving an impression that the clansman in battle array had some resemblance to the White Knight.

"With durk and snapwork and snuff-mill,
A bag which they with onions fill,
And, as their strict observers say,
A tupe horn fill'd with usquebay;
A slasht out coat beneath their plaides,
A targe of timber, nails and hides;
With a long two-handed sword,
As good's the country can affoord;
Had they not need of bulk and bones
Who fight with all these arms at once?"

So runs a contemporary satire, quoted by Mackay, on the Highland Host of 1678. The satirist himself shortly after fell a victim to the Highlander's prowess in arms. Whatever may have been carried in the long march across hill and moor, in the last resort it would seem nearly everything was discarded except sword and targe, for ultimately the Highlander put his trust neither in powder nor shot, but in the quality of his steel and in the strength and skill of his own arm.

Just as Highland weapons were left behind on many a foreign field, so the study of them is no longer confined to Scotland. Many must be rusting even in American soil. The shot that started the American War of Independence may well have been fired by one of them, and many of these lovely war-like relics now rest peacefully in the homes of American collectors.

THE EGLINTON CASKET

NOTES ON OUR ILLUSTRATIONS

Mr Finlay sends us some further notes on our illustrations:

THE SCOTTISH TABARD illustrated probably dates from the early eighteenth or the late seventeenth century. It shows the Royal Arms as borne in Scotland from 1603–1689 – that is, with the Scottish Lion in the first and third quarters, a custom that was not revived till 1924. The embroidery is mainly in silver and silver-gilt thread over string padding on blue and yellow satin. These notes are from Mr W. Cyril Wallis, like Mr Finlay, of the Royal Scottish Museum in Edinburgh.

THE BASKET HILTED SWORD has this legend on the blade over the figure of St Andrew: "With this good sword thy cause I will maintain and for thy sake O James will breathe each vein."

Of the PISTOLS, Mr Finlay says that the one with the heart-shaped butt is more strictly a Lowland type but is in many respects similar to those made in the Highlands. The other is typical of the Highland Dag through the seventeenth and eighteenth centuries.

THE EGLINGTON CASKET in the Antiquarian Museum in Edinburgh is a small box 10 inches long made of whalebone bound with metal. These little caskets seem at one time to have been fairly common, although only two are known to have survived. This example probably is fifteenth century. They were most likely jewel-boxes.

THE BELL-SHRINE OF KIRKMICHAEL-GLASSARY in the Antiquarian Museum is one of two surviving. It is of bronze and is made to hold a holy bell. It is of the twelfth century.

THE HUNTERSTON BROOCH is typical Scoto-Irish work probably of the eighth or ninth centuries. It was found at Hunterston in Lanarkshire in 1826 and at first was thought to be Norse. Later, the inscriptions scratched on the back in runic proved to have been added by two later owners about the tenth century. It is of silver and silver-gilt studded with amber. The Tara Brooch, mainly made of bronze and now in Dublin, is the supreme example of this type of work and makes most delicate use of contrasting textures and colours of different metals. Scotland had her own sources of silver and a good deal of this type of jewellery has been picked up on the plunder route between Ireland and Norway round the north of Scotland. At that time the Outer Isles belonged to Norway.

NOTE

Mr IAN FINLAY, the author of this number, is Keeper of the Department of Art and Ethnography of the Royal Scottish Museum. The illustrations are selected from Mr Finlay's book, "Scottish Crafts" through the kindness of his publishers, Messrs Harrap & Co. Ltd., a book we recommend to all interested in the subject. Unfortunately, we had to translate the illustrations in this volume into black and white. The original "Scottish Woollens" had the privilege of using the original beautifully delicate plates. Not much to do with "Scottish Woollens" you may object, but

"A poor life this, if full of care
We have no time to stand and stare."

THE FINE WOOLS

ERINO or Botany or Saxony. Three names for the same thing. Our mothers, or our grandmothers at any rate, used to wear "Merino" dresses, but for such purposes this name has faded out. Botany has been adopted by the fine side of the English Worsted Trade as the name for yarns made of fine wool and for the wool itself. The name Saxony has been annexed by Scotland for yarn and cloth made of the same wools by the woollen process.

No animal has been so much interfered with as sheep. Everywhere we have tried to modify the beasts to suit our needs. To start with there were many natural varieties of sheep and from the earliest times we have watched over our flocks in every part of the world excepting the tropics. Sheep gave milk and meat and clothing, skins to begin with, wool as we gradually rose in the social scale. Everywhere in ancient days wealth was chiefly centred in our flocks and herds – sheep and cattle, although chiefly sheep.

Today the trade in wools may almost be divided into Cheviots and Merinos – more logically into coarse and fine. There are great quantities of wools that hardly touch our clothing trade, but are made into carpets, felts and such like articles. We in Scotland who own the name Cheviot would by no means admit them to our territory. Cheviots we have already dealt with in two of our papers, so now to complete our work we must deal with the fine wools.

It is a very big subject so we must take it in stages. Merino sheep form the foundations of the world's fine wools. The Merino sheep is Spanish in its origin. In the Middle Ages, English wool was greatly sought after and seems to have been the finest generally available. It was chiefly in wool that English fortunes were founded in the Middle Ages. Most elaborate means were taken to preserve as nearly as possible a monopoly of both the wool and the sheep. But for all this development, we must refer the enquirer to such books as Eileen Powers' "The Wool Trade in Medieval History". This book was a sort of preliminary canter in the Oxford Ford Lectures and was meant to lead up to a general history of the Wool Trade to be undertaken along with Professor Postan – a scheme unfortunately stopped by Miss Power's untimely death.

In 1464 or thereabouts, in spite of all precautions, some Cotswold fine-woolled sheep were taken to Spain. They were crossed with the native Merino sheep and these cross-bred sheep formed the basis of the vast flocks of fine-woolled sheep that gradually spread to Germany, the Cape of Good Hope, Australia, Tasmania, and South America. They were smuggled out of Spain to France and thence to Germany and it was their introduction to Silesia and Saxony that gave us in Scotland our name of Saxony for our fine cloths. It so happened that the first or at least the early introduction of fine wools to the Borders was from Saxony, not from the Colonies.

It is interesting to see how old songs turn up again. Australia is just now taking a plebiscite of their wool men to decide if the export embargo on sheep should be abandoned. Thirty years ago, the Federal Government banned the export of breeding Merinos, following the ancient efforts of Spain, and England and France. In Scotland, perhaps the finest cattle are raised and we make a lot of money from the sale of prize stock. New Zealand is spending vast efforts to tame and to adapt their 300,000 acres of sandhill country to pasture and forestry. They are using the same method we have been using in Scotland for our much smaller problem, the preliminary planting of marram grass to fix the sand and prepare it for trees and sheep. Perhaps some of Australia's Merinos will fly across and populate these wastes.

In 1770, Captain Cook in the "Endeavour" was the first of our people to touch Australia. He landed near where Sydney now stands. In his expedition, Sir John Banks, a wealthy English botanist, voyaged with him. Sir John was so delighted with the innumerable new plants he found when they landed that he named the small roadstead "Botany Bay", and there the first settlement was founded in 1788 just fourteen miles from Port Jackson Heads. A few years later, the settlement was moved to the magnificent site where Sydney now stands. But it was to Botany Bay that the first Merino sheep were brought and so it came to pass quite naturally that Australian Merinos were called Botany wools.

Remember, England – Britain, one might almost say – for centuries was by far the chief wool country in the world, so it was again natural that Britain developed the great prospects of Australia and New Zealand. Now the Commonwealth produces about half the world supply of wool and, at round 1,000 million pounds, Australia produces about half the Commonwealth wool, and most of it is Merino. When the Cape Merinos are added and the small clips from Tasmania, New Zealand, and South America, the importance of the Botany wools can be understood.

So much for the names. It was again natural that London should develop into the chief market centre and in spite of the great rise to importance of local sales all over the world, in the primary markets in America and in Antwerp, London has remained the centre of the distribution trade.

Now it is to the London wool sales that the trade looks for guidance in prices and in supplies. Not only is Britain the chief distribution centre, but until far on in the Great War when the United States displaced us, we were the greatest wool users. We are now once more almost in our old position at the top of the list.

It was an evident convenience in so international and varied a market that some definite method of classifying wools should be devised. Wool and tops went under somewhat vague descriptions as Hog, Super, Wether, Fine, Medium and Low. Then gradually, about 1850, it became the habit to quote the size of yarn to which the wool would spin. The English spinners had a system of stating the size or thickness of their thread by the number of hanks of 560 yards they could spin out of a pound of wool, so it came about that, let us say, 60s meant that 60 hanks of 560 yards each could be spun from a pound. That is theoretically. Actually, the wool merchants being very optimistic men, the spinner would be rather put to it to get all that length of thread from his pound of 60s. Broadly speaking, Botanies come down to 60s, Crossbreds from 56s/58s for fine Cheviot cloths, to 46s for rougher Cheviots, down to the 40s and below that to blankets and such like, down again to carpets about 28s. In spinning qualities, there are many other elements – length, softness and so forth – that modify these standard numbers for the spinner, but broadly speaking they do mean the thickness of the individual fibres. 60/64s is looked upon as average Merino and forms the vast bulk of the wool. It is about 1200 hairs to the inch. 70s Super may be called about the finest ordinarily available in commerce and it is about 1500 to the inch. The finest available in small, very select clips is 90s/100s ranging up to about 2000 fibres to the inch, and at the other end of the scale, the Cheviots range from about 1000 down to about 400. Quite at the top end of the scale stands Vicuna, with about 2500, and Cashmere is not far behind, but these two wonderful wools, though they are actually very fine, do not depend for their exquisite qualities purely on the thinness of their fibres. We have to thank our Research Association in Leeds for finding these figures for us.

Most of this vast quantity of fine wool is made into worsteds – by the way the name comes from Worstead, a small village in Norfolk – and earns the name Botany, but a good part, especially the shorter clips, becomes our Saxonies.

As these papers are primarily concerned with Scottish Woollens, we cannot go through all the complex history of the development of worsted manufacture, which is elaborated in many large volumes. In his "History of Woolcombing", Burnley enumerates 481 patents in the century ending in 1889. Starting with Isaac Mills in 1723, it was not really till about fifty years later that the flood broke out. Almost every major invention in the Woollen Trade dates from that wonderful fifty years shared by the eighteenth and nineteenth centuries, and behind all that progress stood Watt and his kettle – or perhaps it was Voltaire?

A curious and interesting point in all this great development is the number of important inventions devised by men unconnected with the woollen trade or, in fact, with any industry at all. Arkwright the barber sets up his spinning frame and becomes a great industrialist. Hargraves the carpenter invents the spinning jenny. Crompton the small farmer fiddling in the orchestra of Bolton theatre thinks of the self-acting mule. Cartwright abandons Oxford and poetry and the Church to invent the power loom in 1784 and the first moderately successful mechanical comb in 1790 and thereby started the extinction of the ancient trade of hand-combing with its 50,000 combers. After that follows a wonderful list of ingenious men, mostly English. Hawksby in 1783, Toplis ten years later, Passman and Amatt – sometimes engineers like Donisthorpe and Rawson in 1835 and 1840, or men quite outside of the trade like Isaac Holden in his Lanarkshire country school at Hurlet. In all that wonderful procession, Holden is the only important man we can claim as Scottish. His adventures prospered greatly along with Lister at Alston and in France during that most turbulent period. Holden's square motion comb at one time combed about half the tops in the world. Then Noble after fifty years of experiment patented the circular comb in 1853, possibly the most-used comb in this country now. And there were many cross entries in the credits for Donisthorpe and Rawson, and Lister came into the accounts of Noble's invention. There are crowded in such names as Gilpin and Collier in 1814, Platt in 1827, Hitchcock and Donisthorpe again in 1836, and the same recurrent name coupled with that of Lister produced the perfect nip comb in 1843. After that, inventions dealt with details only. Meantime, on the Continent, Josue Heilmann of Mulhausen, watching his daughters combing their hair, thought of a new mechanism and, along with Schlumberger, brought to perfection the third type of comb, which is now the favourite machine used on the continent of Europe.

Although we are dealing primarily with Scottish Woollens, it is interesting to find how the more ancient Yorkshire trade differs from ours. Long before the coming of the Flemings, the West Riding had a large trade in Kersies, heavily milled cloths woven in units of 20 yards, 36 inches wide. Somewhat like our present-day Highland weavers, these weavers were small farmers and weaving was a secondary employment, although practically universal. Their Kersies or Kersimeres were about 26 ounces to our 58-inch yard and were sold white, ready to be dyed. The farm lands were distributed over the uplands and because of the heavy felting the cloth required, from early times power was used for milling or fulling. The many little fulling mills were necessarily set along the small streams and rivers in the narrow valley bottoms. Later to these were added the carding machines for preparing the wool and still later mechanised spinning. The weavers stayed in the uplands and this is the chief reason for the separation of spinning, weaving and finishing which is the usual organisation at the present day. In Scotland our cloths were looser – not beyond the reach of hand milling. Also, as our trade developed much later, power was soon to take over and so our tendency was to assemble our workers in the valleys along the rivers that supplied the only power available. Also owing to the shape of the land, our cultivation was mostly in the valleys, and only the sheep lived amongst the hills. These various circumstances acting together laid the foundations for the very marked general differences in the trade organisation of Yorkshire and Scotland. Our firms are almost all "vertical", buying the wool and turning out the finished cloth. In Yorkshire, that is the exception rather than the rule. Any of our readers who wish to explore these byways of social history further will find a lot of interesting details in such books as Crump and Ghorbal's "History of the Huddersfield Woollen Industry", published by the Tolson Memorial Museum in Huddersfield.

Another useful thing the Merino sheep supplies is the base for nearly all cosmetics – lanoline and glycerine and many things with formidable names besides soda ash and other less-recondite chemicals. These are extracted from the washing water from the wool-scouring machines. The sheep, of course, knew all about it and most successfully invented and produced the kindest and most perfect substance for hair dressing and for keeping their hidden skin soft and pliable. Some fine Merinos lose up to 80 per cent of their clipped weight when washed and not many lose less than 50 per cent. Of course, a good deal of this loss is just sand and general dirt, but there is enough of the "yolk", "suint" or wool grease left to make our ladies both happy and even more beautiful than they were originally.

So we come to the uses of Merino wools. The comb produces a continuous ribbon called a "top", from which worsted yarn is spun. This contains the long part of the wool, and in making this top it discards the short fibres which are called "noils". Strictly speaking, the noil is a by-product, but a by-product so valuable and important to the woollen spinner as to be pretty nearly as expensive as the top. The shorter Merinos are made into a special kind of top for the woollen man. This is broken into short lengths and sold as "broken tops". These, along with much of the fleece wool, are used by the woollen spinner under the name of Saxonies. We have already dealt pretty faithfully with worsteds and woollens and have outlined the different and very fundamental effects of the two preparatory methods of spinning.

So we arrive at the end of our tale. Fortunately for us who live by wool, there seems no chance of our inventing a process for making a fibre that can truly replace wool for the great majority of our clothing needs. Wool has a complex physical structure quite impossible to reproduce. Depending largely on that structure it possesses properties most valuable for clothes. It can absorb up to two-fifths of its dry weight without feeling damp and so can deal with perspiration to an extent which none of the synthetic fibres can manage. Made into thread, it is strong, even if not so strong as nylon. It is elastic – more elastic than any artificial fibre – and thus is comfortable in use. Wool absorbs – and keeps – dyes of many sorts on the whole more firmly than other fibres. The curly and scaly form of wool tends to enclose more little air spaces in a fabric and so gains warmth. Wool contains as part of its normal make-up somewhere about 17 per cent of water, varying with the surrounding atmosphere. Cotton only contains about 6 or 7 per cent. So wool has a far wider margin of variation to compensate for changing temperatures and conditions. It is also a better insulator both from its structure and its composition. Thus it is warmer in cold weather and cooler in hot. In fact – fortunately for us who live by wool – there is nothing that can replace wool – as yet – and it seems most unlikely that there ever will be.

THE PLATES

HE eleven plates that follow illustrate some of the principal processes of woollen manufacture. They were printed on thin Japanese vellum and were intended for framing for office decoration. They were not issued in any particular order or to illustrate any particular numbers of "Scottish Woollens". We have therefore grouped them here for general interest with the short descriptions that went with them.

The series would have included several more illustrations but for the untimely death of our artist, W. R. Lawson, in 1937.

PLATE I

WOOL SORTING

Wool sorting is one of the most highly skilled jobs in the trade. The sorter divides the fleece into the very varying qualities that it contains, from the finest at the neck to the coarsest parts round the tail. The success in spinning fine yarns depends on the care in sorting. As many as six qualities, apart from colour, are sometimes taken from one fleece.

W.R. LAWSON

'1933

PLATE II

SPINNING

This plate illustrates the self-acting woollen mule, or, as it is known for short in Scotland, the "jeeny". It is a machine of wonderful intricacy, the cumulative result of countless inventions and patents. The workers, known as "piecers", mend or "piece" the threads that break, and "strip" or empty the machine when the bobbins are full and put in a new set of bobbins or "pirns".

W.R. LAWSON 1933

PLATE III

WOOL DYEING

This plate shows the dyeing of loose wool in pots – a method by no means superseded by machine dyeing. The dye bath is kept boiling either by a fire underneath or by steam coils. The wool has to be continually and carefully turned or "poached" with big poles to allow the dye to go on evenly. As a rule, this process requires an hour and a half.

W.R.Lawson. 1933.

PLATE IV

DRAWING

This picture illustrates the preparation of a warp for the weaving. Each thread is separately drawn through a cotton or brass eyelet, known in Scotland as a "heddle". The boy in front – the "drawer" – puts his hook through the correct eyelet and the boy at the back – the "in-gie'er": anglice, "in-giver" – puts a thread round the hook. This job is being prepared for a narrow power loom for pattern work.

259

PLATE V

THE HAND LOOM WEAVER

This plate shows the type of narrow hand loom in use throughout the Highlands and Islands of Scotland and on which Harris Tweed and such like cloths are produced. It is a very primitive machine worked by many treadles, but in the hands of a competent craftsman, it is capable of surprisingly intricate work. Excepting for pattern work, hand looms are no longer used in our mills.

PLATE VI

A MODERN POWER LOOM

This elaborate mass of moving parts has superseded the simple hand loom for most purposes. Speed and accuracy are its features. There is little that the power loom can do that is beyond the scope of the primitive old hand loom under the hands of a highly skilled weaver – and almost nothing that we can do that could not be done in the Middle Ages – we are quicker, that is about all.

W. R. Lawson.

PLATE VII

KNOTTING AND PICKING

Knotting and picking or "burling" are really two quite separate processes, but from the pictorial side they are the same. The piece after leaving the loom is gone over and the knots and such like blemishes are removed. In picking, after the goods have been scoured, milled and, in fact, almost completely finished, the cloth is carefully gone over. Little bits of vegetable matter – "burls" – and little irregularities of any kind are picked out.

265

PLATE VIII

HAND SPINNING

This plate illustrates the most primitive method of spinning – with the distaff or rock and spindle. The mechanism required is nothing more than a couple of bits of stick and a weight of some sort, and it is a sad lesson to some of us to compare our efforts, helped by the newest machinery, with the work of a really skilled user of these primitive tools. We have gained speed and little more.

W.R. LAWSON   1936.

267

PLATE IX

MODERN CARDING MACHINERY

These great rotary machines are covered with a kind of fine wire brush, and as the wool passes between the rollers, it is gently disentangled and blended ready for the spinning. It is this process that distinguishes woollen from worsted yarn.

PLATE X

MENDING OR DARNING

The cloth, when delivered from the weavers, is examined both on the face and by looking through it, as is seen at the back of our plate. Every thread missed or misplaced by the weaver is replaced in its correct position. This is one of the most highly skilled crafts connected with the production of Scottish Woollens.

PLATE XI

SCOURING AND MILLING

After the cloth is woven and examined, the knots removed, and any missing or wrongly placed threads corrected, the piece is scoured and milled. This removes the oils used in spinning and generally cleans the cloth. It also felts the fabric and shrinks it anything from 10 to 25 per cent, in length and width, thereby producing the woollen fabrics as we know them.

INDEX

Loom, 49
Lowlander, 20
Lovat, 18, 27

M

Mackenzie, 45
Macleod, 47
MacNab, The, 21, 24
MacRae, 165
Madder, 11, 13
Magenta, 12
Malmaison, 186
Map, 86
Mar, 28, 30
Martin, Martin, 95
Mauve, 13
McKinley Tariff, 194
Menzies, 47
Merino, 75, 245
Meshed, 104
Metachrome, 13
Milling (see also Felting), 143
Minmore, 33
Minto, 36
Mohair, 7
Mollendo, 186
Mombert, 212
Moorit, or Murat, 64
Moray, 66, 87
Quercus tinctoria, 11
Mungo, 212
Munro, Neil, 25

N

Natural Colours, 14
Navaho Indians, 3, 7
New Town of Edinburgh, 160
Netherdale, 227
New Zealand, 246
Noils, 126, 249

Norway, 54

O

Old Tartans, 46
Old Town of Edinburgh, 161
Opals, 8
Orchil, 11
Orkney, 12
Our Office, 159
Overcheck, overplaid, 50

P

Paisley shawls, 65, 213
Pastel, 14
Patterns, 49
Peebles, 67
Pekin, 92
Perkin, 13
Perth, 87
Persia, 103
Peru, 82, 184
Pirn, 59
Plaid, 20
Plain Cloth, 3, 58
Poltalloch, 35
Portland, 66
Powers, Eileen, 245
Prescott, 83
Primaries, 16
Prince Consort, 27
Prince of Wales, 36
Prologue, 5
Purple, 12
"Punch", 203

Q

Quercitron Bark, 11
Queen Victoria, 27, 193, 215